Kingship and Unity

Scotland 1000–1306

Kingship and Unity

Scotland 1000–1306

G. W. S. Barrow

Edinburgh University Press

© G. W. S. Barrow 1981

First published 1981 in The New History of Scotland by
Edward Arnold (Publishers) Ltd
and reprinted (with corrections) 1989 by
Edinburgh University Press
22 George Square, Edinburgh

Printed and bound in Great Britain by
Billing and Sons Limited
Worcester

British Library Cataloguing in
    Publication Data
Barrow, Geoffrey Wallis Steuart
Kingship and unity.—(The new history of Scotland; 2)
1. Scotland—History—1057–1603
2. Scotland—History—To 1057
I. Title   II. Series
941.102   DA780

ISBN 0 7486 0104 X

Contents

Orkney
(to Norway)

S

Caithness E

Moray Firth

Ross E
Cromarty (S)
Dingwall (S) ●
Forres (S)
Inverness (S) ●
Elgin (S) ●
Banff (S)

Skye

④

Buchan E

M o r a y

R. Spey

Mar E
R. Don
Aberdeen (S) ●

R. Dee

Angus E
Kincardine (S) ●

Atholl E
Forfar (S) ●

R. Tay

Gowrie
Perth (S) ●

Strathearn E E
Menteith E
①
Fife E
②
Dunfermline ●
Crail ●

Firth of Forth

E A
Lennox
Stirling (S) ●
Dumbarton (S) ●
Linlithgow ●
Rutherglen ●
Haddington ●
Edinburgh (S) ●

D E

Berwick (S) ●

Mull

Islay

Arran

Lanark (S) ●
Peebles (S) ●
Roxburgh (S) ●
R. Tweed
Jedburgh ●

Ayr (S) ●
Selkirk (S) ●

Carrick
Galloway
Dumfries S

Wigtown (S) ●

Carlisle ●

Newcastle
upon Tyne ●

Solway Firth

Tir
Conaill

Tir
Eoghain

Ulster

Kintyre

A r g y l l

U D

(To Scotland 1266)

R. Clyde

Firth of Clyde

I n n s e g a l l o r
O u t e r I s l e s

S

IRELAND

Man

(To Scotland 1266)

ENGLAND

0		60 ml
0		100 km

Key

Atholl Province   E Earldom   ● King's burgh   (S) Seat of sheriff

D Area of main lands of non-provincial earldom of Dunbar

Small sheriffdoms   ① Auchterarder
   ② Clackmannan   —·— Southern limit of King David I's
   ③ Kinross   authority 1153
   ④ Nairn   --- Inter-regnal boundary 1286

Map I **Scotland in 1286** Provinces, Sheriffdoms, King's Burghs

1

Land and People

From the summit of Carter Bar, where the modern A68 road crosses the Border between Scotland and England, the view to east and west is closed in by green bracken-clad hills, but southward and northward the eye is carried to distant horizons. The deep valley of the little River Rede running down into England is rugged and desolate. Like much of the widespread river system of North and South Tyne to which it belongs, Redesdale cuts its way through high moorland plateaux, now largely planted with imported species of conifer which give the landscape an aspect profoundly different from the way it appeared only 50 years ago and for centuries before that — wastes of heather, birch, scrub oak, and peat hag stretching as far as the eye could see. To the north the view presents a startling contrast. On a clear day one may take in a sweep of country some 30 miles by 60, from the second highest hill in south-east Scotland, Broad Law, on the west, to the rolling slopes of Lammermuir in the north-east. Everywhere hills break the view, gently curving like the Moorfoots or rearing sharply from the plain like Rubers Law and the Eildons. But unlike the Tyne basin to the south, the basin of Teviot and Tweed to the north drains a land overlying Silurian and Devonian measures (greywacke and sandstones) and its broad valleys are green and fertile. Of course the neatly hedged fields and noble woodlands and windbreaks of fir, beech, and elm are not immemorial, but the result of careful planning and investment by lairds and farmers and of many generations of hard work by grieves, foresters, and farm servants. The A68 road, which gives us this splendid prospect, is itself the product of nineteenth-century 'improvement'. But the shelter, rich pasture, and fertility are ancient and have made this region especially favourable to human settlement for at least 3,000 years. The paradox of the Border at this point is that it is English Northumbria that appears stern and wild, Caledonia smiling and gracious.

Fertile though it may be, the Tweed basin is today severely depopulated. Most of modern Scotland lives in a narrow corridor running from Greenock and Dumbarton on the west to Edinburgh and Kirkcaldy on the east, or in a few outlying pockets of true urbanization such as Aberdeen and Dundee. The contrast in this respect with Scotland in the Middle Ages, indeed in any period down to the middle of last century, is striking. In the thirteenth century (as, probably, in the eleventh, and certainly in the eighteenth) the population lived in small communities, towns of no more than a few score houses, villages of 20 or 30, above all in hamlets and farmsteads of perhaps five, ten, or a dozen households, scattered widely across the country, often extremely isolated with neither road nor navigable waterway to link them with the outside world. Naturally enough, such settlements were thickest in the lower-lying districts wherever the land could be drained, but in the twelfth and thirteenth centuries permanent habitation was pushed far up the river valleys, along difficult coasts, and even on to the hills above the 600–700 foot contour. On the higher ground, however, the characteristic type of dwelling was the seasonal pasture station to be found in every corner of Scotland. Depending on which language was spoken locally, this pastoral encampment was known as a shiel or shieling (English), *airigh* or *longphort* (Gaelic), *pebyll* (Cumbric), *saetr* or *skali* (Old Norse). When the monks of Arbroath Abbey were given some land in the parish of Fordoun (Kincardineshire) towards the end of the twelfth century, their benefactor conceded that they and their peasant tenants might have 'skeling' (shieling) for the nourishment of their cattle beasts, from Easter to All Saints (1 November), in Tipperty, Corsebauld, or Glenfarquhar, an area about the upper waters of the Bervie where the land rises to just over 1,000 feet.

If, by a reasonably well-informed guess, we put the population of Scotland in 1300 at about half a million, that is, a tenth of the present-day total, we would certainly not be guessing if we envisaged that population distributed much more evenly across the country than its larger counterpart is today. In the earlier Middle Ages the obstacles to permanent habitation were too cold a climate (ruling out most land above 1,000 feet), too ill-drained or infertile a soil (excluding, therefore, much low ground which nowadays is either covered with buildings or grows good crops), shortage of fuel – but peat, wood, or coal were to be had in most parts of Scotland – and density of forest growth which may have been an adverse factor in a few areas.

Our view northward from Carter Bar encompasses a surprisingly large part of what may be called the Lothian–Tweed Valley triangle, a tract of country that had an outstanding rôle to play in Scottish history throughout the period dealt with in this book. I shall call the triangle simply 'Lothian', which is not only convenient but finds plenty of support in the usage of that period. By Lothian will be meant the country bounded on the north-east by the Firth of Forth, on the south-east by the line of River Tweed–Cheviot Hills–River Esk, and on the west by a line drawn north-westward from Canonbie to Stirling. The inhabitants of this fertile triangle, overwhelmingly English-speaking, were not thought of as 'Scots' much before the middle of the thirteenth century. Nevertheless, the political and economic importance of the region, historically the northernmost section of the old kingdom of Northumbria, was so pervasive throughout our period that it will hardly be distorting our picture of early medieval Scotland if we begin with an account of Lothian and its people.

Like the rest of Scotland, Lothian was a pastoral region. The grazing of cattle and sheep on the flat 'haughs' or 'holms' beside the rivers or along the grassy hillsides, and the fattening of pigs on woodland 'pannage' (chiefly acorns and beechmast) constituted the economic staple. Cattle, sheep, and pigs were all more slender and smaller boned than their counterparts in southern England and on the continent. Many of the cattle were killed off about the feast of Martinmas in winter (11 November), hence their popular name of 'marts'. What little winter feed there was had to be carefully husbanded for the vitally important cows and plough oxen, the main source of winter food and tractive power respectively. Milk was taken from ewes as well as cows and cheese was a principal item in what must have been a monotonous though not unhealthy diet. Goats were also kept, both for their skins and for eating, but documentary sources, perhaps from a feeling among clerks that such homely animals were beneath notice, reveal almost nothing about them. Many goats, of course, would have been wild, and the feral aspect of the countryside can hardly be exaggerated. Much hill ground was technically 'forest', that is, it formed a zone set aside for the hunting of wild beasts, mainly red deer and boar, by the king or by those few great lords to whom royal forest privileges had been delegated. The dales of Yarrow and Ettrick in particular formed 'The Forest' *par excellence*, quite simply known as such until the later Middle Ages. Forest did not exclude the grazing of domesticated animals, although at certain seasons it might restrict it. Nor did it preclude a little local industry, for Cappercleugh by St Mary's Loch in the heart of The Forest means the 'ravine frequented by the makers of wooden cups'.

In the flatter and lower-lying country between Stirling and Dunbar, in modern Berwickshire south of Lammermuir ('the Merse'), and in every river valley where there was enough level ground, the ox-drawn plough had for many generations before our period created a big tract of arable on which to sow and harvest cereal crops, oats and bere (the northern six-rowed barley) and (though rarely) a little wheat and rye. In those settlements, often marked by compact ('nucleated') villages, where the plough was drawn year after year across the same stretch of ground, big 'fields' — that is, areas of unfenced, hedgeless arable — came into existence, gradually growing larger as the population increased, or shrinking again if the population dwindled. In Scotland, these areas, the 'open fields' of the agrarian historians, should be pictured as something of a patchwork made up, often very irregularly, of 'furlongs'. These were arable units in which the plough invariably followed one axis of direction. Furlongs varied in shape and size depending on how far a team of oxen, from four to eight strong, could drag the heavy wooden wheelless plough and how soon their course would be obstructed by a steep bank, watercourse, or rocky outcrop. Within each furlong the earth was ploughed in long narrow strips, hump-backed in cross section, known by the French words *selion* or *raie* or, in popular usage, 'acres' or 'rigs'. A 'full' acre measured some 200 yards by between 20 and 30, but uneven ground evidently gave rise to many 'half acres' and other fractions. The actual ploughing unit, the 'rig' strictly so called, would normally be a quarter acre. A single draft ox was notionally reckoned to be capable of ploughing 13 full acres in a year (an 'oxgang'), and a full team of eight oxen should have managed 104 acres (a 'ploughgang', 'ploughgate', or simply 'plough').

It seems that a village would normally have two big fields ('north' and 'south' or 'east' and 'west' are commonly found), and it is likely that as much as practicable of the dung from sheep and cattle was concentrated on these fields, the 'infield' of later record, while less attention was paid to the 'outfield', the more distant ground where 'intakes' for cropping would be made by extra ploughing every few years. Within the infield some ground was no doubt left fallow each year and as such contributed to the pasture available for the villagers' livestock. Such fallow would necessarily have been composed of a given number of furlongs each year. Most of the pasture was not provided by the annual fallow but was derived from three other sources: hay meadows after the hay crop had been lifted in July, cornland opened up as stubble after the late northern harvest in September or even October, and the more or less permanent rough grazing afforded by unplough-able pieces of village territory and by the villagers' share of some not too distant stretch of moorland or hill pasture, the 'commonty' or 'common' familiar in seventeenth- and eighteenth-century Scotland. Common grazing rights, however, were not apportioned primarily village by village but shire by shire, and this fact calls for some expla-nation of a social and economic arrangement of great antiquity which will be essential for an understanding not just of Lothian but of Scot-land as a whole.

In the twelfth century, conservative Wales, northern England, and the whole of Scotland (except possibly the west highlands and the isles) retained a system of lordship (including the lordship exercised by the king) that almost certainly went back to the period of Roman occu-pation, when it was probably general throughout Britain. Under this system, the kings resided from time to time at any one of a large number of centres or strongholds. At these centres they would exercise royal power and authority, holding courts, dispensing hospitality and patronage, consuming with their officers, servants, guests, and hangers-on vast quantities of foodstuffs and provender. To these centres would be brought the revenues exacted from the king's subjects: cattle, cereals and some honourable services from the free-born, further food-renders and more menial and laborious services from the unfree. Each royal centre would form the chief place of a district or little 'province' in which there might be a considerable number of dependent or satellite villages and hamlets. Under the direction of one or more responsible royal officials, the men and women of such a district would not only share in the rendering of goods and services to their lord ('soke') but would also have the use of a common mill, common grazing for their beasts, and common rights of cutting peat for fuel (where this existed) and turves for the building of cottages and boundary walls. In Scotland during our period, the com-monest word in use to describe an administrative unit of this archaic kind, which was also a socio-economic unit, was 'shire'. Very rarely, we also find the word 'soke' which was used much more frequently in mid-land and southern England to describe surviving or residual units of the same type.

In Lothian we can see the implications of this old shire system soon after King David I had founded an abbey for Augustinian canons at the foot of Arthur's Seat near Edinburgh in 1128 (Holyrood Abbey). The new abbey was planted in the middle of the 'shire' of Edinburgh, a district reaching from the boundaries of Kirkliston on the west to those of Inveresk or Musselburgh on the east, from the sea on the north perhaps as far as the boundaries of Dalkeith and Penicuik on the south. King David wished his favoured canons to enjoy outright possession of the extensive lands he had given them, and so we find him addressing a command to all his men of 'Edinburgh shire' forbidding any of them to take peats or exercise grazing rights in the land granted to Holyrood. The king was not contemplating theft or casual encroachment but the much more serious problem of fitting a completely new kind of institution into an age-old framework of common rights and expectations. In the very same year as he founded Holyrood King David also transferred the French monks whom he had brought from Thiron near Chartres to Selkirk in 1113 to a more congenial monastic site at Kelso on the north bank of the Tweed near the royal stronghold of Roxburgh. Almost certainly the new site lay within the ancient shire of Ednam, whose men had to learn to share their rights and easements with a privileged corporation of monks who grew more and more demanding.

The men of the shire could band together on occasion and speak with one voice, but they lacked any strong leadership. The person in charge of a shire was not a peasant foreman or headman but a royal officer. The word generally used to describe him was 'thane' or 'thegn', derived from the Old English verb *thegnian*, 'to serve'. Essentially, as well as by origin, the typical Scottish thane was the active and dependent minister of his lord, even although his rank was aristocratic and he held for his own support and enjoyment an estate amounting to at least one village, perhaps several. In the early twelfth century one Thor 'the long' was apparently thane of Ednam, which had been given to him by King Edgar (1097–1107) when it was 'waste', perhaps devastated by some border raid or by one of the Norman kings of England in a punitive expedition. Two letters of Thor have luckily been preserved in which he proudly writes that he has built a church at Ednam at his own expense, but he also says that it was the king who gave this church its endowment of one ploughgate, and no doubt it was also the king who made sure that the new church was promptly bestowed upon the Benedictine monks of Durham cathedral priory 80 miles to the south. If there was still a thane at Ednam as late as 1128 he was clearly unable to prevent the new king, Edgar's younger brother David, annexing much of the shire for Kelso Abbey.

Immediately west of Ednam was the larger and far more important shire of Roxburgh, which unlike Ednam probably boasted several families of thanely rank. Nevertheless, there seems to have been one thane in particular whose job it was to administer the shire for the king and to whom (as was true of northern England in equivalent circumstances) the title *scir-gerefa*, 'sheriff', literally shire steward or shire officer, was applied. The sheriff of Roxburgh in the early decades of the twelfth century, Cospatric son of Uhtred son of Ulfkil, is the first sheriff known to Scottish record but was surely by no means the earliest in Scottish history. Cospatric was a prominent member of what a contemporary called the 'lesser rank of nobility', whose pedigree takes his ancestry back to the mid eleventh century. His father had served two bishops of Durham as thane of the shire of Hexham in Northumberland. The mixture of personal names in this one family, Cumbric (Brittonic or 'Old Welsh'), Old English, and Anglo-Scandinavian, should be set beside the evidence from many other Lothian personal names, Thor son of Swein (thane of Tranent?), Malbead (thane of Liberton?), the Ulfkil who has left his name in Oxton ('Ulfkil's toun') in Lauderdale, the Liulf whose name is preserved in Lyleston ('Liulf's toun'), the countless Orms, Uhtreds, Waltheofs, Osulfs, and Eadulfs, the wealthy Maccus son of Undweyn who seems to have founded or at least owned Maxtoun and Maxwell and conceivably even Longformacus (respectively the toun, well, and shieling of Maccus). Three things must be emphasized in respect of this solidly native Northumbrian aristocracy: its names demonstrate an appreciable intermingling of Gaelic (i.e. Scottish) and Scandinavian blood with a basic Celto-Germanic stock of Britons and Angles of Bernicia; its solidarity was such that there could be no question of its arbitrary removal or demotion as a class; nevertheless, its position was official, dependent in the last resort on the will of the king, and to that extent precarious.

The thanes did not quite form the topmost stratum of the aristocracy of Lothian, for late in his reign King Malcolm III 'Canmore' (1058–93) had granted to the refugee Cospatric son of Maldred, a representative of the ancient earls of Northumbria who had had to flee from the wrath of William the Conqueror, the estate of Dunbar (which must surely have been an old royal 'shire') along with much other land in East Lothian and Berwickshire. On this Cospatric based the dignity of a new earldom which came gradually to be called Dunbar or March. The earldom of Dunbar was and remained unique, and even thanes can hardly have been a numerous class (although in the customary English fashion the rank may have been passed on by a father to all his sons). The backbone of the gentry or freeholder class in Lothian consisted of men variously called 'hiredmen' or 'drengs', the equivalent of the very large class of small freemen and 'sokemen' in northern and east midland England. A 'hiredman' (Old English *hired*, 'household') was in origin a freeborn retainer of some lord, an honourable (as distinct from menial) servant. Unnamed individuals of this class have left some trace of their presence in places called Hermand, Hermiston, and Herdmanston. 'Dreng', a loanword from Scandinavian, has much the same meaning, a young man performing honourable or quasi-military service. These were the tenants, not ungenerously endowed with land, who performed the routine tasks required to administer the shires under king and thane, seeing to the regular renders of foodstuffs, collecting money rents, keeping the lord's hunting hounds, overseeing the seasonal work of ploughing, haymaking, and harvest which had to be performed on the king's demesne estates, arranging transport by sumpter horse and wagon, replenishing the lord's fuel stocks or logpile, carrying important messages, riding on escort duty, summoning those whose attendance was needed in court, arresting malefactors and suspects. As with the thanes, from whose younger sons they may well have been partly recruited, the king's drengs formed a solidly based class far too numerous to be eliminated by the pressure of feudalism. They passed imperceptibly into the general class of Lothian freeholders for whom we find abundant evidence in the later thirteenth century. When, in 1291, the officials of Edward I of England (who had just pressed home his claim to be overlord of Scotland) took fealties at Berwick from Scots gentry, they encountered one man they could not easily classify, Edmund of Bonnington. They described him as *simplex patriota*, 'mere countryman'. It may be guessed that Edmund, apparently landless, was descended from a line of drengs or hiredmen.

Not every village would have a family of thane's rank, but we can reasonably presuppose a more widespread distribution of drengs, hiredmen, or substantial freeholders. The tenure by which they held their land was called drengage or socage, and it usually involved a money rent in addition to a burdensome round of services. Today we might scarcely consider a dreng's life truly 'free', but he undoubtedly counted as a free man, indeed even a member of the noble class which in 1100 was much larger proportionately than it had become by 1300. Also free, at least in law and theory, was the peasant farmer to whom the words husbandman, bondager, or bonder were applied (Latin *bondus*, from Old Norse *bondi*, a free yeoman farmer). His characteristic holding was as much as 26 acres (two oxgangs) of arable, a sizeable farm if the accompanying grazing and other rights are added.

The tenant of a husbandland was expected to pay taxes and perform military service in the 'common army'. In time, however, the husband-man or bondager often fell into a dependence on his lord from which it would be difficult for him or his heirs to extricate themselves. It might be virtually impossible to evict him, but he could certainly not prevent the transfer of lordship over himself and his family from one lord to another, possibly on harsher terms. Thirteenth-century courts and lawyers made effective play with a false etymology deriving bonder from the verb 'to bind', in order to emphasize this dependence. In a society where everyone was enmeshed in a complex of obligations the bonder came to be thought of as 'bound' to his lord in exceptionally restrictive ways, not free to leave his holding, nor to have his daughter married or his son enter holy orders without paying a fine, nor even to leave his own possessions by will, save for the simplest household utensils. But though depressed into excessive dependence the Scots peasant farmer was not completely deprived of his voice. In 1305 the 'poor husbandmen of the king in Scotland' were able to complain to Edward I (who by this time had conquered their country) about the one grievance that probably irked them more than any other, the pre-cariousness of their tenure: 'they ask that they may enjoy the position of peasants holding of the royal demesne in England, so that they shall no longer hold their land, as hitherto, from one year to the next'.

The bonder class was no doubt largely recruited by straightforward inheritance, as well as by misfortune or excessive sub-division of patri-mony in the class above and occasionally by lucky marriage or skill in husbandry in the class below. The existence of this lower class cannot be doubted, even though the outright slavery which English chroni-clers lead us to expect as one consequence of Malcolm III's savage raids into Northumbria has left practically no trace in surviving record. What we do hear of are cottars or cottagers, men and women with very small arable holdings or no more than a plot attached to their dwel-lings, and also gresmen (literally 'grass' or 'grazing' men). Cottars and gresmen paid appreciably lower rents than bonders and many must have earned part of their livelihood by working for wages. In origin the gresman (who can be found in England as far south as Lincolnshire) was a landless man, perhaps a young man migrating from one village to another, who was offered pasture on which he could raise stock, and in some cases pioneer by breaking out new arable from waste ('assarting'). The gresman may sound archaic but as the gerseman (girseman) he survived in parts of the Highlands and the north into the eighteenth and nineteenth centuries, a poor tenant who had a house from the laird but no land.

In even greater dependence, though not necessarily poorer, than cottars and gresmen were those described in Latin documents as *servi*, literally 'slaves'. It is not easy to see their status as that of outright chattel slavery, for sometimes they appear to hold land and they may not always have been at the mere beck and call of their masters. But when we find Richard de Morville granting to Henry Sinclair of Herdmanston in East Lothian Edmund son of Bonde and his brother Gillemichel and their sons and daughters and whole progeny in return for three merks (i.e. two pounds), on condition that if they 'leave' Henry they must return to Richard, or Adam of Prenderguest (Berwickshire) declaring 'I have sold Stephen son of Waltheof my former serf and his offspring and chattels to Alexander the almoner of Coldingham Priory, and whoever else shall be almoner, for a certain sum of money which I have been paid in my state of need', we are surely learning about people so dependent that there can have been little practical distinction between their condition and chattel slavery. Often enough, we hear of their existence only at the moment of their emancipation.

So far, most of what has been written in this chapter about land and people has related to Lothian. In proportion to population and area, Lothian was the richest region of Scotland and without question we possess the richest documentary evidence for it in our period. If we extend our survey into south-western Scotland and into the country north of the Clyde—Forth line we ought to avoid making any over-simple assumptions, whether of contrast or of similarity. At one time it used to be thought that variations in social organization and economic structure within medieval Scotland could be explained quite simply in racial terms. Lothian, as part of Northumbria, had a Germanic or Anglo-Saxon pattern of villages and lordship closely comparable with that prevailing in England. The far north and the western isles had been given a Scandinavian settlement pattern by Norse incursions. As for the country in between, and the south-west (or at least Galloway), it was Celtic in speech and race and its way of life was specifically Celtic. While it would almost certainly be wrong to deny the importance of racially-determined variations, especially in regard to the Scandinavian north, the overall truth seems to be a good deal more complex. It may be helpful to distinguish between, on the one hand, underlying and long-term features which were shared by all or most of the major regions of Scotland, and, on the other, those features, often points of detail or emphasis, which show up as genuine regional variations.

Moreover, beyond these considerations it is as well to remember that two influential historical divisions in Scotland have been the essentially geological line of the great Highland Boundary Fault, running from the Firth of Clyde to Aberdeen, and the more notional division between the 'Atlantic' and 'North Sea' zones, neither of which had any racial significance in medieval times.

As far as the basic facts of economic life were concerned the whole of Scotland should be seen as a pastoral country with an essential agricultural component which was naturally strongest in the Lowlands, north and south, but shrank almost to vanishing point in many mountainous and hilly areas not only in the Highlands proper but also in Galloway. The need to keep herds of cattle and flocks of sheep and goats must have enforced a similarity in way of life between Lothian and the south-west, or between both these regions and the north, overriding many points of contrast. The church was realistic enough to require its chief upkeep tax of 10 per cent of animals, animal products, and crops (teind) to be paid in goats as well as other animals in Carrick and Lennox during the 1220s. Possibly fishing and hunting were rather more important for the maintenance of life in the north and the Highlands, but this can only have been a matter of degree. Everywhere we have evidence that butter and cheese, oatmeal, barley, malt, cattle and pigs, eels, salmon, herring, and venison were used in the payment of rents, in renders of tribute (what we should call 'taxes') to kings, earls, or the church, and in judicial penalties.

South-western Scotland, including Galloway, continued throughout our period to show traces of its lengthy earlier history as Cumbria or Strathclyde, a Celtic land using the Cumbric variant of Brittonic speech, organized on the basis of kindred-groups with a recognized position accorded to the 'head of the kindred' (Welsh, *pencenedl*), and divided into districts which in size and physical character strongly resembled the 'cantreds' or historic divisions of Wales. This picture, however, had been greatly complicated well before the twelfth century by a fairly thoroughgoing Gaelic-speaking settlement of the southwest extremity, Galloway, possibly brought about by migration from the Hebrides, Man, or parts of Ireland, and by a curiously rapid thinning out of Cumbric speech and social custom within the broad swath of territory stretching from modern Renfrewshire southeastward to the Solway Firth. In this area a slight but unmistakable Gaelic settlement and an appreciably denser settlement of people of English (or Anglo-Scandinavian) speech seem to have taken place in fairly quick succession between the mid eleventh century and the end of the twelfth. By 1200, at latest, south-west Scotland had become a true melting-pot of races and languages, with English beginning to dominate in the valley of the Clyde (save for Lennox, north-west of Glasgow) and already fully dominant in Eskdale, Annandale, and lower Nithsdale, while Gaelic remained the ordinary language of Carrick and Galloway. As late as the second half of the thirteenth century the senior member of the Kennedys (the chief family of Carrick) was formally recognized as 'head of his kindred' in a document using the Gaelic form, *ceann cinéil*, of the Welsh *pencenedl*. In 1296 a conquering Edward I took the fealty of 'the chief men of the lineage of Clan Afren' in Galloway, just as he would have done from their counterparts in Wales.

Galloway, already famous for its cattle, was so overwhelmingly pastoral that there is little evidence in that region of land under permanent cultivation, save along the Solway coast. Cumbria proper, on the other hand, was markedly agricultural. Dumfriesshire (especially Annandale) and much of Ayrshire, Renfrewshire, and Lanarkshire were richly fertile districts in which the arable unit familiar in Lothian, the ploughgate, looms large in surviving sources. Yet nucleated villages, with their houses huddled together in the midst of large open fields, were by no means typical of Cumbria. A few might be found in south Annandale and in the plain of Kyle in mid Ayrshire, probable instances being Hoddom near Annan and Prestwick near Ayr, both with strongly Anglian associations. We should envisage most of the arable made up of separate plots scattered here and there wherever the plough could conveniently be taken, interspersed with clusters of peasant dwellings and stretches of rough pasture and other uncultivated ground. In this region the power of the king and of a handful of great lords was exercised from fewer centres, and those more widely dispersed, than in Lothian. Some of their names, e.g. Dumfries, Dunscore, and Dundonald, bear witness to the fortified residences (Gaelic *dún*, Cumbric *din*) from which these potentates, or at least their ancestors, were wont to hold sway. Most, however, seem peaceful or neutral enough: Lochmaben, Lanark ('grove'), Cadzow, Rutherglen, Renfrew ('promontory by river current'), and Irvine, which is simply a river name.

If Lothian tended, in matters of social organization, to go with English Northumbria east of the Pennines, Strathclyde tended to parallel English Cumbria and Wales. But it would be wrong to draw too sharp a distinction between 'Anglian' Lothian and 'Brittonic' Cumbria. Although the word 'shire' was rare in west-country sources it can be found in neighbouring north-west England, where we also find thanes and drengs forming an aristocratic semi-official class which is not likely to have stopped abruptly at the Solway. Admittedly, the districts of south-west Scotland were generally larger than their equivalents in the east, but in other respects they must have been very similar – Lauderdale, for example, cannot have differed much from Eskdale or Douglasdale. In each district a number of scattered settlements contributed, at some centre of Cumbrian royalty, the annual round of foodstuffs and services to the king or to some lord to whom royal powers had been delegated. In every district there would certainly have been free men of 'noble' birth from whose ranks the king would draw the officers needed to collect tribute, give judgements in the courts and perform police and peace-keeping duties. A fleeting glimpse in our sources of the titles given to these officials suggests that the 'managerial class' of Scottish Cumbria was virtually identical with its Welsh counterpart, and it may even be that the word *kadrez* applied in twelfth-century documents to the districts of Cumbria is the Welsh word *cantref* (literally, 'district of 100 homesteads') as modified by Gaelic speakers. As in Wales, the general-purpose administrator was the *maer* ('mair' in later Scots); pursuit and arrest of suspected criminals was carried out by serjeants entitled to free hospitality; and the traditional law was pronounced and interpreted by apparently hereditary judges. The chief of the Kennedys was hereditary bailie of Carrick, an office resembling that held by the *rhaglaw* in comparable districts of Wales.

It is clear too that there was a sizeable class of unfree or at least extremely dependent peasant farmers. In the 1170s the king quitclaimed to the cathedral church and bishop of Glasgow his rights to lordship over a man named Gillemachoi (his name, aptly enough, means 'Saint Mungo's servant') and all his offspring and the entire following who ought rightfully to follow him – very likely a kindred-group of Welsh type. Perhaps the king was only saying that in future not he but the bishop of Glasgow would be Gillemachoi's employer, but if words mean anything this royal charter undoubtedly conferred upon the chief church of Saint Mungo, in perpetuity, a lordship bordering on possession over an obscure Clydesider and all his descendants.

If we turn our gaze from Lothian and Cumbria to the country north of the Clyde–Forth isthmus, without doubt an important boundary in Scottish history, we find no abrupt transformation in the twelfth century, either in the way people lived or in their social organization.

A gift made between 1059 and 1093 by Fothach bishop of St Andrews to the religious community established on St Serf's Inch in Loch Leven (Kinross-shire) nicely conveys the flavour of a simple, not to say spartan, pastoral existence. The bishop's benefaction consisted of the parish church of Auchterderran (West Fife), together with the customary dues which had been paid to that church from olden times, that is, 30 baked loaves (along with the ancient measure of flour permanently kept at the church), 30 cheeses each weighing one stone, 8 bolls of malt, and 30 and 4 bolls respectively of commodities whose names are now missing, probably oatmeal and barley. What was true of Fife held good, as far as our evidence takes us, for the whole eastern seaboard up to and including the Moray Firth, and also for the central Highlands. For the west Highlands documentary sources are much less adequate, but geographical factors alone would suffice to prove that this region was even more strongly pastoral than the east.

What is undeniable is that north of Forth and Clyde, until one reaches north-east Caithness and the Northern Isles, where Scandinavian peasant colonization had been so intensive that it had practically obliterated all trace of earlier cultures, Scottish society was profoundly Celtic in speech, culture, and social organization, more emphatically Celtic than was the society of Lothian or Cumbria. Even the mixture of features that we find in Lennox was a compound of Cumbric and Gaelic elements, just as elsewhere we find a compound of Gaelic and Pictish. As far as language is concerned, there is unequivocal evidence that Gaelic was the normal, in most areas the sole, speech in use from the Mull of Kintyre northward to Lewis, including all the islands, and from the west right across to the North Sea coast from the Ord of Caithness southward to the northern shore of the Firth of Forth. No doubt some use of Norse remained in the isles, where in any case the prevailing Gaelic would show strong Norse influence, and no doubt there was some infiltration of English speech into the coastal parts of Fife and Angus. But this cannot contradict the fundamental truth that the country from Cape Wrath to the Clyde—Forth line, Alba in the tongue of its own natives, Scotland to the English speaker, Scotia in the Latin of school-bred clerks, was a land whose inhabitants, the Scots, were overwhelmingly Celtic, speaking almost universally the 'Scottish', i.e. the Gaelic language, and observing social and religious customs that must be explained largely in Celtic terms.

That said, we may at once note comparisons and similarities among the contrasts. The ploughgate of Lothian and Cumbria shows up in Lennox as the 'arachor' (a word ultimately of Old Irish origin) which, whether or not it contained 104 acres, lent itself easily to division into halves and quarters. Elsewhere in 'Scotia' the universal arable unit was the davoch (from a Gaelic word meaning 'vat' or 'tub') which seems to represent a unit already known in Pictish times, when it would presumably have had a different, Pictish name. The davoch cannot have been identical with the southern ploughgate, but it was sufficiently like it to be given the alternative name of 'Scottish ploughgate'. Instead of being thought of primarily as a measure of arable scattered in rigs and furlongs across two or more big fields, the davoch was a relatively fixed, compact piece of ground, so permanent in fact that it would normally be given a definite name in the way that a farm is given a name. Indeed, in the north of Scotland a few named davochs still survive. In origin the davoch may not have been made up of 'acres' and there is uncertainty about how many acres a normal davoch contained in medieval times. It seems to have been readily divisible by two, three, and four, and there is some evidence to support a figure of 192 acres, with the caveat that we do not know what size those acres were. A davoch constituted a farm of respectable size, to which the common Pictish word *pett* (e.g., Pitbladdo, Pitfour) or the still commoner Gaelic word *baile* (e.g. Ballenbriech, Balfour) was often applied. Such a farm would support at least one family of free birth, perhaps several such families holding jointly, for we have cases of pit- and bal- names compounded with *mac*, meaning 'of the sons of', joined to a personal name, e.g. Pitmacdufgil, 'farm of Dugald's sons', or Balmackewan, 'farm of Ewen's sons'.

The topmost stratum of the free population consisted of about a dozen provincial rulers called mormaers ('great officers'), or earls as they came to be called in English usage, together with a small number of great landowners lacking any official status. Beneath this small group were numerous small gentry closely comparable to their Northumbrian and Cumbrian counterparts. The word *satellites* (plural) often used in Wales to denote the native *cais* or serjeants who carried out much of the day-to-day work of local administration occurs in an early-twelfth-century Fife document, and may point to the existence there of officers of the same type. Throughout central and eastern Scotland north of Forth the word thane was used of higher officers who seem precisely equivalent to their southern counterparts. Thanes administered portions of royal demesne within which they would themselves hold substantial estates and enjoy lucrative perquisites, usually hereditarily. Earls and bishops – but apparently no one lower down the social scale – also employed thanes. The estates they simultaneously held and administered were known as 'shires', precisely as in Northumbria, English Cumbria, and Lothian, and in exactly the same way as in those regions further south, the inhabitants of shires in Scotland north of Forth enjoyed or were subject to rights and duties in 'shire mills' and grazing on 'shire moors' of which the famous Sheriffmuir is one example. The sources reveal a strongly conservative quality in these customary rights and duties. Thus the thanes of Fochabers in Moray enjoyed a salmon fishing in the Spey in the twelfth and thirteenth centuries, while a similar fishing in the Deveron at Banff was still called 'Thanesnett' as late as the seventeenth century. The king's thanes at St Cyrus, Laurencekirk, and Arbuthnott (Kincardineshire) had common grazing in the pasture of their shires along with the men under them, while in southern Perthshire the men of Muthill and Blackford defended an immemorial right to pasture their beasts on the Muir of Orchill where they claimed that no one was allowed to take a plough. At the end of the thirteenth century, two neighbouring barons in West Fife shared the common mill of Lochoreshire.

We do not know how or why the English words 'shire' and 'thane' came to be used so widely in Celtic-speaking Scotia, but they serve to underline the common social heritage of Scotland proper and Northumbria. The shire was the prevailing unit of social and economic organization, not only circumscribing the annual sequence of tribute and service due to the king but also providing common pasture and a common mill. The unity of the shire was demonstrated north as well as south of Forth by the office of sheriff, a title that was presumably bestowed on shire thanes as some use of English began to spread among Gaelic-speakers. Scone, for example, hallowed as the place where the Scots kings were solemnly enthroned, was administered for the Crown by a thane who seems to have borne the alternative title of sheriff – hence the farm of Sheriffton between Scone and the Tay, which used to have a salmon fishing attached. Under David I the sheriff of the 'shire' of Dunfermline, a man named Swein, was instructed to assist the Benedictine monks whom the king had brought from Canterbury to serve his new abbey of Dunfermline. Swein was rather exceptional in having an Anglo-Scandinavian name, for most of the earliest known sheriffs north of the Forth bore Celtic names, among them Gillebrigde of Dunfermline, Gillemore and perhaps Gilleserf of Clackmannan, and Malotheni, Ewen, and Macbeth of Scone. These names confirm the belief that as with Cospatric of Roxburgh we are dealing with an old-established native official gentry, and that the shires they managed were of an ancient type. These shires were generally very much smaller than the sheriffdoms created between 1124 and 1286, but an extremely interesting overlap led to a few of the old shires or thanages surviving as historical sheriffdoms, Auchterarder till after 1300, Clackmannan and Kinross until the present day.

It is much harder to give an adequate account of the typical peasant of early-twelfth-century Scotland north of Forth. The evidence is too patchy and jejune to allow us to make any generalizations. Much land was owned by the church and on its estates we know of three classes of lower tenant, all likely to have occupied their holdings or offices heritably. The origins of these rather specialized categories of 'cumelache' (Old Irish *cumalacht*, 'female servitude'), 'cumherba' (O. Ir. *comarba*, 'heir') and *scoloc* (O. Ir., referring to the lowest grade of pupil in a monastic school but ultimately coming to mean a poor farming tenant) must surely be sought in the Ireland from which the Scottish church had drawn so much inspiration between the ninth and eleventh centuries. Just as the 'gresman' survived as the gerseman in the north of Scotland, so also the *scoloc* clearly appears in the Highlands as late as the eighteenth century as the 'sgalag', a particularly despised and depressed species of farm servant.

All three specialist categories would have been included within the portmanteau description of the unfree peasant beloved of the clerks and lawyers of the time, namely 'neyf' (*nativus*, one born within an estate or shire, not free to leave it without the lord's permission). The difficulty here is a lack of precision in our sources, for the word neyf was used with a wide range of meaning, although the essence of his status seems always to have been subjection and dependence *vis à vis* the lord but relative freedom and security *vis à vis* anyone else. The neyf's tenure was precarious, on a short lease or on a year-to-year basis. At the same time, most lords would not wish to evict their neyfs or weaken a class of tenant forming the backbone of their labour force. Surviving documents include a high proportion that show lords going to some lengths to hold on to their neyfs, who in the twelfth century (still more in the next) were easily tempted to abscond and seek better paid jobs or greater freedom in towns or rural industries or merely in another lord's estate. Early in David I's reign a lady named Leviva, whose home was probably somewhere near Dunfermline, seems to have been experiencing precisely this problem of a flight of labour from her estate. She was well-enough connected to be able to seek the king's help to get her farm servants back. 'I command you' (so runs the

royal writ addressed to all the king's loyal subjects throughout his land)
'that wherever this woman Leviva may discover any of her runaway
neyfs they are to be justly restored to her, and no one is to detain them
improperly'. But though the writ would have borne the king's great
seal and was issued at his castle of Edinburgh, we may doubt if it
brought back a single one of Leviva's fugitive servants against their
will, or proves anything but the ease with which they could slip from
her control.

In much of southern Scotland the bonder or husbandman with his
husbandland of 26 acres was probably not a rarity. In the Northern
Isles and Caithness the free bonder was the normal peasant farmer,
almost certainly enjoying greater independence than his namesake in
the south and doubtless having slaves attached to his household to
carry out menial tasks. In the large intervening territory of Scotland
proper it is doubtful whether this type of small peasant, essentially or
theoretically free, existed at all until landlords began to encourage the
formation of such a class during the twelfth and thirteenth centuries,
either through deliberate immigration or by offering better terms to
the sons of existing neyfs. There was also some assimilation in this
period, for we begin to get evidence of gresmen north of the Forth (as
the place-names Grassmiston in East Fife and Grassmainston in Clack-
mannanshire bear witness), and it may be that they took the place of
the *scolocs* who belonged to the old order. Even so, it seems likely that
as late as *c*.1200, in all the provinces of mainland Scotland between
the Clyde−Forth line and Sutherland, the farms held by the smaller
freeholders and the more complex groupings of estates held by great
secular lords, by the earls, by bishops and important churches, were
actually worked, in tillage but more particularly in the grazing of
cattle, pigs, and sheep, by a peasantry enjoying little if any legal
freedom. In practice, the extent of their servitude would have been
lessened　by two things, first by the comparatively high degree of
personal freedom conferred by the pastoral way of life (men whose
wealth is on the hoof can more easily take refuge from oppression than
men who depend on harvesting field crops), and secondly by the
markedly vertical structure of Scottish society. This meant that in
every shire and region what counted was the lineage and kindred to
which a man or woman belonged. Freedom was neither absolute nor
homogeneous, but was experienced and enjoyed at different levels and
in different milieux. This can be illustrated by two pieces of twelfth-
century evidence, one from south of Forth admittedly, but demonstrating conditions that are not likely to have been in sharp contrast

with those to the north. King David I gave the land of Carberry in Midlothian to Dunfermline Abbey, together with certain men of Tweeddale, surprisingly distant, with their descendants, who were to pay a rent to the abbey of one two-year-old ox or four shillings. Clearly the men so dealt with were hardly 'free' as far as the king was concerned. But later in the century Abbot Archibald of Dunfermline, referring to these very same men or their successors, declared: 'Mac Cormi and Edmund, and Edmund's son and heir Michael, and Michael's brothers and sisters, and Mervyn, Gillemichel, Malmuren, Gillecrist and Gillemahagu and all their progeny are *our free men*, dwelling in our peace and by our leave wherever they may be'. The north-country evidence is contained in a charter of King William the Lion in which he includes his thanes of Birse in Aberdeenshire among his *nativi* or neyfs, a sharp reminder that our modern notions of an unbridgeable gulf between a free and privileged aristocracy on the one hand and an oppressed peasantry on the other cannot be squared easily with the concepts actually prevailing in the twelfth century. In any case we should do well to recall the underlying harshness of life in our period. The absence of legal freedom would often have seemed a small enough matter when set beside the threat of harvest failure or epidemic disease among the livestock upon which the very survival of a peasant family depended.

On the threshold of the feudal age Scotland, at the extreme northwest corner of Europe, was a more remote country than it became in the era of sea-borne empires. It was also, however surprisingly, more remote than it had been in earlier centuries when Irish missionaries and Viking raiders were venturing across the ocean. The Scots lords, writing in their famous letter to the pope (1320) of 'This little land of Scotia beyond which there is no human habitation', may be forgiven their hyperbole. Scotland faces west and east, not south, and in consequence historical movements and influences originating in the heart of the west European continent have nearly always reached Scotland slowly and indirectly. Those that have sprung from across the North Sea, from Ireland, or from the far south-west coming by way of Ireland, have made much more rapid progress.

Without any doubt, poverty went with isolation. We must, however, be wary of this word, applied so readily to Scotland by English observers and historians, many of whom believe that to have called Scotland a poor country is to say all that needs to be said. This somewhat grotesque generalization has found a ready echo among those many Scots of the past two centuries whose view of their own country has been informed by a complacent defeatism. Men and women of the medieval centuries were infected neither with misplaced optimism nor fashionable pessimism, but were forced to take life as they found it and make the best of things. Poverty is always relative. Today when we speak of a wealthy country, in popular usage, we may mean a small country where incomes *per caput* are high (as, for example, Sweden or Switzerland), a large country with great capital accumulation and industrial potential, where nevertheless there may be extremes of individual wealth and poverty (e.g., the U.S.A.), or even a country such as the U.S.S.R., where enormous natural resources contrast with very low individual incomes. Such measurements are hardly ascertainable, even roughly, for most medieval European countries. What objective evidence we have indicates that Scotland made no coin of its own before the reign of David I, that foreign money (mostly English and Scandinavian) had a limited circulation, that money rents before 1150 were few, small, and almost confined to Lothian, that an economy based on cattle, pigs, spring-sown cereals, and inshore and river fishing was unlikely to make much headway against the Malthusian checks of famine and disease. On the other side of the balance we may point to the fact that within the limits set by a primitive technology a largely self-sufficient population had succeeded in settling permanently almost every part of the country. In striking testimony to their success, the overwhelming majority of habitation names in the rural areas of Scotland either still in use or at least surviving on the modern map had already come into existence before *c.*1250. Moreover, as far as can be judged the net flow of migration was inward until about the same period, in marked contrast with the position at almost any time since the later fifteenth century.

Beyond the objective evidence we may allow our imagination to wander more freely without verging on fantasy. Scotland in our period was, for a start, a wonderfully quiet country, where nearly all sounds would have stemmed from natural causes like weather and running water, from farm animals, the barking of dogs, the shouts of village children, or the songs of men and women as they worked. The loudest artificial sound familiar to ordinary people may well have come from church bells. Moonlight and starlight would have been much more keenly appreciated than they can possibly be by a generation that takes electricity and the sadly inescapable sodium lamp for granted. There would also have been an immediate and continual assault upon the nose in what was quite literally a stinking country: the warm homely smells of cattle, horses, and hay, of food cooking in stone ovens or on open hearths, mingling unavoidably with the acrid reek of peat fires, the putrid odour of rotting meat and fish or of untreated skins and hides, and in every inhabited locality the stench of animal and human ordure. All but the richest families lived in low houses thatched with turf, heather, or reed, built wholly of timber or perhaps more commonly of turves and rubble fitted round a timber frame. At night and in winter the most valuable beasts occupied one end of the dwelling, the humans of both sexes and all ages finding what living space they could at the other end. The degree of social mobility was slight, and even geographical mobility would have been confined to a minority. Skills of every sort, from husbandry to literacy, were expected to be transmitted from parent to child or at least within an hereditary caste. Sickness and disease were ever-present problems in a hard life, and to remedy them people of all classes had recourse to medical lore which was hardly more than traditional, and to seeking the intercession – or even the frankly magical, superstitious powers – of innumerable saints whose shrines were visited by lepers, by pregnant women hoping for a safe childbirth or barren women hoping for children, by those sick unto death and those with reasonable hopes of a cure. The veneration of some saints was extremely local, of others remarkably widespread, transcending racial, linguistic, and geographical boundaries. For example, a famous Irish saint named Findbarr or Finnén was revered at Kilwinning ('Saint Finnén's church') in Ayrshire, where typically there were his 'seat' (*Suidhe Fhinnein*) and his well; at Kirkgunzeon ('Saint Finnén's church') near Dumfries; and at Dunlichity south of Inverness, where the local people treasured a wooden image of the saint as late as 1643. We may be sure that scores and hundreds of the faithful frequented all three places hoping for a remedy which herbs and simples had failed to provide.

We began our account of Scotland at the turn of the eleventh and twelfth centuries by calling to mind one of the finest views in the modern Scottish landscape. Let us conclude it by evoking another prospect, equally magnificent and certainly much wilder. From Dúnan Mór, the hill that rises from the black promontory of Cape Wrath at the north-west extremity of the Scottish mainland, the view southward takes in five miles of rocky shoreline before ending in the gleaming white beach of Sandwood Bay. Just out of sight, the crofts of Oldshore More and Oldshore Beg preserve in their doubly disguised names the sojourn of some unchronicled Norseman called Asleifr, whose *vík* or inlet this briefly became. To the north-west, if the day is clear, the lonely island of Rona rises into view 40 miles away on the

Atlantic horizon. Long deserted, in 1550 it was 'inhabite and manurit be simple people scant of ony religion' (although they had a chapel dedicated to St Ronan). Eastward the eye is confronted by starkest grandeur, the cliffs of Cló Mór, the highest on the main island of Britain, towering beyond the little Norse-named cove of Kearvaig and terminating in the storm-beaten islet of Garbh-eilean. Cape Wrath might itself be an island, for it cannot be reached save by an atrocious road which floats or sinks, according to the state of the weather, across eight miles of desolate peatmoss. Until recently, even this bad road was accessible only by crossing the Kyle of Durness in a rowing boat. Of course we must allow that even by the standards of Scotland in 1100 the old hunting-ground of the 'Parph' (as the hinterland of Cape Wrath is known) seems bleak, remote, and inhospitable. And yet, if we are to recapture anything of the quality of that still more remote country, we are surely closer to it in the far north of Sutherland than in the douce landscape of Teviotdale with its substantial stone-built farms, trim hedgerows, and big tractor-ploughed fields.

2

Kings and Kingship

Kingship proved to be the most enduring contribution made by the earlier medieval centuries to the common stock of west European political experience. It reached its zenith in the twelfth and thirteenth centuries, although the Carolingian and Ottonian monarchies of the Franks and Germans had been remarkable forerunners of the type of kingship which was then to emerge in its fullest development in several different countries or groups of countries. The shortest list of examples would be found to include Sicily under its most brilliant kings, Roger II and Frederick II, France under Philip Augustus and Louis IX, the Angevin empire under Henry II, England under Edward I, and Castille under Alfonso X. The roots of this kingship were manifold, for the rulers themselves and those who, as theoreticians or executants, advised and supported them drew readily for their models on the Bible, on Greek and Roman history, including the Christian empires of Constantine, Theodosius, and Justinian, as well as on the earlier kingdoms of western Europe going back to the age of barbarian invasions. At its height, the kingship of the medieval west was atavistic and tribal, feudal yet also bureaucratic and centralized, sacred and intensely personal. Saint Louis (King Louis IX of France) styled himself 'king of the Franks', was counselled by powerful territorial magnates called 'peers' (i.e. 'equals'), governed remote provinces through *baillis* and enquêteurs, dispensed justice to his people while sitting under an oak tree at Vincennes, cured the scrofulous by a touch of his fingers, and died at Carthage personally leading a Christian army against the Muslims.

Kingship of this distinctive type had attained such resounding success by the end of the thirteenth century that it made all other kinds seem old-fashioned or peculiar. In 1050, however, it had hardly begun to be recognized. From Scandinavia to the Iberian peninsula, from Ireland to Hungary, western Europe could show a wide variety of royal government. A barbarian, iron-age strain was never far distant from the monarchies of Scandinavia and the British Isles until the end of the eleventh century. The north-country English historian William of Newburgh remarks that down to his own time (the 1180s) it was usual for every king of Norway to reach the throne by killing his predecessor. Ethelred II of England became king because his half-brother was treacherously murdered. Of his sons, Alfred was killed in the interests of Harold I, grandson of Swein Forkbeard, the king of Denmark whose conquest of England had driven Alfred's half-brother Edmund Ironside to defeat and early death. Swein's son Cnut had Edmund's two sons exiled, intending them to be killed. Harold II was slain defending his kingdom against William the Conqueror. William Rufus, the Conqueror's heir, met his death in the New Forest in circumstances that point to murder rather than accident. In contemporary Ireland, where there were scores of kingdoms, it was normal for every king to have a named successor (*tanaise*, 'second man') during his reign. This may have been meant to reduce the threat of casual regicide, but surely gave impatient tanists a dangerous incentive to cut short the natural term of their predecessors. It was in any case not uncommon for Irish kings who escaped being killed outright by their rivals to be blinded or otherwise mutilated.

The kingship of eleventh-century Scotland had been formed three centuries earlier by the fusion of an ancient Pictish monarchy and a specifically Scottish kingship brought from north-east Ireland early in the sixth century. Despite the careful preservation of the presumably Pictish practice of inaugurating a new king at Scone near Perth, Scottish (i.e., historically speaking, 'Irish') features were predominant in this mixed monarchy. This can be seen not only in the Gaelic personal names favoured by the kings (Malcolm, Kenneth, etc.) but also in the enthronement ceremony itself, at which a new king was symbolically 'married' to his kingdom by being placed on the Stone of Destiny, and in the succession customs by which adult, able-bodied males within one generation – brothers or first cousins – were preferred to sons or nephews under age. There had been total rejection of the Pictish practice, unique in the British Isles, of restricting the royal succession to the sons of women, not men, belonging to the royal lineage, so that no king of the Picts could be the son of a previous king of the Picts. It is noteworthy that all the kings were buried on Iona, the holiest sanctuary of the Gaelic west, strongly Scottish, not Pictish, in its associations. An element of tanistry may have been present in the early eleventh century, but from Malcolm II onwards there was a clear tendency for kings to secure the succession for their own direct descendants rather than allow it to pass to collaterals, whereas in true Irish custom it was rare for any son of the reigning king ever to be the tanist.

Three exceptionally long-reigning and powerful kings dominated Scotland in the eleventh century, Malcolm II Mackenneth (1005–34), Macbeth Macfinlay (1040–57), and Malcolm III Macduncan, nicknamed Canmore ('large headed'), who ruled from 1058 to 1093. Malcolm II, who had duly slain his predecessor Giric at Monzievaird near Crieff, belonged to what may be called the main Scottish royal line. The base of his power was the heartland of the Scoto-Pictish kingdom, formerly called Fortriu, the country between the Clyde–Forth line on the south and, on the north, the principal east–west mountain range of Scotland, the 'Mounth', reaching from Ben Nevis to the North Sea near Stonehaven. By winning the battle of Carham on Tweed in 1018 Malcolm II made sure of permanent Scottish possession of Lothian and brought strong pressure to bear upon Cumbria, hitherto a distinct kingdom fluctuating between dependence on the Scots to the north and being a satellite of the powerful West Saxon monarchy advancing from the south. When the native Cumbrian dynasty became extinct, Malcolm II set up as ruler of this region his grandson Duncan, son of his only firmly recorded child Bethoc and her husband Cronan or Crinan, abbot (i.e. head of the secularized monastery) of Dunkeld in central Perthshire. Contemporary writers, Scandinavian and Norman, differ as to whether Malcolm II was subject to the lordship of Cnut, the extremely powerful king of Denmark and England who died in 1035. Without resolving the conflict we may take seriously their statements that King Malcolm had his headquarters in Fife (at Dunfermline?) and that he was both a pious Christian and an effective warrior – after all, he was the victor of Carham and found time to give his royal revenues from Biffie in Buchan to the little community of monastic clergy settled near by at Old Deer.

Contrary to Scottish custom, Malcolm II was followed on the throne by his daughter's son Duncan, ruler of Cumbria, but the attempt to establish a single linear dynasty was thwarted by intervention from the north. In earlier generations a few kings of Scots had been drawn not, like the majority, from the senior 'line of Fergus', but from the junior 'line of Loarn' (both Fergus and Loarn were sons of Erc, traditional ancestor of the Dalriadan royal house). The line of Loarn was still represented in the eleventh century by the rulers (mormaers) of the large province of Moray which stretched from east of the River Spey right across to the west coast at Loch Alsh and from the Mounth northward to Ross. In 1040 King Duncan, apparently on an expedition against the men of Moray, was defeated and killed at Pitgaveny near Elgin by the mormaer Macbeth Macfinlay. Macbeth was at once accepted as king of Scotland and drove into exile Duncan's two eldest sons, Malcolm and Donald Bán. Despite his Moray origins, Macbeth took over the strongholds of royal power in the south, good evidence that the political centre of gravity for a viable Scoto-Pictish kingdom lay in the region between Perth and Edinburgh. Almost certainly, Macbeth campaigned against the Norsemen of Caithness and Orkney, the old enemies of Moray, but it was the security of his southern frontier which was to prove more critical in the long run. The earldom of Northumbria, temporarily weakened by the battle of Carham, had been given by Cnut to the doughty warrior Siward, who may have been King Duncan's brother-in-law and lived until 1055. It was in any case natural that King Duncan's elder son Malcolm should take refuge with Siward, and because of his political importance he went on to become the protégé of the English king Edward the Confessor, who granted him the rich manor of Corby in Northamptonshire. In spite of threatening clouds on northern and southern horizons King Macbeth ruled firmly for more than a decade. Following Cnut's example, in 1050 he travelled as a pilgrim to Rome where, perhaps with the remote barbarian's anxiety not to seem penurious, he scattered largesse 'like seed' to the poor. This we learn on the good authority of an Irish monk named Marianus (Maelbrigte) who from his austere Rhineland cell took a keen interest in the doings of his fellow countrymen (as he saw them), the Gael of both Ireland and Scotland. The native Irish annals likewise pay much attention to Scottish affairs in this period. To at least one Irish writer, whose history is thinly disguised as 'prophecy', Macbeth was the 'generous king of Fortriu', the 'ruddy-complexioned, yellow haired tall one in whom I shall rejoice'.

If Macbeth represented Scottish conservatism he ought not to have objected to the manner of his downfall. In 1054 the normally pacific Edward of England commanded Earl Siward to invade Scotland, drive out Macbeth, and establish his protégé Malcolm Macduncan on the throne. In a battle fought at Dunsinnan Hill north-east of Scone, Malcolm and Siward led a mixed Anglo-Scandinavian and Scottish army to decisive victory over Macbeth, even though the king had stiffened the ranks of his own force with Norman mercenaries, the first ever seen in Scotland. Macbeth was put to flight and Malcolm acknowledged as ruler over most of southern Scotland. Three years later, on

15 August 1057, Macbeth met his doom at Lumphanan north of the River Dee, but even then his supporters, presumably still strong in the north, chose the late king's stepson, Lulach Macgillecomgan, as king of Scots. The reign of Malcolm Macduncan, better known as Malcolm III Canmore, may be formally reckoned only from March 1058, when King Lulach was ambushed and killed at Essie in Strathbogie, Aberdeenshire, and was duly buried on Iona.

For eight years it looks as though Malcolm III's most serious problems were concerned with the internal pacification of Scotland and its defence against Scandinavian pressure. For half a century the dominant figure in the north had been Thorfinn Sigurd's son, earl of Orkney and Caithness, founder of the remarkable church of Christ at Birsay in the west of Orkney where he lies buried. Thorfinn was probably the enemy of Macbeth, and in any event his friends tended to be the friends of Malcolm III. On Thorfinn's death in (or before?) 1065, King Malcolm married his widow Ingibjorg, daughter of Finn, Arni's son. The marriage was a shrewd move calculated to neutralize some of the potential hostility that any king of Scotland might expect from the far north. In fact, it had more lasting consequences, bringing the earldom of Orkney into close relationship with the central province of Scotland, Atholl, whose ruler was Malcolm III's brother Maelmuire.

On Earl Siward's death in 1055, Edward the Confessor ill-advisedly chose in his place the West Saxon trouble-maker Tostig, brother of Harold, Godwin's son, already immensely powerful as earl of Wessex and the obvious native English choice to succeed the childless Edward as king. The raid which Malcolm inflicted on Northumbria in 1061 may have been partly in support of Siward's son Waltheof or the kindred of the ancient earls, but in general Malcolm's relations with England and Tostig remained peaceful. In 1065, however, Tostig was ejected from his earldom by a violent Northumbrian revolt and fled to Flanders. After Harold had become king in 1066 a bitter quarrel between the brothers led to Tostig's appearance first in Scotland to win King Malcolm's support and then at the court of the king of Norway, the fierce Harald Hardrada. There they planned a massive invasion of England, to be launched from Orkney, designed to allow Hardrada and Tostig to divide England south of the Tees between them, while their Scottish ally Malcolm would presumably have annexed English Northumbria north of the Tees. From a northern standpoint, the autumn onslaught upon Harold of England should be seen as the attempt of the Scandinavian world to re-assert its dominance in the rich country of southern Britain, lost after Cnut's death. The quite separate onslaught being carefully prepared by William the Bastard duke of Normandy must have appeared to the northerners as a wholly unwanted and irrelevant nuisance, and it may reasonably be guessed that had the Norwegians won the battle of Stamford Bridge they would have bargained with Duke William for at least the northern two-thirds of England or else have fought him for the whole. If that had happened it is hard to see how Malcolm of Scotland could have avoided becoming a Norwegian vassal.

The event, as everyone knows, turned out quite otherwise. On 23 September 1066 Hardrada and Tostig were killed and their shattered army compelled to withdraw. Within three weeks (14 October) King Harold, the victor of Stamford Bridge, was himself laid low on the hill north of Hastings where now stand the ruins of Battle Abbey. Within four years William of Normandy had made himself master of England from the Channel to the River Tees. From 1066 onwards, Scottish relations with England were relations with Norman England. For the rest of King Malcolm's life they were bad, open hostility alternating with sullen suspicion. For this, the Scots ruler's personal attachment to the old West Saxon house may be partly to blame. Nevertheless, the Norman Conquest had produced a fundamentally different situation. We cannot doubt that Malcolm was aware of the change or blame him for fearing that it would lead to the destruction of his kingdom. For his part, William the Conqueror, although probably not the conscious exponent of a new type of monarchy, was a sure judge of contemporary politics. He would not have considered the kingship of the Scots as the equal of the royal dominion and authority he had won for himself in England. That authority was already conceived of in English clerical circles as 'imperial', conferring lordship over all Britain, although this was not an aspect which the Conqueror himself ever emphasized. But he would have known that quite apart from the scores of tribal kings in Ireland there were in the Britain of his own time kings of the south Welsh and of the north Welsh, kings of Powys and Ceredigion, kings of the Manxmen and of the Isles, kings of the men of Galloway and at least a strong memory of kings of Cumbria. In his eyes the king of Scots was not different in kind from these other kings, merely different in the extent of his territory and number of fighting men.

In 1057 Edward the atheling ('prince'), the elder of Edward the Confessor's two nephews, sons of Edmund Ironside, whom Cnut had sent into exile in eastern Europe, returned to England from a lengthy sojourn in Hungary. There he had been treated with honour and had found a wife, Agatha, probably half-niece of the Emperor Henry III the Salian[1]. He might have been preferred to Harold or any other candidate for the throne, but died soon after his return, leaving a young son, Edgar the atheling, and two older daughters, Margaret and Christina. Probably Margaret was the oldest, born in the 1040s during the reign of the strongly Christian but also strongly nationalist King Andrew, founder of the monastery of Tihany on the north shore of Lake Balaton. Margaret was brought up in the evangelical atmosphere of a Hungary only recently and by no means completely converted from paganism to the Catholic faith by Saint Stephen (died 1038). We may safely assume that her strict and pious religious education would have begun early and would not have been relaxed after she came to England.

In the aftermath of William of Normandy's victory at Hastings many Englishmen in the midlands and north refused to submit to the Conqueror and naturally chose the young atheling Edgar as at least their symbolic rallying-point if not their actual leader. In 1068, when it appeared that William would gain control of northern England, several Northumbrian diehards fled to Scotland taking Edgar and his sisters with them. King Malcolm, by now evidently a widower, was captivated by Margaret and, allegedly to the dismay of the English refugees, who could hardly refuse him, insisted on marrying her. The marriage had enduring significance in the history of Scotland for two reasons. In the first place, it brought down on Malcolm the suspicion, not to say the wrath of William the Conqueror, although in the longer term a close family relationship between the Scots and English royal houses was cemented with the marriage between the Conqueror's youngest son Henry I and Edith the elder daughter of Malcolm and Margaret. Secondly, and no less formatively, the marriage of Malcolm and Margaret initiated and inspired a drastic reorientation of Scottish society. The way was opened up for continental and English influences of every kind to pour into Scotland, most conspicuously in the life of the church but by no means confined to religious faith or ecclesiastical organization. Perhaps the most important consequence of the marriage, however, lay in the fact that Margaret bore her husband six sons and two daughters. Of the daughters, the elder, changing her name from Edith (which the Normans could not pronounce) to Maud or Matilda, became queen of England, while the younger, Mary,

[1] I owe this suggestion to the investigations of Mr Gabriel Ronay.

married the count of Boulogne and was mother of another Queen Maud of England, wife of Stephen of Blois. As for the sons, the first-born Edward was killed by treachery, with his father, in 1093, the second, Edmund, allied himself to his uncle Donald Bán and ended his days in prison, while Ethelred, the third son, although permitted to hold the secularized abbey of Dunkeld (of which his great-grandfather had been lord), along with Fife, the premier earldom of Scotland, was never a candidate for the throne. But the three youngest, Edgar, Alexander, and David, who were successively kings from 1097 to 1153, all showed in their lives the decisive influence of their mother and a marked attachment to the Norman royal house.

Once English Northumbria had fallen to the Normans it must have seemed clear to Malcolm III that its neighbours Cumbria and Lothian were at risk. He can have needed little encouragement from the English fugitives at his court to embark on a savage raid in 1070 which took the Scots as far as Cleveland and Harterness. In 1072 William I, who could not ignore this provocation, brought a large army, supported by a fleet, into southern Scotland and pursued Malcolm as far as Abernethy on the Tay. There the Scots king, in the heart of his own ancestral kingdom, bowed to William and became his vassal, agreeing at the same time to give shelter no longer to any of William's enemies, including Edgar the atheling. Not surprisingly, the ceremony at Abernethy was to be recalled long afterwards by English kings as proof of Scotland's subjection to England, and at the time of the Union of 1707 a perfervid Scots patriot went so far as to excise the offending words 'became his vassal' from an early chronicle which narrates the event. But it is doubtful if to Malcolm the homage was more than recognition of the harsh fact that his army was no match for Norman mailed knights. Instead of going down in glory like the heroically suicidal English at Maldon and Hastings, Malcolm would give up his eldest son Duncan as a hostage and live to raid another day.

Malcolm's third invasion of England came in 1079 when he was at the height of his power. King William's response was surprisingly muted: he despatched his eldest son Robert Curthose to Lothian in 1080, admittedly at the head of an army, but also with a team of diplomats, including the abbot of Abingdon. The failure of their conference with the Scots at Falkirk is underlined by the fact that on his way south Robert built, by way of frontier defence, the 'New Castle' at the north end of the vital Tyne bridgehead, 80 miles south of the Tweed. It was not the Conqueror but his son William II Rufus who proved to be Malcolm's undoing and converted Scotland into a client kingdom for some 30 or 40 years.

After William the Conqueror's death in 1087 Duncan of Scotland, King Malcolm's heir, was set free and knighted by Robert Curthose. Three years later, Edgar the atheling, spurned by William II, paid the last of his many visits to Scotland and persuaded Malcolm to invade Northumbria for the fourth time. Rufus led an army north as his father had done in 1072, and somewhere in Lothian he forced Malcolm to renew the pact of Abernethy, apparently in an atmosphere of friendship. But in 1092 the English king seized Carlisle, built a castle there to match Newcastle on the east, and drove out the provincial ruler of Cumbria appointed by Malcolm. Since this was precisely the aggressive 'forward policy' the Scots must have feared, it is hard to know what satisfaction Malcolm can have hoped to obtain from a conference Rufus agreed to hold with him at Gloucester. When Malcolm arrived, however, Rufus simply refused to see him, and the infuriated king of Scots returned north to lead his last raid into Northumberland. As he and his second son, Edward, were riding homeward they were attacked treacherously, on the hill north of Alnwick, by Robert de Mowbray, the Norman to whom William I had entrusted the Northumbrian earldom. Robert's nephew Arkil Morel, King Malcolm's 'sworn brother' (who was afterwards to betray his uncle and many fellow-knights to Rufus), slew the Scots king and his son. When the news was brought to her at Edinburgh, Queen Margaret died of grief, and a violent reaction against new-fangled Norman ways brought to power the king's brother Donald Bán. Obviously at the bidding of a resentful native aristocracy, he expelled the Normans and southern English brought in under Malcolm and Margaret. Malcolm's eldest son Duncan, trained by the Normans in the art of knighthood of which they were the acknowledged masters, rode to Scotland at the head of a force supplied by his patron Rufus. Driving out King Donald, Duncan held the throne for almost a year (1094) in a reign as uneasy as it was short-lived, for the new king was forced to dismiss the very Anglo-Norman retainers on whom he depended. He was murdered at Mondynes near Stonehaven by Maelpetair, mormaer (or thane?) of Mearns, and Donald Bán was restored. It was now the turn of Edgar, oldest of Margaret's sons to be *persona grata* at the Norman court, and with more active help from Rufus than Duncan had enjoyed he took an army to Scotland in 1097, captured and blinded Donald (the last Scots king whose remains were buried on Iona), and ruled for 10 years. The peacefulness of his reign proved Edgar's ability, but he was clearly the dependent client or vassal of the Norman kings of England.

Edgar died unmarried and the succession passed to his next brother, Alexander I, whose name, unprecedented in Scotland, was probably in honour of Alexander II, pope at the time of Queen Margaret's marriage. Although he must have done homage to Henry I, whose bastard daughter Sybil he took as his wife, Alexander I seems to have taken a more independent line than Duncan II or Edgar. Instead of relying on mercenaries or other temporary foreign support, Alexander began to build castles (e.g. at Stirling) and allot lands out of royal demesne to men who would settle permanently, performing military service in return for their estates which thus became the 'knights' feus' or military fiefs destined to fill an enduring place in the Scottish social and political landscape. Alexander had probably been allowed during Edgar's reign to rule much of southern Scotland between Forth and Solway. Certainly such an arrangement was envisaged by Edgar, in respect of his two younger brothers, for the years following his own death. We are told that when it came to the point Alexander was reluctant to transfer so much territory to his brother David, who threatened to seize it with a stronger force of Norman knights than the king himself could muster.

With the 29-year reign of David I, beginning in April 1124, the kingship of Scotland moves at once into a new epoch. The change is neatly symbolized by the earliest charter to survive from the reign, issued at Scone probably on the occasion of David's enthronement. By this charter the king granted to one of the senior Normans in his entourage, Robert of Brus, lordship over the whole of Annandale, a district of 200,000 acres adjacent to the English border north of Carlisle. Brus, now spelled Brix, is a small village near Cherbourg in western Normandy, and Robert had won the favour of Henry I who gave him Cleveland and Harterness in north-east England. This first Robert of Brus, thus shown equal favour by Henry I and his protégé David of Scotland, cannot have considered himself either an Englishman or a Scot, but his younger son Robert inherited Annandale and the lordship remained with the family of Bruce (to give them their familiar spelling) till the fourteenth century, long before which they had become thoroughly Scottish. David's charter for Bruce is written in the professional 'shorthand' of a full-time royal scribe. There were nine witnesses, of whom eight were incoming Normans and the ninth a household official from David's English estates, probably himself an Englishman.

At first glance, therefore, it might seem that David I, knighted and educated by Henry I of England, was merely completing what his brothers had embarked on half-heartedly, a Norman conquest of Scotland. That impression is reinforced by considering the other things that King David either introduced or developed further than his predecessors. He was the first king of Scots to employ moneyers to strike his own coinage, silver pennies or 'sterlings' which enjoyed parity with English sterlings (as, indeed, Scots currency was to do until the mid fourteenth century). He established a new type of sheriffdom closely resembling that employed by the Norman kings of England, so that it is from his reign that we can date the familiar 'counties' of Scotland which lasted until 1975, though only about half a dozen of them had been created before David I's death. These new sheriffdoms or counties were much larger than the old shires or thanages which they gradually replaced, and the new sheriffs were intended to deal with much of the business of royal government including the supervision of the new baronial class of feudatories who could well have overawed the older thanes. As a complement to the sheriff David I introduced the office of 'justiciar', a title held by the highest administrative and judicial officer under the crown – again, clearly modelled on Norman England. David increased the total of royal castles, constructed in the most up-to-date Norman fashion. This normally combined an essential *motte*, or ditched and palisaded mound surmounted by a timber *donjon* or keep, with an optional outer court or *bailey*, separated from the *motte* by an internal ditch but defended externally by its own ditches and palisades.

King David greatly accelerated the process of feudalization, so that by the end of his reign a vast area of Scotland south of Forth had been allocated to tenants (almost all newcomers) holding by military service, who enjoyed the right to transmit their estates to their sons or other heirs by blood or family relationship. Even Moray in the far north was rapidly feudalized. Its native earl Angus, grandson of King Lulach, rebelled in 1130 and when his army had been defeated and himself killed at Stracathro near Brechin, David annexed the whole province for the crown and set up foreign feudatories there. Of even more lasting importance, however, than coins, castles, or feudalism were the burghs – privileged, corporate merchant communities – which King David founded in almost every part of his kingdom outside the essentially highland area. 'He illumined in his days his land with kirks and with abbeys', says the fifteenth-century chronicler Andrew Wyntoun. Religious illumination must be left for a later chapter, but it would be no flight of fancy to add that David I brought light into

Scotland through the many trading communities he founded or
favoured, from Berwick at the mouth of the Tweed to Aberdeen and
Inverness in the north, from Roxburgh and Edinburgh on the east to
Rutherglen, Renfrew, and Irvine on the west. Jealous, quarrelsome,
and monopolistic they may have been, but the new burghs opened up
the country to a profitable intercourse in which raw materials
provided by Scotland crossed the sea to Flanders and northern
Germany while manufactured goods and new skills and techniques
were brought to enrich native society.

Such an explosion of new ideas, policies, and practices could hardly
have happened within a single generation unless Scotland had had a
king of exceptional energy and determination, backed up by a cohort
of like-minded strangers wielding, or protected by, formidable
military power. And yet it would be wrong to see David I as no more
than a Scottish counterpart of William the Bastard. Even though he
found the undisguised paganism of the inauguration ceremony abhor-
rent, he showed consistent reverence for many of the native saints of
his realm, Mungo of Glasgow, Fechin of Lesmahagow, Cuthbert of
Melrose, and Columba of Iona, to name only four among a multitude.
David may have destroyed individual native magnates or even dynasties, such as the earls of Moray and Ross, but he made no attempt to
replace the native aristocracy as a class. On the contrary, some 10
provincial earldoms which either certainly or very probably existed in
the eleventh century were still occupied in the 1150s and '60s by heads
of native families, and with the earls of Fife and Dunbar the king seems
to have enjoyed a close and friendly relationship. When the king went
to war against Stephen of England it is noteworthy that he led no mere
force of Norman knights and mercenaries but a national army
composed of men drawn from Lothian, Galloway, Argyll, and the
north, whose reported warcry of 'Albannaich' ('Scots') was a truly
national slogan. This 'common' or 'Scottish' army, as it was known,
could not have been called up for service save with the full co-
operation of the earls whose immemorial right it was to raise the men
of their provinces for war. Within his own royal household the king
introduced many new offices, filling them with foreigners such as the
Breton Walter son of Alan, first of the Stewarts, or the Norman Hugh
de Morville, the first hereditary constable of Scotland. But David I
continued to be served by a Gaelic-speaking *rannaire* or 'divider of
food' and by doorwards (Durwards, or royal bodyguards) whom he
must have inherited from his Celtic ancestors.

King David may have owed his own name (never before used in

Scotland, but from his time onward the best-loved of Scottish men's names) to his mother's regard for the royal house of Hungary, if, for example, King Solomon or his brother David (mentioned in early Hungarian chronicles) had been her godfather. Perhaps it was due merely to her wish to honour the Old Testament ruler most admired by Christians. It is, however, significant that David gave his first-born son his own father's wholly Scottish name of Malcolm ('servant of Columba'), emphasizing the continuity of the dynasty. The child was murdered in infancy by a clerical psychopath, and the king's second son was named after his patron Henry I of England. Nevertheless, respect for the dynasty and its Scottish character was again shown in the next generation, when Henry's eldest son was christened Malcolm.

We ought therefore to see David MacMalcolm as a man of two worlds, conscious that the roots of his own kingship lay far back in the past of Scotland, but even more aware that in Norman England and on the continent there was being demonstrated a quite different kind of kingship which he had to imitate if he and his dynasty were to survive. Imitation was made easier by the circumstances of David's upbringing and marriage. Educated from his teens and trained as a knight in the household of Henry Beauclerk, David served his patron on both sides of the Channel and was, it seems, rewarded with a small lordship in the Cotentin. At Christmas 1113, Henry I gave him in marriage the rich heiress Maud (Matilda), widow of Simon de Senlis and daughter of Waltheof, Siward's son, earl of Northumbria (who had been beheaded for rebellion in 1075) and his wife Judith, the Conqueror's niece. With the marriage David was given not the earldom of Northumbria, which Henry took care to keep in his own hands, but the vast complex of estates in east midland England known as 'Waltheof's earldom' or more commonly the 'Honour of Huntingdon', based chiefly on Huntingdon, Bedford, and Northampton.

The possession of such a large stake in the Norman kingdom of England brought with it both advantages and disadvantages. Being lord of the Honour of Huntingdon made David of Scotland wealthy even by English standards – certainly putting him at the head of the second rank among the greatest English magnates. These south-country assets, moreover, could often be realized in the form of cash, which was far from true of the royal demesnes north of the Border. The Honour also provided a convenient catchment area within which to recruit men (often younger sons) to come north and settle permanently in Scotland as military tenants of the crown. Even if the importance of Huntingdon in this respect has been exaggerated, nevertheless the lengthy sojourns that David was encouraged to make at the attractive manors within his English lordship (for example, Earls Barton and Fotheringay, Yardley Hastings and Tottenham) led to innumerable contacts with young hopefuls of the feudal class who were in no way daunted by a colder climate, foreign languages, and a strange culture if there was a prospect of being promoted in the Scottish realm to power and wealth they could not hope to achieve in northern France or England. The later Scots proverb 'Ane crook of the Forth is worth a kingdom in the North' was not one that would have appealed to these eager adventurers who from the earlier decades of the twelfth century began to flock into Scotland from western Wessex (especially Somerset), the east midlands, Yorkshire, and certain continental districts, in particular Normandy, Picardy, and French Flanders.

Migration, however, could bring problems of divided loyalty. As long as Scotland continued to seem very remote from England and David I remained on good terms with the English king, as was the case until Henry I's death in December 1135, such problems can hardly have been acute. But as more and more links were forged between Scotland and the south and as relations between David and Stephen worsened from suspicion to outright enmity it must often have been difficult for one individual to stay loyal to both kings or even for a family to hold together if one member was a landowner in England or Normandy while another had become a Scottish baron. The problem was of course most serious and urgent at the highest level: the relations of King David himself and his son and heir Henry with the kings of England. For a century, from 1136 to 1237, the English estates held by the Scottish crown played a part in Anglo-Scottish relations closely comparable to that played in Anglo-French relations by the lands that English kings held south of the Channel in the twelfth and thirteenth centuries.

On New Year's Day 1127 Henry I, holding a great council at London, commanded the leading magnates of his realm, lay and ecclesiastical, to swear fealty to his daughter Maud (widow of the Emperor Henry V, king of Germany) as rightful heir to the English throne and Norman duchy. Since Adeliza of Louvain, Henry's second wife, was still alive, there was a proviso that any son of the king yet to be born would take precedence of the empress. The marriage proved childless and the oath to Maud was repeated in 1131, three years after she had married Geoffrey Plantagenet (soon to be count of Anjou) but two years before the birth of her oldest child Henry, afterwards King

Henry II. David of Scotland was the first lay magnate to swear fealty to the empress in 1127. There is no reason to disbelieve the statement of a contemporary chronicler that David remembered his oath nine years later, when instead of Maud succeeding peacefully to the English realm on her father's death her cousin Stephen of Blois seized the throne. His *coup* had the support of many Anglo-Norman barons who hated the thought of being ruled by a woman and the prospect of the renowned line of Rollo descending through a female to the despised Angevins.

Stephen had also taken the oath to the empress in 1127, so that it was an easy matter for David I to represent him as a perjured usurper and invade northern England as a gesture of support for his niece. It is probable that David was entirely sincere in upholding her claim but what must have been uppermost in his mind was the recovery of south Cumbria (from Solway southward to the River Duddon and Stainmore Common), lost to Scotland in 1092, and gaining control of the earldom of Northumberland from Tweed to Tees, perhaps in the name of his son, a grandson of Earl Waltheof. In other words, he genuinely wished to see Maud on the English throne but only on condition that she accepted Scots suzerainty over Cumbria and acknowledged Henry of Scotland (and presumably future Scottish kings) as earls of Northumberland. It is a measure of David's consistency that these were the terms he obtained from the 16-year-old Henry of Anjou in 1149, and these seem to have been the terms sought by William the Lion, David's grandson, when he joined the great revolt against Henry II in 1173.

David's dealings with Stephen and the Empress Maud reflect realism rather than duplicity and are especially important as evidence of how the Scots saw their kingship during the first of the three medieval periods (1136–53, 1266–86, and 1314–29) in which it was at the height of its power and authority. In particular David's assertion of independence against any claims that Stephen might put forward shows that he had repudiated the status of client king. This is confirmed by what we know of David's unsuccessful attempt, to be discussed in a later chapter, to have St Andrews recognized as a metropolitan see. By the first treaty of Durham (February 1136) David retained Cumbria, restored Northumberland and Newcastle upon Tyne, and, refusing homage to Stephen on his own part, nevertheless allowed his son to do homage in respect of the Honour of Huntingdon. At Stephen's Easter court Henry of Scotland, probably because he was already 'king-designate', was given the place of honour at the king of

England's right hand, deeply offending the archbishop of Canterbury who claimed the place as his by ancient right. Thereafter, relations with Stephen deteriorated rapidly. The empress appealed to her uncle for help and the Scots invaded Northumberland early in 1138, ravaging the country with fire and sword. The language in which the monastic chroniclers describe the invasion is so hysterical and uncircumstantial that it suggests a good deal of exaggeration, but we need not doubt that terrible crimes were perpetrated by the heterogeneous army, English, Norman, Flemish, Scots, and Gallovidian, called up by King David's 'general edict' and unleashed upon northern England in the depth of winter. It is, however, noteworthy that while the chroniclers are eloquent about the atrocities committed in districts remote from their own monasteries, they admit, when dealing with events nearer home, that David I granted his special protection to churches such as Hexham Abbey and Tynemouth Priory. While besieging Norham Castle on the Tweed, on 11 June 1138, the king addressed a 'brieve' (a written, sealed command) to his French, English, Scots, and Gallovidian lieges in which he declared: 'Know that I, with the consent of my son Henry, have granted my peace to the church of Saint Mary and Saint Oswin the martyr at Tynemouth, its monks and domestic servants and all who on Saint Barnabas' Day, 1138, were under the protection of that church, for the souls of my father and mother and King Alexander my brother and of my sister Maud queen of England, as long as the monks and men of that church conduct themselves peaceably towards us'. The continental quality of David's entourage is typically emphasized by the letter's witness list which, in addition to the native Northumbrian Earl Cospatric II of Dunbar, names Hugh de Morville the royal constable, Manasser Marmion, Robert Foliot, Hugh of Eu, and Hugh le Breton. It is in documents such as this, many of which survive, that we hear the authentic voice of King David I.

The spring and early summer of 1138 were spent by the Scots devastating Northumberland, killing and burning, while King Stephen, combining great energy with lack of any clear strategy, took an army to kill and burn in Lothian. In the later summer, one month after raising what was probably the largest force ever taken into England by a Scottish king, David I suffered a full-scale military defeat at the hands of an Anglo-Norman army fighting in the name of Stephen but in truth to save Yorkshire from the fate which had befallen Northumberland. The battle, fought (22 August) on Cowton Moor between Northallerton and the Tees, was made memorable by the erection on a waggon of a high mast or 'Standard' (French, *étendard*) on which were displayed a casket with the consecrated host and the banners of Saint Peter of York and other northern English saints. Only a small and indecisive part of the battle took the form of a cavalry engagement. The main encounter was between knights, dismounted but clad in mail, and well combined with archers, on the English side, and unarmoured, half-naked infantry, mostly spearmen, on the Scots side. It was body-armour and accurate shooting, coupled no doubt with Norman self-confidence, that won the day. King Stephen, however, hard-pressed in southern England and influenced by his wife who 'greatly loved her uncle the king of Scots', was unable to exploit the victory. Forced for a time to withdraw to the present Border line, David was still strong enough to obtain, in the second treaty of Durham (9 April 1139), terms that on balance were actually more favourable than those of 1136. David did no homage to Stephen, while his son was given the earldom of Northumberland and allowed to keep the Honour of Huntingdon. The Scots' only sacrifice was to give up a quartet of nobly-born hostages. Stephen may have thought it a gain that with his approval Henry of Scotland married into the great Norman house of Varenne (Warenne) which supported him against the empress, but David I remained firmly attached to the Angevin cause and found many friends in England throughout the 1140s. He took part in Maud's unsuccessful bid for the throne in 1141, and although her failure led to the Scots losing the Honour of Huntingdon King David and his son effectively ruled over the whole of England north of Tees and Duddon until 1152, when Earl Henry, a young man of high promise approaching his prime, tragically died before he could succeed his father.

It was therefore to a Scottish ruler at the height of his prestige that the youthful Henry of Anjou turned for help in 1149, coming to Carlisle at Whitsuntide and being welcomed and knighted by David I in a ceremony of some splendour. David's military assistance proved feeble but his moral encouragement was undoubtedly valuable. Henry went so far as to promise that if he gained the English throne (which he did in 1154) he would leave the Scots in possession of Cumbria and Northumberland, a promise he broke as early as 1157.

In the decade preceding the death of Henry of Scotland we can see how David viewed the monarchy which he had now held with enough distinction to excite the notice and admiration of western Christendom. In his hands the kingdom of the Scots (for he never attempted to call it by any other name, despite the importance of Cumbria,

Lothian, and even English Northumbria in his scheme of things) reached from Caithness to Westmorland, from Argyll and Kintyre to Berwick and in a sense to Newcastle and Durham. The dynasty was to descend lineally like that of the Capets, which he admired and imitated, from father to son. By 1144 (very possibly by 1136) his heir Henry was acknowledged as *rex designatus*, king-designate, and indeed shared much of the work of royal government. The queen of Scots, Maud, daughter of Waltheof, had died in 1131, but Henry's marriage to Ada de Varenne produced three sons and three or four daughters. As soon as Henry died David commanded Earl Duncan I of Fife, the senior magnate of Scotland, to take the king's 11-year-old grandson Malcolm through the different provinces of the realm and show him to the people as the king's heir — in other words, to 'designate' him. To secure his new southern frontier of the Tees, King David personally invested Henry's second son William (named after his maternal grandfather) with the earldom of Northumberland. The boy was received reluctantly by the local Norman baronage, suspicious of Scottish aggrandisement.

The prestige of the monarchy was enhanced by the formation of a court and council comparable, though obviously on a smaller scale, with those of Norman England and Capetian France. The household was provided with hereditary offices of a continental, feudal type: a *dapifer* or steward to supervise the king's hall and the household personnel, a constable to command the king's knights, one or more marischals to assist the constable, and a butler to ensure supplies of good wine. Among the non-heritable offices, exclusively or customarily held by churchmen, the most important was that of chancellor, who supervised the court chaplains, had charge of the king's 'chapel' or writing-office and was responsible for the king's seal by which, in an age when kings were not supposed to be, and normally were not, literate, all charters, brieves, and letters were authenticated. The chancellor ranked as one of the leading councillors of the king and would normally expect to be rewarded with a bishopric at the end of his term of office. Royal finances, rapidly growing in importance in the twelfth century as coin and money of account began to supersede foodstuffs and other commodities in all but the lowliest and most local transactions, were the business of the chamberlain. Some chamberlains were clerics but more were laymen, although the office was slow to become hereditary. Strictly speaking, the king's chamber was where he slept, ate (save on solemn occasions), and led what little life he had that could be called private. That the chamberlain who had charge of this part of the household was responsible for the king's rents and treasure is a reminder that although Scottish kingship under David I might have been brought into line with the most up-to-date European models it remained in many ways intimate and domestic.

The north-country Englishman Ailred of Hexham who became famous as abbot of the Cistercian monastery of Rievaulx in Yorkshire began his working career in King David's household and has left us a vivid, though perhaps slightly idealized, portrait of life at the Scottish court. He tells us that it was the king's custom to sit at the door of the hall at whatever royal residence he happened to be, so that he could hear and deal personally with the grievances brought to him by widows, the poor, and the afflicted. In similar vein, we have a story from one of the senior chaplains of William I, King David's grandson, that on one occasion King William overslept and his household officials, anxious to get on with their duties, urged the reluctant clerks of the king's chapel to celebrate the first mass of the day even though the king was not yet awake and the chapel was only a short distance from the royal bedchamber. It is thus that we should see the itinerant royal household of twelfth-century Scotland as the king and his relations, his friends, guests, knights, retainers, and hangers-on travelled the length and breadth of the country with court officers who were simultaneously domestic servants and national administrators. This sizeable community, at once family and government, sojourned for a few days at a time, while food supplies lasted, at the newly-built castles and royal halls of Carlisle, Cadzow, Peebles, · Roxburgh, Berwick upon Tweed, Edinburgh, Stirling, Perth, Forfar, Aberdeen, Inverness and a number of other centres favoured by the kings because of their good communications, secure defences, or quiet seclusion as hunting lodges.

By remarkably good fortune we possess a contemporary double portrait of King David I and his eldest grandson King Malcolm IV. It is incorporated within the initial letter M of Malcolm's great charter for Kelso Abbey, dating from 1159 and now preserved at the National Library of Scotland. The portrait shows the recently deceased King David as a venerable figure with a long beard and a decidedly biblical air of dignity and even sanctity, whereas his grandson, as befits a 17-year-old who has been but six years on the throne, has no trace of beard or moustache on his fresh young face. There can be little doubt that the artist intended a direct comparison with the great King David of the Old Testament, while the youthful Malcolm was to be welcomed as a second Solomon: 'Furthermore, David the king said unto all the congregation, "Solomon my son, whom alone God hath chosen, is yet young and tender, and the work is great". . . . And David died in a good old age, full of days, riches and honour: and Solomon his son reigned in his stead'.

King David of Scotland died at Carlisle on 24 May 1153, and his body was carried to Dunfermline Abbey in Fife to be buried beside those of his mother and brothers. Many years earlier, he had taken steps to ensure that his parents and sister, Maud queen of England, would be commemorated annually by the monks of Westminster Abbey, Edward the Confessor's foundation, as befitted men and women closely associated with the West Saxon royal house. His son Henry had been buried at the abbey of Kelso which David I himself had founded for monks from Thiron in the heart of France. Although David Macmalcolm was not buried on Iona (whose church his mother is said to have restored), nevertheless his funeral at Dunfermline identified his dynasty with the old Scoto-Pictish kingdom as clearly as did the careful inauguration of his young grandson at Scone a few days later. It has been well said that among the gallery of European notables who died about the middle of the twelfth century 'in some ways the most characteristic figure . . . was King David. Many aspects of the twelfth century were summarized in the career of this cultivated and attractive man, son of the learned Margaret, patron and friend of Saint Ailred, founder and benefactor of over half the monasteries in Scotland, and patron of the bloodless Norman conquest of Lothian, the man who girt the sword of knighthood on the young Henry of Normandy and Anjou'.[2]

[2] C.N.L. Brooke, *Europe in the central Middle Ages* (1964), p. 381.

3

The Feudal Settlement

Military feudalism was a continental, west European phenomenon and because it came from the south it reached Scotland late. Wherever feudalism prevailed there was a tendency for the merely political lordship wielded by a ruler over his greater subjects in virtue of his royal authority to be converted into the strongly proprietary control exercised by a landlord over his tenants. For their part, the wealthiest and most powerful of the king's subjects, his 'vassals', acknowledged that they held their lands of the crown in return for performing a military service which was far from honorific, being expensive of money, time, and manpower. The benefits for the vassal were comparative security of tenure and title to his lands, a right to enjoy the lord's protection and patronage, and the keeping of peace within the lordship, among vassals of roughly equal power who might easily quarrel among themselves. The vassal would also acquire tenants or lesser vassals of his own and govern his fief with authority delegated to him by the king or other lord of whom he held. Feudalism was thus an aristocratic arrangement of landownership and the ordering of power which provided for a gradation of aristocracy from the highest lord – usually a 'king' – to the lowest, a 'knight' (horsed warrior). 'esquire' (shield-bearer), or even merely a substantial freeman or 'franklin'. In the process the highest was inevitably brought a little lower and the lowest somewhat raised. When Richard de Lucy, a great English baron of Henry II's reign, indignantly exclaimed 'These days every petty little knight seems to possess his own seal!' he was unconsciously paying tribute to the levelling effect of feudalism. The military quality fundamental to feudalism also played a leading rôle, for it implied that a particular skill in fighting on horseback was common to the entire ruling class. It permitted, indeed encouraged, lords and even knights to build castles, that is fortified residences, for themselves and their retainers.

Originating in the region between the Loire and Rhine as early as the eighth and ninth centuries, feudalism had only been faintly prefigured in southern Britain before the Normans conquered England in 1066. William I and his followers were therefore able to introduce it in a highly developed form, and it came into southern and midland England with a rush during the first decade of the Conqueror's reign. It is necessary to dwell for a moment on this phase of Anglo-Norman feudalism because all the feudalism that came into Scotland was brought by men on horseback riding up from the south. In spite, or to some extent because, of the Conqueror's ruthless suppression of northern English revolts in 1069–70, feudalism penetrated the country north of Trent very slowly, although by 1086 most of Yorkshire had been feudally allocated. English Cumbria (after Rufus's annexation of 1092) and Northumbria were feudalized only gradually between the last decade of the eleventh century and 1135. It is significant that whatever claims of overlordship William I and his sons asserted or vindicated over the Welsh princes, there was no effective or permanent feudal settlement west of Offa's Dyke before the thirteenth century save in those districts, chiefly in mid and south Wales, that had been conquered, usually on their own account, by Norman, Breton, and Flemish adventurers. And although it is true that the vast estates of the ancient, privileged churches of England were not immune from the feudalizing process, even being compelled to furnish knight service by William I, some of the ecclesiastical landowners proved much slower than others to adapt to the new system. The English medievalist's regrettable habit of always viewing events from the standpoint of the crown has made us exaggerate both the tidiness and the thoroughness of the military feudalism of England in the age of the Norman kings.

If feudalism came ready-made into England, it was brought into Scotland very much as a finished article in the last stage of refinement. David I and the two grandsons who followed him successively on the throne, Malcolm IV (1153–65) and William I 'the Lion' (1165–1214), not only made the incoming Anglo-Normans and Flemings feudal vassals of the crown in the strictest sense, they also expected the native magnates (including even the earls) to become feudal vassals by assimilation. Within 12 years of his grant of Annandale to Robert Bruce, David I gave Fife, pre-eminent among the earldoms, to Earl Duncan I to be held as a fief by royal charter for service which, if not specifically military, was at least formally defined. It is true that in marked contrast with England the earldoms remained surprisingly intact and still identifiable as provincial governorships until the fourteenth century. But if the earls preserved their position in the front rank of the aristocratic class, they were nonetheless included by the twelfth-century kings among the 'barons and knights' of the crown.

Four fundamentals have been listed by which we may test the feudalism of post-Conquest England: the knight, or mail-clad soldier trained to fight on horseback; vassalic commendation, or mutual acceptance of lordship and homage between two free persons; the fief, or estate (usually land) granted by the lord to be held of him and his heirs by the vassal and his heirs as long as the due service was performed; and the castle, a fortified residence, in practice invariably constructed as a 'motte' or earthen mound surmounted by a timber tower or keep, with or without a 'bailey' or court defended by earthwork banks and ditches. All these are certainly to be found, taken as it were for granted, in Scotland between 1124 and 1286. At the same time it is important to bear in mind three notable contrasts with the situation in Norman England which go far to explain contrasts still to be drawn between the Scotland of Alexander III or Robert I and the England of Edward I. First, feudalism in England was imposed as a consequence of harsh military conquest, scores and hundreds of baronies or other fiefs being created out of the Norman kings' forfeiture of the native ruling class and because of the importunate pressure of knightly adventurers expecting rich rewards. Secondly, outwith the kingdom of England strictly defined, the invading feudal warriors fought their way into the marches of Wales, including purely Welsh territory, in a series of miniature Norman conquests for which they seem to have had only the vaguest permission from the kings, creating a unique complex of lordships and principalities which were half Welsh, half feudal. In Scotland, on the other hand, the introduction of feudalism, although it could obviously never have been accomplished by David I and his grandsons without the threat of superior military force, had in practice to be carried out peacefully. Instead of being able to impose feudalism at a stroke upon most of Scotland the kings had to establish fiefs piecemeal and feudalize existing landowners gradually. On the other hand, there is little evidence that the Scottish realm was threatened with anything comparable to the Marcher lordships of Wales, even in Galloway where the earliest-known feudatories arrived in the wake of King Malcolm's expedition of 1160. Finally, we should note that, doubtless owing to the deeply religious outlook of Queen Margaret's sons and Malcolm

IV, no attempt was made in Scotland to require knight-service from land held by the church. Such land remained liable only to the ancient common army service from which there were scarcely any exemptions.

In order, therefore, to introduce the knight and the knight's feu or fief the kings exploited the royal demesne available to them in Lothian, Cumbria, Fife, Gowrie, Angus, the Mearns, and Moray. What seems to have happened in detail may be illustrated by a few examples. In Lothian most of the shires held and administered by thanes were small or readily amenable to subdivision. Whenever a thane died his heir might expect, but probably had no clear legal right, to succeed. In such a case, or where there were no heirs, the king could take the shire into his own hands and grant out the whole or a convenient part of it to one of his favoured Anglo-Norman or continental immigrants. These men would insist on secure, permanent, hereditary tenure as an inducement to settle so far from home. They undertook to perform knight-service, including garrison duty at the nearest king's castle ('castle ward' or simply 'ward'). Since they had no standing in their new country, belonged to no recognized kindred group, and had no known blood-price or 'wergild', it was difficult to fit them into the existing framework of popular courts and traditional, customary law. It is likely that this problem was solved by means of the new type of sheriffdom with its regular courts to which the tenants of newly-created baronies would come as of right. The intermediate phase, before the new families had had time to become acclimatized, is nicely shown by the division of the witness-list of King David's foundation charter for Melrose Abbey into two groups, the first naming 18 men most of whom were foreign settlers and household officers, the second naming 14 'men of that land' (i.e. the valleys of Tweed and Teviot), of whom only three were foreigners.

In this way it was possible for King David to grant the shire of Yetholm to Robert or Walter Corbet, the lands of Lilliesleaf to Walter of Ryedale, most of Lauderdale (an exceptionally large shire) to Hugh de Morville, and the lands of Linton in Roxburghshire and Carnwath in Lanarkshire to William de Somerville. The typical pattern of feudal settlement in Lothian was determined by the granting out as military fiefs of estates consisting of a single village and its territory, two villages constituting a normal maximum infeftment and half a village a normal minimum. Often the new lord's estate would be formed into an ecclesiastical parish. Further west, in Cumbria or Strathclyde, it was the much larger districts which set the pattern, e.g. Liddesdale, Eskdale, Annandale, Kyle, and Cunningham, resembling the cantreds or commotes of Wales. Thus the first of the Stewarts, Walter son of Alan, was made lord of almost the whole of what later became the sheriffdom of Renfrew (composed of the districts of Renfrew, Mearns, and Strathgryfe), together with the north half of Kyle in Ayrshire (Kyle Stewart), whereas on the east he had only been able to acquire single villages such as Hassendean, Legerwood, Mow, and Stenton. Hugh de Morville or his son Richard got the whole of Cunningham with Largs, Robert Avenel was given half Eskdale and Ranulf de Soules received Liddesdale. Looking further north we see that an adventurous Fleming named Freskin was given Duffus and other lands near Elgin (but with a safer foothold at Uphall in West Lothian), while, perhaps before 1153, Alan de Lascelles got the shire of Forgan or Naughton – ecclesiastically the parish of St Fillan's – in the north-east corner of Fife.

Under Malcolm IV, who found nothing incompatible in being simultaneously a deeply devout and celibate upholder of the Christian faith and an ardent feudalizer, new baronies and knights' feus spread rapidly in the valley of the Clyde as well as in Fife and Moray, and they even began to creep tentatively along the shores of Galloway. There were strong reasons for the Scots king to try to modernize his defences. In 1157 Henry of Anjou, who had needed only two years on the English throne to emerge as one of the most powerful rulers in western Europe, met Malcolm IV at Chester and imperiously deprived him of all the territory south of Esk and Tweed which David I had striven so laboriously to annex to Scottish rule. Thus by *force majeure* Henry repudiated the oath he had sworn before King David in 1149. He softened the blow by restoring to the king of Scots the Honour of Huntingdon, lost in 1141, while to his brother William he gave back not the earldom of Northumberland which had been his but only the lordship of Tynedale, the valleys of North and South Tyne. Malcolm desired ardently to be knighted by his cousin, who had himself been knighted by Malcolm's grandfather. Henry astutely postponed the favour until he had induced both brothers to bring a force of knights in 1159 from Scotland to Aquitaine where the English king was trying to bring a disobedient vassal, the count of Toulouse, to heel. The Scots were obviously meant to be seen in the rôle of obedient vassals. The point was not lost on the native magnates at home in Scotland, because as soon as their young king returned, full of pride in his newly-acquired knighthood, they besieged him in the castle of Perth, 'angry', as a contemporary puts it, 'because he had gone to Toulouse'. It is hardly an exaggeration to say that King Malcolm's defeat of this group of recalcitrant earls, followed as it was by a successful campaign to reduce Galloway to submission, formed a crucial turning-point both for the dynasty of Malcolm III – the 'House of Canmore' as it is often called – and for the future of military feudalism as the basis of Scotland's landholding class and common law. In dramatic testimony of the king's triumph, the lord or self-styled 'king' of Galloway abdicated in favour of his sons Gilbert and Uhtred and became an Augustinian canon at the royal monastery of Holyrood.

At the outset of his 12-year reign, Malcolm IV had to fend off attacks by Somerled Macgillebrigte lord of Argyll and suppress a minor rebellion by some native gentry of middle rank who were probably alarmed at the onset of foreign settlement and feudal practices. At the end of his reign, the king was again confronted by a dangerous manifestation of conservative revolt, an outright invasion of south-western Scotland by Somerled of Argyll, who in 1164 brought a fleet up the River Clyde as far as Renfrew. The invaders were repulsed and Somerled himself slain by royal troops probably under the command of the king's steward, Walter son of Alan, though the clergy of Glasgow cathedral did not hesitate to give the credit for victory to Saint Mungo and their bishop Herbert, formerly a monk of Kelso. When Malcolm died in December 1165, not yet 25 years old, he bequeathed to his brother William a legacy of strength and weakness. In Scotland itself royal authority, which for the first time in the history of the country had been sufficient to allow the succession of a youth of 12 in 1153, had never been more firmly established. Malcolm IV's reign saw important developments, to be discussed in the next chapter, in the formation of a distinct Scottish church. Marriage alliances were made in 1160 and 1162 with Brittany and Holland respectively, the latter a county owing no allegiance to the Angevin ruling house. Foreign feudatories and at least a majority of the native magnates were ready to welcome William to the throne he would occupy for nearly half a century. But beyond the southern border the Angevin colossus maintained its pressure. In 1163 Henry II had followed up his seizure of 'English' Cumbria and Northumberland by extracting a homage from King Malcolm at Woodstock which, however personal in its terms, almost certainly went further in the direction of feudal dependence than David I would have been prepared to go after 1135.

The king whom we know as William 'the Lion' (an epithet never used by contemporaries) was cast in a very different mould from either his grandfather or his elder brother. He was impetuous and warlike, occasionally high-handed, determined to cut a figure as a knight of renown, determined also with an almost fanatical singleness of purpose to recover the earldom of Northumberland held by his father Henry, his great-grandfather Waltheof, and his great-great-grandfather Siward. Although a conventionally dutiful son of the church who founded the noble abbey of Arbroath (1178) and was actually revered in his declining years for personal sanctity, William began his reign with a markedly secular look. Neglecting marriage till he was over 40, he had numerous mistresses and fathered a large brood of bastards. Himself a devotee of chivalry and jousting, he drew to his service a vast following of hopeful young knights, many of them younger sons without prospects at home in Flanders, Normandy, Brittany, or England. They belonged to that class of *juvenes, les jeunes*, whose disproportionate influence within the feudal aristocracy of western Europe has been noted by modern students of the period. Under William the feudalization of Galloway was resumed, although it was interrupted by a violent anti-foreign reaction lasting some 10 years from 1174 to 1185. The rest of southern Scotland was already thoroughly feudalized at his accession, but William pushed feudalism further and further into the country north of Forth, creating knights' feus in Strathearn, Fife, Gowrie, Angus, and Mearns and eventually finding landed estates well to the west and north of Inverness for such families as Bisset and Freskin.

The two leading themes of Scottish history between the end of the eleventh and the beginning of the fourteenth century are sharply exemplified in William the Lion's reign. On the one hand we see the shaping and consolidation of Scotland as a feudal kingdom with clearly defined territories, throughout which (very much on the Angevin or Capetian model) royal power and authority were deliberately stressed and exalted. On the other hand we see the integrity and independence of this realm being defended against the aggressive claims of Angevin kings of England, claims that were formulated in feudal terms and backed by a military force that could seldom if ever be matched by the Scots.

To understand the political geography of twelfth-century Scotland we should note the division of the realm, small though it was, into two zones. One stretched from the English border (which did not fluctuate significantly after 1157) across to the Firths of Clyde and Forth and thence northward in a broad sweep to the southern shore of the Moray Firth. It included on its western fringe the southern and central highland earldoms of Lennox, Menteith, Strathearn, Atholl, and

Mar, and it fully embraced the earldoms of Dunbar, Fife, Gowrie (in the king's hands throughout our period), Angus, and Buchan (Map I). Beyond this 'inner' zone, in which the king spent most of his time and where his commands were effectively enforced, lay an 'outer' zone, not regarded as any less integrally a part of the realm, but seldom if ever visited personally by the king and apt to be unreliable in its obedience to royal commands. The outer zone included the larger Galloway (from the River Nith round to the River Doon), the whole western highlands from Kintyre to Sutherland, and the far north-east mainland from the Dornoch Firth to Dunnet Head. Throughout our period Galloway showed strong signs of separatism, but, if independent of Scotland, the province was not consistently dependent on any external power. The southern and western highlands, including the important lordship of Argyll, were closely linked, geographically and in their ruling families, to the western isles. The isles in turn were formally subject to the crown of Norway and ecclesiastically within the province of Trondheim. It should be remembered that these Norwegian 'western isles' included the Isle of Man, strategically placed between England, Scotland, and Ireland though in fact nearest to Scotland. As for the far north, especially Caithness and what is now eastern Sutherland, this territory had long possessed close associations with the strongly Norse islands of Orkney and Shetland. The earldom of Caithness in Scotland was actually ruled by the same family that held the Norwegian earldom of Orkney, causing serious problems of divided loyalty. What we see in the reigns of William I, Alexander II, and Alexander III is a consistent effort by the crown to assert its authority not only within the inner zone as David I had done but equally in the outer zone. Logically, the effort culminated in the acquisition of the western isles in 1266; it was to be another two centuries before the northern isles also were brought within the Scots realm.

Consolidation of the realm and of the dynasty went ahead together. It was only to be expected that threats to the dynasty would come from areas such as Argyll, Ross, Moray, and Caithness. In particular Ross and Moray proved fruitful sources of disaffection. Ross was not the larger county familiar today but the district between the Beauly and Inverness Firths on the south and the Dornoch Firth on the north, including the valleys of eastward-flowing rivers in between. Moray, one of the largest provinces of Scotland, stretched from east of the River Spey across to the western sea by Knoydart and Glenelg, and included the mountain fastnesses of Lochaber, Badenoch, and the Rough Bounds.

David I, despite his power and prestige, was beset by rebellion. Throughout his reign rivals contended for the throne. King Lulach's grandson Angus earl of Moray was killed leading a dynastic revolt in 1130. An ally of Angus was Malcolm Macheth, whose father Heth or Aed had perhaps been deprived of the earldom of Ross. Malcolm also allied himself to Somerled of Argyll and persisted in his rebellion until 1134 when he was captured and imprisoned at Roxburgh for 28 years. His sons, Somerled's nephews, joined their uncle's revolt against King Malcolm IV, but the eldest, Donald, was imprisoned with his father in 1157. By 1162 the king was ready to be generous, setting both Macheths free and restoring the earldom of Ross to the father, who died in 1168. Ross seems to have been taken back into direct royal possession for no more earls are heard of before *c*.1215, when the honour was given to a local nobleman, Farquhar Mactaggart, who had just helped to defeat a revolt by Kenneth Macheth, Earl Malcolm's great-grandson.

Moray posed a more serious threat than Ross. There is surely no stranger figure in twelfth-century Scottish history than Wimund, who began his career in the Savigniac abbey of Furness in north Lancashire, transferred to its daughter-house at Rushen in Man, and *c*.1134 was chosen bishop of the Isles, apparently with the support of King Olaf I. Wimund claimed to be the son of Angus Earl of Moray, and for years he waged war against King David, aiming to seize the throne. At last he was captured, removed from his bishopric and blinded. He lived on for years at the Yorkshire abbey of Byland, where the memory of his past exploits would occasionally stir him to fierce excitement. In King William's time the most serious Moray threat came from the line of Macwilliam. Duncan II, eldest son and successor of Malcolm III, had left a legitimate son named William (presumably in honour of Rufus or the Conqueror). This son was well-treated by David I and obviously not regarded as a potential rival. He is known to have married an Anglo-Norman heiress, Alice de Rumelli, who brought her husband the northern English lordships of Craven in the West Riding and Coupland in west Cumberland. They had a son William, born at Egremont, who was not yet 21 when he died unmarried, and three daughters who each inherited an equal portion of their mother's estates. None of these individuals ever put in a claim to the throne or to compensation for abandoning such a claim. But William son of King Duncan had another son, Donald, popularly known as Macwilliam. From the 1160s till his death in 1187, Donald Macwilliam persistently claimed the realm of Scotland. The probability is that Alice de Rumelli was the second wife of William son of Duncan, and that Donald was the son of an unrecorded earlier marriage to a kinswoman of Earl Angus of Moray, who transmitted the Moray claim to the throne to her descendants. At this remove of time Bishop Wimund and Donald Macwilliam may appear mere oddities. In their day they were taken very seriously. They may have been close kinsmen, and they undoubtedly believed passionately in their dynastic claims.

It is some confirmation of this suggested origin for Donald Macwilliam that his rebellion, which called for urgent action in 1179, was based on the northern highlands and led to the building of two key castles north of Inverness, one in the west of the Black Isle and the other on the north side of the Cromarty narrows. Donald put forth his greatest effort in 1187, ill-timed from his point of view since King William had recently been reconciled with Henry II and had pacified Galloway. Its lord, Roland (otherwise Lachlan) son of Uhtred, experienced in hill warfare, played a crucial part in defeating Macwilliam. An army was taken north in the summer and while the king stayed at Inverness a force of young warriors under Roland discovered Macwilliam on a moor called 'Mam Garvia' (north-west of Dingwall?), inflicted a decisive defeat, and brought Donald's head to the king in triumph. Although Donald's son Guthred was capable of raising a major revolt in the north from 1211 to 1212, and yet more Macwilliams were active against the crown as late as 1230, it was unlikely after 1187 that the Canmore dynasty would be toppled from the throne by these Moray claimants. Before 1214, feudal settlement was being pushed into the highland parts of Moray beyond Inverness.

The pacification of Moray and Ross brought the crown into immediate contact with Caithness, compelling King William to assert royal authority over a remote province which David I had claimed to rule but can hardly have governed directly. Military expeditions in 1196–7 brought to heel the ambitious Harold Maddadson earl of Caithness and Orkney (Orcadian only on his mother's side, his father having been the Scots earl of Atholl, Maddad, or Madet). Paradoxically, the humbling of Earl Harold, accomplished by 1203, was accompanied by the aggrandizement of an incoming feudal family of Flemish origin, the sons of Freskin who adopted the surname *de Moravia*, 'of Moray', or in modern form Murray, to whom so much power was delegated by the crown that in course of time they would themselves pose some threat to royal authority. By the mid thirteenth century various members of the Murray family held the lordships of

Duffus near Elgin, Petty near Inverness, and many lands in Strathspey; they had acquired the earldom of Sutherland, carved out of the older and larger province of Caithness; and marriage to an Olifard heiress had brought to the family the great feudal lordship of Bothwell on the Clyde. Powerful as were the Murrays, however, they were never simultaneously major vassals of the king of Scots and of a foreign king (for in England they held only a small estate in Northamptonshire), and their lands in Scotland were held for knight-service, binding them in strict loyalty to the crown.

The feudal bonds by which William the Lion linked the majority of his greatest subjects to the throne could be invoked against the monarchy as well as in its support. The homage which David I had performed to Henry I and Malcolm IV to Henry II was too vague and personal to satisfy the ambition of Angevin kings who wished to be overlords of the whole island of Britain and even (after 1171) of Ireland as well. When in 1173 the 'Young King Henry', Henry II's eldest son, plotted with his mother and brothers and Louis VII of France (his mother's former husband) to overthrow Henry II and partition the vast Angevin empire, the king of Scots foolishly allowed himself to be led into a trap, tempted by the offer of his lost earldom of Northumberland. The Scots were regarded by the conspirators as a crucially important element in the great revolt. Henry II kept his nerve, realizing that he had the loyalty of most of his great feudatories and the support of the vast majority of his humbler subjects. He also judged correctly that his enemies were too scattered and disparate to be capable of organizing a co-ordinated campaign. After indecisive warfare in northern England in 1173 and the spring of 1174, William I brought a large army to Northumberland in July 1174. With the greater part of his troops dispersed on plundering raids, the king himself with a small escort of knights was surprised and captured while engaged on a leisurely siege of Alnwick castle. William was taken south, first to Northampton (his feet tied together beneath his horse's belly to emphasize the humiliation of his captivity) thence to imprisonment in the dungeon of Falaise, the strongest castle of Normandy.

The great revolt promptly collapsed, and Henry II exploited his triumph methodically and thoroughly. William was not deprived of his realm, but he was made to do homage to the English king explicitly 'for Scotland and his other lands', and henceforward he and his greatest feudatories would acknowledge that they were directly subject to the overlordship of the king of England and his heirs. The bishops of Scotland, in addition to swearing fealty to King Henry personally, were forced to agree that their church would give such obedience to the English church as it owed by right and custom — though they were able at once to lobby successfully at the papal court against this claim, vague as it was. The sons of important Scots nobles were taken as hostages, and English garrisons were installed in the three key castles of Berwick, Roxburgh, and Edinburgh. The new relationship, although recorded in a written document (the 'Treaty of Falaise', 1174), was not totally feudal, for Henry II did not seize the Scottish realm and grant it back to William to be held as a fief for some fixed service. Nevertheless, William was now unequivocally the liege vassal of the king of England in respect of Scotland. In the Treaty of Falaise Henry II put on record his ideas about different grades of kingship, for the document mentions no fewer than three kings, himself as 'lord king', his son and heir apparent as 'King Henry the king's son', and William as 'king of Scots'. It is interesting to compare the Treaty of Windsor made in 1175 between Henry II as conqueror of Ireland and Ruairi ua Conchobair, claimant to the 'high kingship' of Ireland. This provided that Ruairi should be king of Connacht under Henry II, as long as he should serve Henry faithfully and render an annual tribute of cowhides.

There are signs that Henry II was prepared to interfere in the domestic affairs of the Scots realm on the strength of his newly-defined lordship. In restoring Edinburgh castle to William as a cheap wedding present in 1185 Henry emphasized the Scots king's subordinate position by choosing as his bride Ermengarde, the daughter of a comparatively minor vassal, Richard *vicomte* of Beaumont. It has been said that what really irked William was not his feudal subjection but only the loss of his castles. This is plainly contradicted by the fact that as soon as Henry II died in July 1189, the Scottish king applied successfully to Richard I not only for the restoration of Berwick and Roxburgh but also for the complete cancellation of the Treaty of Falaise, 'which our good father Henry extorted from (William) by new documents and by his capture'. In future, kings of Scotland would do to kings of England whatever King Malcolm IV justly did to Richard I's predecessors. In other words, homage would revert to a personal and undefined relationship, no longer involving the Scottish kingdom. The store which King William set by this 'Quitclaim of Canterbury' may be gauged by his readiness to pay 10,000 merks for it, a sum that may be seen as an equivalent to the ransom he ought to have paid in 1174, which was not demanded by Henry II because a ransom might have implied that William was an independent king.

On the terms restored in 1189 William was ready to do homage in 1200 to Richard's brother and successor John Lackland, although he continued to importune John as he had importuned Richard for the return of Northumberland. All he could extract from John was the lordship of Tynedale. John was ambitious to re-assert the overlordship won by his father from 1174 to 1189. Now in his 60s William suffered from increased ill health. He was reluctant to contemplate armed resistance against John who was thus able to reimpose a degree of subjection upon the Scots between 1209 and 1212. He built a new castle at Tweedmouth, facing Berwick, and when William protested John brought a large army to Norham which the Scots king judged too strong for the host he had summoned to risk a battle. We do not know the detailed terms of the peace then made, but William agreed to pay John 15,000 merks and to hand over his two elder daughters, Margaret and Isabel, to be married under John's supervision. Evidence from the reign of Henry III suggests that John had agreed that one or other of the Scots princesses was to marry either Henry or Richard, the former destined to be king of England for 56 years, and the latter to be elected king of Germany. Tweedmouth castle was dismantled, and it may be that William formally abandoned his claim to the northern counties of England. In 1212 John was able to exploit William's weakness in the face of Guthred Macwilliam's revolt, obtaining a confirmation of the peace of 1209 and the right to arrange the marriage of William's only legitimate son Alexander, whom he knighted in March 1212. The Scots gained little and lost much by the transactions of 1209 and 1212. It is true that Alexander II married the young King Henry's sister, Joan, in 1221, and it is true that troops provided by John helped to suppress the Macwilliam rising. But the English left Margaret and Isabel of Scotland on the shelf until they were eventually married beneath their rank to English barons. The treaties must have given the impression that both William and Alexander were as much subject to John as William had been to Henry II. It is not surprising that as soon as his father died Alexander II allied himself to the rebellious English barons who in June 1215 wrung the Magna Carta from an extremely unwilling King John. Chapter 59 of the 1215 version merely states that right shall be done to the king of Scots in the matter of his sisters, which Alexander must have found inadequate for he not only adhered to the baronial diehards who remained in arms against John but actually did homage to their patron Louis, heir to the French throne. From them Alexander won promises of all that his father had striven for in vain.

The political setbacks of the period 1209–14 did not mean that the

Scottish monarchy was in decline. There is abundant evidence that royal government had never been so effective over so large an area of Scotland as it was between 1189 and William the Lion's death. Galloway, the far north and much of the western seaboard (including the islands of the Firth of Clyde), were now as fully within the realm as Lothian, Strathclyde, Fife, Angus, or Buchan. Almost everywhere, feudal tenure and service constituted the norm of relations between the crown and its substantial free subjects. The earldoms survived for some purposes as provincial units of government, and the earls enjoyed a special relationship with the crown. Nevertheless, this relationship came to be expressed in increasingly feudal terms, and the new sheriffs had taken over much of the earls' power. A few earls (most notably Fife, Dunbar, and Strathearn) played an active part in royal government as justiciars, along with barons and royal servants who were mainly of Anglo-continental origin. Before the end of William I's reign the justiciarships were based on a division of the kingdom into two or occasionally three regions, i.e. 'Scotia', the country north of Forth, 'Lothian', normally meaning the whole of southern Scotland, and 'Galloway' which, when applied to a justiciarship, seems to have meant much of the south-west.

The crown obtained its revenues from a variety of sources, the overall pattern undergoing a marked change during the twelfth century. Customs duties were levied at seaports on wine and imported manufactured articles. Exports were not yet taxed. At fishing havens on royal demesne the king took either a proportion of the catch or a cash equivalent. Royal demesne estates yielded large revenues in kind, chiefly cereal crops (barley, oats, and wheat), cattle, pigs, salmon, and eels. The kings of the Canmore dynasty did not relinquish their immemorial right to periodic hospitality ('conveth', 'waiting') or its commutation into money. Probably the levying of this ancient due was already organized on the basis of sheriffdoms by 1214. In earlier centuries the companion levy of conveth was 'cain' or 'geld', a tribute normally payable every three years (possibly biennial in some districts), equivalent to the tax called cornage in England and commorth in Wales. Cain was usually paid in cattle and the other farm livestock, and in certain basic foodstuffs. It was levied on the basis of the ploughgate (*carucata terra*) south of Forth and its counterpart in the north, the davoch (also often latinized as *carucata*). As with the common army service, which was also levied on a ploughgate/davoch basis, there seem to have been few or no exemptions from cain before the advent of knight-service tenure. Thus, when King

William confirmed a grant made to the pilgrim hospice of St Andrews by Simon son of Michael of a davoch of land at Kedlock, Fife, with common pasture for 26 cattle and 80 sheep, he took care to add that Simon himself would be responsible for the army service and public labour services (on bridges and royal castles) due from the land, but the hospice would be answerable to the king for the royal geld 'which is commonly levied from lands and eleemosynary estates (in effect, church lands) throughout the Scottish realm'. The importance of cain as a universal and dependable source of revenue declined sharply in the thirteenth century. The reason for this seems to lie in the crucial decision of twelfth-century kings to exempt from cain nearly all land granted out for knight-service. When William of Malmesbury tells us that David I exempted from the triennial tribute all those willing to be civilized he was probably referring to the new feudal class. It might seem reckless for the crown to make so large a tax concession to its new aristocracy and gentry, but at the time it probably calculated that the fiscal 'incidents' of feudalism would amply compensate for a land tax that may have been growing less profitable with increased prosperity. Moreover, south of the border the English kings exempted feudal barons from cornage, and the Scots kings could hardly offer less favourable terms if they wished to attract new feudal settlers.

The 'incidents' of feudalism were broadly the same in Scotland as in England. Tenants in chief paid a premium or 'relief' before they could succeed to estates, even when these were acknowledged to be hereditary. If under age, the crown could control their marriages and exploit this right by selling marriages to the highest bidder. Again, if an heir was under age the estate he or she expected to inherit was kept in the king's hands. If the heir were male the crown would not relinquish the estate until he was 21; if female, then not before she was married. The crown was entitled to what were euphemistically called 'aids', payments made by vassals usually in money. By custom (already evidenced in Scotland by c.1210), the vassal had to offer an aid to his lord on three occasions without needing to be consulted — the knighting of the eldest son, the first marriage of the eldest daughter, and the ransoming of a lord careless enough to be captured by his enemies. It was generally understood that any other aids were subject to bargaining between a lord and his vassals. In England the necessity for the vassal's consent to extraordinary aids was expressly mentioned in Magna Carta, and during the thirteenth century the English practice of converting extraordinary aids into ordinary taxation, coupled with the freeholders' insistence on consent to such taxation, led to a remarkable development of parliament as a negotiating forum between the crown and its most substantial subjects. No such development took place in Scotland before the fourteenth century. From time to time William I, his son Alexander II, and his grandson Alexander III managed to raise extraordinary aids from their subjects, but it seems clear that the practice remained infrequent and was fraught with difficulty. In fiscal matters, feudal custom could work as powerfully in favour of the tenant and vassal as of the lord. The kings of later medieval Scotland may have regretted their predecessors' readiness to abandon the levying of cain, which might have proved a solid fiscal asset if it could have been converted from kind to cash.

To a much greater extent than his grandfather or elder brother, William the Lion accustomed his subjects to the use of money and the circulation of a standard royal coinage. The steady production of Scots sterlings over the half-century of William's reign facilitated the transition to a money economy and the collection of royal revenues. The king's moneyers worked mainly in a handful of south-country and midland burghs, Berwick upon Tweed, Roxburgh, Edinburgh, Stirling, and Perth. They were probably recruited from the goldsmiths' trade, and it is noteworthy that in 1296 the chief burgess ('alderman') of Roxburgh was Walter the Goldsmith. They struck silver pennies closely resembling, in pattern and fineness of silver content, the coins of Henry II and his sons. Since it was Scottish policy to maintain the currency at parity with that of England, changes in English coin had to be matched in Scotland. It is curious that the Scots did not at once follow suit when the Angevin single 'short-cross' penny was altered to the voided short-cross type in 1180, but waited till 1195. Half a century later, when Henry III's coinage underwent the radical renewal of 1247 as the famous 'long-cross' penny, the Scots took less than three years to bring their coinage into line, despite the sudden death of Alexander II and the succession of a minor. A comparably rapid adjustment was made when Edward I renewed his coinage in 1279.

William the Lion, suffering for many years from ill health and in his old age enjoying a reputation for personal sanctity which spread far beyond the borders of Scotland, died at Stirling on 4 December 1214. He was buried in the abbey church which he had founded at Arbroath 36 years earlier. In spite of the humiliation to which his cousin Henry of Anjou had subjected him and the rebuffs he had suffered at the hands of King John, William had performed a notable service for the feudal kingship of Scotland. His long reign saw military feudalism reach the high-water mark; thenceforward, although feudal tenure and custom were irreversibly entrenched within the law of Scotland they would be interwoven with traditional rules and practice to form a distinctively Scottish common law. The most intensively Celtic and Scandinavian parts of the kingdom, which had been peripheral in David I's scheme of government, were brought effectively within the reach of royal authority. Celtic Scotland had been familiar with one version of the oldest European idea of royalty, that of the king as a native-born member of his own people, upon which the church had successfully overlaid the notion of the king as upholder of Christianity. This strongly traditional kingship is clearly demonstrated by John of Hexham's account of the succession of Malcolm IV in 1153: 'and so all the people of the land, raising up Malcolm, son of Earl Henry, King David's son (a boy still only 12 years old), established him as king at Scone (as is the custom of the Scottish nation)'. To this traditional kingship William I was able to add the more modern idea, conspicuously favoured by the relatively upstart Normans and Angevins, of a king who was above all a territorial lord and a governor of subjects, a ruler who once lawfully appointed could exercise authority by his mere royal will.

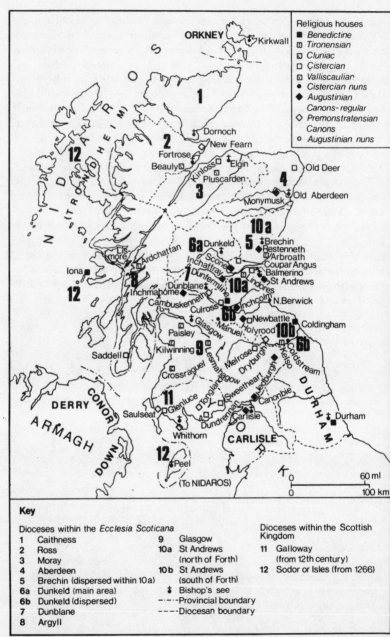

Religious houses

- ■ *Benedictine*
- ◧ *Tironensian*
- ◪ *Cluniac*
- □ *Cistercian*
- ◩ *Valliscaulian*
- • *Cistercian nuns*
- ◆ *Augustinian Canons-regular*
- ◇ *Premonstratensian Canons*
- ○ *Augustinian nuns*

ORKNEY — Kirkwall

1

Dornoch
New Fearn
Fortrose
Beauly — Elgin
Kinloss — Old Deer
2
3 — Pluscarden
4
Monymusk — Old Aberdeen

10a — Dunkeld
6a — 5 — Brechin
Restenneth
Scone — Arbroath
Inchaffray — Coupar Angus
7 — Balmerino
Dunblane — Dunfermline — St Andrews
Inchmahome — 10a
Cambuskenneth — Inchcolm
Culross — N. Berwick
Lismore
Ardchattan
Iona
12
8

Glasgow — Newbattle — Coldingham
Manuel — Holyrood
Paisley — 10b — 6b
Kilwinning — Melrose — Coldstream
9 — Lesmahagow — Dryburgh — Kelso
Crossraguel — Tongland — Jedburgh
Saddell — Sweetheart — Canonbie
11 — Glenluce — Dundrennan — Carlisle
Saulseat
Whithorn — CARLISLE
DERRY
CONOR
ARMAGH
DOWN

Durham
DURHAM

12
Peel
(To NIDAROS)

60 ml
0 — 100 km

Key

Dioceses within the *Ecclesia Scoticana*

1 Caithness
2 Ross
3 Moray
4 Aberdeen
5 Brechin (dispersed within 10a)
6a Dunkeld (main area)
6b Dunkeld (dispersed)
7 Dunblane
8 Argyll

9 Glasgow
10a St Andrews (north of Forth)
10b St Andrews (south of Forth)
⸸ Bishop's see
–·–·– Provincial boundary
– – – Diocesan boundary

Dioceses within the Scottish Kingdom

11 Galloway (from 12th century)
12 Sodor or Isles (from 1266)

Map II **The Church in the Twelfth and Thirteenth Centuries**

4

The Church Transformed

One fundamental obstacle threatens to frustrate all attempts to assess the quality of religion in medieval Europe and to estimate the importance of Christianity in society. Almost all our documentary sources and a surprisingly large proportion of our unwritten evidence, such as buildings and works of art, were produced by or for the church which was at once the guardian and the propagator of the Christian faith. It is not just that explicitly religious works — homilies and sermons, liturgy, theology, saints' lives, and miracles — occupy a dominant position in surviving literature. The difficulty for the present-day historian arises from the fact that so much secular literary material was composed by church-educated clerks whose basic assumptions about the eternal validity of Christianity unconsciously colour much of their writing. It is as though we were trying to understand the character of a great painter of whom the sole evidence we possessed lay in his paintings, including a number of self-portraits. Some non-Christian or anti-Christian modern writers have reacted to this difficulty by boldly defying the source material. They have postulated, on scarcely any evidence, a vast popular religion of the Middle Ages, conducted conspiratorially and preserving a hotch-potch of primitive and sophisticated paganism. Other historians, with a committed Christian belief, especially those writing from a Protestant or post-Reformation standpoint, have accepted the apparently all-pervasive Christianity of the Middle Ages as genuine and not an illusion created by skilful propaganda. But they have emphasized the contrasts between the primitive church evidenced, e.g., by the Acts of the Apostles and Saint Paul's letters, on the one hand, and, on the other, the powerful and triumphant church of twelfth- and thirteenth-century western Europe. They have urged that however universally this splendid institution was accepted by the people, it was living a life and preaching a doctrine far removed in substance and spirit from the gospel of Jesus

61

Christ. Naturally enough, modern Roman Catholic historians have seldom launched radical attacks of this sort. They have stressed the enormous variety of religious experience and expression to be found in medieval Christendom and have defended the church against ignorant misrepresentation, partly by pointing out that there were plenty of vociferous critics of that church within its own ranks, by no means all of whom were driven into the wilderness of unforgiveable heresy.

If we look at the Christian church of Scotland from the eleventh to the fourteenth century with these considerations in mind, we must first of all admit that our fundamental obstacle, the clerical origin of so much of the source material, poses as much of a challenge here as elsewhere. But we can also see that many of the more detailed points, whether of criticism or of defence, that figure in the debate about medieval Christianity in the west either do not apply to Scotland or apply only with qualifications. Our biggest difficulty lies not in the bias but in the inadequacy of the evidence. This is true for most aspects of church life, but is perhaps most noticeable in connexion with popular religion and the church's intellectual activity. The only sensible course for the historian to adopt is to use the available sources as fully and sympathetically as he can, applying nevertheless his critical faculty and common sense.

The first point to be made can hardly be over-emphasized. In its structure and organization the Scottish church underwent a thorough-going transformation in the course of the twelfth and thirteenth centuries. Scotland was by no means peculiar in this respect. A high degree of uniformity was imposed generally upon the whole of western Christendom under the authority and leadership of a revived and exalted papal monarchy. As a result the peculiarities of many regional churches of the west, that of Scotland among them, were ironed out.

The second point is not so obvious. As far as we can judge, the doctrine upheld by the church of eleventh-century Scotland was orthodox, conforming in all essentials to the Catholic faith. Had it been otherwise the papal letters addressed to Scottish rulers and church leaders in the time of Saint Margaret and her sons would have insisted above all on compliance with the teaching of the universal church. Instead, they dealt with matters on the fringe rather than at the heart of doctrine, or with observance and jurisdiction. The *ecclesia Scoticana* may have appeared a little odd in the eyes of reformers based upon or originating in continental church centres, but they do not seem to have had any doubt of its true Christianity.

Once its governmental framework had been reorganized it could, in their view, function as an effective member of that much larger body familiarly known as Holy Mother Church. When, for example, under Pope Innocent III the fully-developed doctrine of transubstantiation was promulgated, the Scots, inclined neither to theological controversy nor to heresy, simply accepted it as part of received teaching.

The third and last general point to be made concerns the historical development of Christianity in Scotland since its earliest beginnings. The great variety of channels through which the Christian faith reached northern Britain was still reflected in the character of the Scottish church at the end of the eleventh century. An Irish strand was strongly marked but not quite predominant. This strand derived only indirectly from the mission of Saint Columba and the prestige of the church of Iona, important though these were. It was rather that with the merging of Scots and Picts in the ninth century there had been a revival of Irish influence generally, and in the church this affected worship, observance, organization, and even architecture. Queen Margaret's debates with church leaders and letters addressed to Scotland by Popes Paschal II and Calixtus II as late as the second and third decades of the twelfth century dealt critically with what were regarded as errors or abuses of an Irish type. For example, marriage customs were so lax that they seemed to condone a kind of polygamy, and it was easy for husbands to divorce their wives. To outside observers such practices, probably dating from pre-Christian Irish society, were hardly compatible with Christianity. Again, the laity only rarely confessed their sins, and with infrequency of confession went infrequency of communion. The Scots were reluctant to receive communion even at Easter, the culminating feast of the Christian year. The actual form of the eucharist was suspect to reformers who criticized what they called a 'barbarous rite' in the celebration of mass. Moreover, it seems that children were admitted to communion, contrary to what had become the normal practice of the church. The annual cycle of fasts, involving four seasons of solemn fasting, was not observed in Scotland, where the Irish custom of observing only three major fasts was followed. The Scots began their Lent four days after Ash Wednesday and reckoned the six Sundays before Easter as fast days, another archaic observance in line with the unreformed· Irish church. Sundays generally were not kept as rest days, a surprising fact when one considers the strength of sabbatarianism in Scotland from the seventeenth to the twentieth century.

There were irregularities in the ordination of priests and consecration of bishops. In most of Christendom new bishops were appointed in the context of an orderly hierarchy and provincial system, so that a metropolitan bishop (head of a province and usually an 'archbishop') performed consecrations with the assistance of at least two suffragan (i.e. subordinate) bishops, and in a solemn and public manner. The charge against the Scottish clergy was not that familiar in Germany, France, and England, namely that lay rulers interfered too much in the appointment of bishops, but the surely less serious charge that in the absence of any metropolitan in Scotland the bishops simply took it upon themselves to consecrate new recruits to their order, perhaps without insisting that at least three bishops should participate. For a single bishop to consecrate a priest to the episcopal grade was undoubtedly contrary to canon law as observed in the eleventh century.

Other Irish features of the Scottish church included the cult of innumerable saints of Irish name and origin, ecclesiastical dignities and offices found also in the Irish church, and a variety of customs and institutions of an Irish nature to which surviving place-names still bear witness. Irish missionaries widely venerated in Scotland since early Christian times included one or more of the many saints named Fáelán and Colmán respectively, Saint Findbarr, Saint Finán, Saint Donnán of Eigg, Saint Moluoc of Lismore, and Saint Maelrubha (Maree) of Applecross, after whom Loch Maree is named. The early saints of Iona were of course revered, not only Columba himself (at Dunkeld and Inchcolm) but also several of his successors as abbot, among them Saint Cumméin and Saint Adamnan who wrote biographies of Columba. The most famous reliquary of Columba in Scotland, the little house-shaped casket known as the *Brecbennach* (now the Monymusk Reliquary), enjoyed a truly national status and was solemnly borne into battle with the armies led by kings of Scots.

There can be no doubt of the Irish origin of dignitaries such as the *ab* (*abbe*), the head or abbot of a monastic church of Irish type, holding an office that had usually become secularized before the twelfth century; or the *fer léighinn*, literally 'man of reading', who taught the younger clergy in all large monastic churches. A distinctively Irish monastic reform movement of the eighth century, that of the *Céli Dé*, 'clients' or 'vassals' of God, was strongly represented in central and eastern Scotland north of Forth, as well as in Iona. There were communities of *Céli Dé*, or culdees as they have been known in later times, at such notably 'Pictish' churches as Abernethy, St Serf's Inch in Loch Leven, Muthil in Strathearn, and St Andrews. At a humbler level there were the *deòradh* or 'dewar' whose duty was to guard a church's holy relics, the *scoloc*, or small tenant on church lands, and the servile *cumherba* and *cumelache* apparently confined to ecclesiastical estates.[1]

Place-names such as Appin (Argyll, Perthshire), Abdie and Abden (Fife), Dysart (Argyll, Perthshire, Fife and Angus), Scryne (Angus) and Elie or Eliebank (Iona, Fife, Peeblesshire, Strathspey) all show the ubiquity of Irish usage. An 'appin' (Irish, *apdaine*) was the jurisdiction and thus the territory of an *ab* or abbot; a 'dysart' was the *díseart* or *desertum*, a cell set apart for the contemplative solitary monk; a *scrín* was the *scrinium* or shrine of a locally venerated saint; while the *ealadh* was the landing place or bank that received corpses being carried to some hallowed cemetery. The round towers at Brechin and Abernethy, built of good squared ashlar, are reminiscent of round towers at Cashel and Glendalough in Ireland. And yet, when Irish influence is given its due emphasis, our picture of the Scottish church must allow for important characteristics derived from other sources. For a start, we should bear in mind that throughout Celtic-speaking lands the church had a general similarity of character. Some of the apparently Irish features may have been Cumbric or Welsh in origin, easily assimilated to an Irish form after the Scots gained political ascendancy in the ninth century. In Galloway and Clydesdale there are traces of a church structure analagous to that of Wales, based on the *clas* or enclosed clerical community. The Welsh word *llan*, originally meaning 'enclosure' but acquiring an ecclesiastical sense of 'enclosed church' at an early date, occurs occasionally in Scotland, in such names as 'Planmichel' (the older form of Carmichael in Clydesdale), Lumphanan, and Lumphinnans – though in these last two instances we cannot be sure whether the first part is Welsh and not Irish. The mixed nature of churches at the start of our period, some obviously monastic, many others serving secular communities, may be compared to the situation in South Wales.[2] In southern Scotland, where at least two Northumbrian saints, Oswald and Cuthbert, were greatly revered, the church had a good deal in common with that of Northumbria as a whole. In this area the beginnings of a true parochial system, alien to Irish practice, may be inferred from what the sources tell us of the clergy, local in origin and forming a substantial

[1] These last three classes are noticed above, p. 17.
[2] Wendy Davies, *An early Welsh microcosm* (Royal Historical Society, 1978), p. 123.

stratum among the region's freeholders or gentry. Many of these priests would have been married and would expect sons or other close kinsmen to succeed them in their benefices. It is not necessary to look to Ireland for the origins of this state of affairs, for a married rural clergy was normal throughout western Europe until the late-eleventh-century reformers began to impose celibacy upon the priesthood. As late as 1220 the abbot of Jedburgh complained to the pope that bishops of Carlisle had actually granted the reversion of parish churches to the sons of rectors during their fathers' lifetime. If this happened in Carlisle diocese it may have happened in Scotland also.

It is probable that throughout Scotland the clergy formed an hereditary caste, many of whose members would rank as free men, while others were lowly enough to be included among the neyfs or *nativi* tied to the estates of their birth. Free or unfree, the clergy would not have enjoyed much mobility, whether social or geographical. Often they bore names that indicate devotion to the cults observed at their own churches, e.g. Cosmungho ('Saint Kentigern's servant') at Eddleston in Peeblesshire, or Gilise ('Jesus's servant'), who seems to have been hereditary priest of the ancient church of Saint Mary the Virgin at Stow, north of Galashiels.

Because Scottish society was much less tribal than Irish and much more territorial, the church in Scotland was not organized into great tribal monastic federations as happened in Ireland. It had therefore been possible for some kind of episcopal structure of church government to survive from the days when Pictish kings had adopted the 'Roman' system in the early eighth century, in the wake of the Synod of Whitby (664). However attenuated this episcopal structure had become, it is clear that the Scottish church in the reign of Malcolm III was still led by bishops. The bishop at St Andrews was even distinguished by the title *árd escop*, *summus episcopus*, not indicating metropolitan status but acknowledging a sort of primacy or seniority. Again the parallel with South Wales in the same period is suggestive, for there the situation 'appears to have been strictly comparable neither to the Irish nor the English pattern. . . . There were species of monastic federation and of bishopric in Wales'.[3] Alexander I and David I could base their reform of church government on existing practice, although they emphatically shifted the balance in favour of episcopacy.

We are able to infer continuity in this vitally important matter of

---

[3]W. Davies, *An early Welsh microcosm*, p. 139.

church government because several of the earliest twelfth-century bishops of whom there is any record had native Scottish names such as Cormac, Nechtan, and Macbeth, proving that David I did not start from scratch by bringing in exclusively English and continental clergy to rule over Scottish dioceses. A more decisive piece of evidence is to be found in the complex diocesan pattern of medieval Scotland (Map II). In 1155 there were 10 dioceses in the kingdom: St Andrews, Glasgow, Dunkeld, Aberdeen, Moray, Brechin, Dunblane, Ross, Caithness, and Galloway (Whithorn). Of these, Whithorn was clearly a revival, if not a continuation, of the see founded by the Northumbrians *c*.700 in deference to the still earlier tradition of Ninian as already a bishop there in the fifth century. Glasgow, the see of Saint Mungo or Kentigern (sixth century), corresponded to the historical kingdom of Strathclyde or Cumbria, and its bishops even claimed episcopal authority as far south as Westmorland in the mid thirteenth century. In practice, Henry I's creation of the diocese of Carlisle (1133) fixed the southern limit of the large bishopric of Glasgow at the Solway Firth. Whithorn and Glasgow were therefore both ancient and territorial, corresponding respectively to the lordship of Galloway (which survived till 1455) and the kingdom of Strathclyde (which disappeared in the eleventh century).

The remaining dioceses of Scotland fall into two groups. The first were based on ancient churches of a Celtic monastic type. These churches already owned large endowments of land, often widely scattered. St Andrews, for example, had estates as far north as Aberdeenshire and as far south as East Lothian and the valley of the Gala Water. The lands of the old 'abbey' of Dunkeld lay as far apart as Bunkle in Berwickshire and Loch Etive in Argyll, although most were concentrated in the provinces of Atholl, Gowrie, and Fife. Brechin and Dunblane had lands scattered through Angus and Perthshire respectively. The territory of Aberdeen, though more compact, still reflected a diocese whose see had been moved to the mouth of the River Don from the upland site of Mortlach, now Dufftown, in Banffshire. These dioceses are characterized by an extraordinary intermingling of territories and a profusion of detached portions often remote from the mother church. Had the twelfth-century kings been starting from scratch it is inconceivable that they would have produced such complexity.

The second group was more explicitly the creation of Alexander I and David I, although even here they must have made use of some existing churches. The dioceses of Moray, Ross, and Caithness were clearly provincial or territorial, and the same was roughly true of Argyll when that completely new diocese was carved out of the sprawling bishopric of Dunkeld *c*.1190. There was surely a strategic aspect here, a desire to give each frontier province a strong secular government and a bishop to match. It is true that the first three recorded bishops of Ross — Macbeth, Simon, and Gregory — may have been the last of an old episcopal succession. Their cathedral church at Rosemarkie on the Black Isle (later transferred to nearby Fortrose) had ancient traditions, but the diocese corresponded to the earldom of Ross and the western seaboard known as 'North Argyll'. In Moray there is no record of any early bishop's church and the see was not fixed permanently at the royal burgh of Elgin until the thirteenth century. The splendid new cathedral was built there in the course of that century, obviously as an after-thought, for its site is outwith the old burgh limits. King David's first bishop of Moray, Gregory (later promoted to Dunkeld?), was almost certainly titular, and we may regard Richard of Lincoln, appointed in 1187, as the first effective resident bishop. Likewise in Caithness the first known bishop, Andrew, a Scotsman who had been a Benedictine monk at Dunfermline, was largely an absentee. He possessed many estates in central Scotland and attended the king's court assiduously. Andrew's appointment by about 1147 as titular bishop must be seen as part of David I's policy of detaching this remote and partly Norse-speaking Scottish province from the Norse-ruled earldom of Orkney. Not until the thirteenth century was the see moved from Norse-dominated Halkirk to the more southerly church of Dornoch in the Gaelic-speaking part of the diocese.

If Scotland was to be brought into line with western Christendom the setting up of an effective diocesan system was of crucial importance. But it immediately raised the problem of church government at the highest level. The papacy was well aware that in asserting its own authority throughout the church it could not simply ignore the entrenched claims of lay rulers nor overlook the emergence of more or less permanent kingdoms, often the future 'national' kingdoms, which can be seen as the most significant long-term trend in twelfth-century Europe. The popes, themselves bishops among a great host of brother bishops, were prepared to recognize, above the level of the diocese, a grouping of dioceses under a metropolitan archbishop, that is, a 'province', and also, perhaps more reluctantly, to acknowledge that those metropolitans who were accepted as 'senior' within territories enjoying national or political unity should be accorded the rank of 'primate'. Thus, primacy was granted to Toledo for all Spain, to Canterbury (under protest from York) for all England, to Armagh for all Ireland, to Gniezno for Poland, to Esztergom for Hungary, and to Lyons for much of France. It is noteworthy that since France was too extensive to form a truly national territory in the earlier Middle Ages, the primacy of the French church was claimed by other provincial sees, especially Bourges.

For Scotland, the twelfth-century papacy produced an unsatisfactory compromise, yet the policy of several popes, notably Alexander III (1159–81) and Celestine III (1191–8), strongly favoured the Scots crown in its bid to preserve the separate identity of the *ecclesia Scoticana*. David I and Malcolm IV wished to have St Andrews recognized as the metropolitan church of their realm. This was refused by the papacy although in 1152 it promoted Trondheim to be metropolitan for the scattered sees of Norse lands and at the same time grouped the 39 dioceses of Ireland into no fewer than four archbishoprics under Armagh. The popes' reluctance to give official approval to a distinct identity for the Scottish church sprang from their attachment to the master-plan of Pope Gregory the Great as reported in Bede's *Ecclesiastical History of the English People*. This provided for the division of Britain into two provinces each of 12 dioceses, headed respectively by bishops at London and York. Although never implemented the Gregorian plan was attractive to the Norman conquerors of England and their archbishops. A council at Windsor in 1072 actually assigned the whole of Scotland as far as the Pentland Firth (and probably the Northern Isles as well) to York province. If enforced this would have made Canterbury's claims to jurisdiction as far north as the Rivers Trent and Ribble less aggressive than they afterwards appeared. But the Windsor ruling was probably not widely known in Scotland and was certainly never put into effect. Alexander I and David I refused to countenance any interference by York or Canterbury in the government of the Scots church, save in the case of Galloway whose 'special relationship' of dependence on York was not only allowed but lasted until the fourteenth century.

After a series of tentative but important moves in the 1160s and '70s generally confirming the ecclesiastical autonomy of Scotland, Pope Celestine III in 1192 took the unusual step of declaring that all the Scottish sees except Galloway were collectively the 'special daughter' of the Roman church, immediately subject to the papacy. The bull to this effect, known from its opening words as *Cum universi*, was reissued by Innocent III and Honorius III. It should have included

Argyll, omitted in error no doubt because its creation was so recent. It rightly omitted Galloway, though within the Scottish kingdom, and the Isles ('Sodor and Man') which covered far-flung territories subject to Norway until 1266. The diocese of the Isles became increasingly Scottish from the later thirteenth century and had ceased to be subject to Trondheim by *c*.1350. By that time Galloway had in effect broken away from York, so that the later medieval *ecclesia Scoticana* was made up of 12 dioceses, to which Orkney was added in the later fifteenth century.

Over a remarkably long period from the 1080s to the middle of the thirteenth century the bishops gradually provided their sees with cathedral churches and established chapters of dignitaries and other senior clergy to serve as their governing bodies. Naturally enough this long-drawn-out process began with the two richest and most important sees of St Andrews and Glasgow. St Andrews had two successive cathedrals on closely adjacent sites, the first (now 'St Rule's') dating from *c*.1070–80, the second, very much larger, indeed by far the largest single building in medieval Scotland, founded *c*.1162 by Bishop Arnold. Solemnly dedicated in 1318, it was not structurally complete before the later thirteenth century, though it was in use by the 1230s. At Glasgow veneration for the traditional shrine of Saint Mungo beside the Molendinar Burn meant that the successive cathedrals of Bishop John (*c*.1115–47), Bishop Jocelin (1174–99), and Bishop William Bondington (1233–58) were all constructed on the same difficult sloping site, involving an elaborate undercroft or lower church. Unlike St Andrews, where the major cathedral is a ruin, Glasgow cathedral has survived largely intact and well restored, even if visually overborne by the bulky Royal Infirmary building. Most of the Scottish cathedrals as we have them today, whether beautiful even in ruin, like Elgin, or splendidly restored, like Dunblane, belong structurally to the period *c*.1220–80, a wonderfully busy time for the Scots stonemason. In many ways the finest of the Scottish medieval cathedrals to survive substantially unaltered is the beautiful red sandstone church of St Magnus at Kirkwall in Orkney, which was not in the realm of Scotland when it was being built, between 1137 and the end of the thirteenth century. This impressive church shows three main building phases, a simple and dignified romanesque of the mid twelfth century, a phase of transition towards the gothic pointed style, and some fine pure gothic work especially at the east end. Taken together, the cathedral churches of medieval Scotland constitute a remarkable and too much neglected monument of north European architecture.

All but two of the Scottish cathedrals had chapters of secular clergy, sometimes explicitly on the model either of Salisbury (as at Glasgow) or of Lincoln (as at Elgin), The head of the chapter was the dean — 'parish priest of the cathedral clergy' — assisted by the subdean. The other principal officers were the chancellor (in charge of legal and written business), treasurer (finance), and chanter or precentor (responsible for the music, choir, and liturgical offices). All would normally have deputies, and the rest of the chapter would consist of secular canons, often reinforced, in the poorer sees, by the heads of the richest religious houses of the diocese. The two exceptions to this pattern were St Andrews and Whithorn. The former had a convent of Augustinian canons-regular for its chapter, as was true of Carlisle which may have had some influence on St Andrews. The latter, most unusually, had a chapter of Premonstratensian or 'White' canons, an austere reformed order which had several houses in Galloway. Although there were famous monastic cathedrals in England, they were mostly old Benedictine houses which do not seem to have provided the model for the two Scottish 'quasi-monastic' cathedral foundations.

Transformation by no means ended with the creation of a diocesan system, although by *c*.1250 Scotland might be justifiably proud to have a church governed neither by too few bishops (like England) nor by too many (like Ireland), divided into dioceses that did not show too gross an imbalance between the populous and unpopulous parts of the country. Within each diocese the bishop appointed a number of officers to help him perform his rôles of pastor of the Christian flock, corrector and judge, and landowner. For example, archdeacons begin to appear in Scotland between *c*.1126 (Glasgow) and *c*.1144 (St Andrews). These two large dioceses came to have two archdeaconries each, but single archdeaconries sufficed for the other sees. Trained ecclesiastical lawyers known as Officials began to be appointed in the later twelfth century. They acted as presidents of the bishops' ordinary courts of jurisdiction where lawsuits concerning what were classified as spiritual and ecclesiastical matters were heard and decided and where transgressions against Christian law were dealt with and if necessary punished. At parish level the bishops chose certain members of the clergy (often closely associated with their own households) to act as leaders of groups of parochial incumbents. Such a group, usually containing between a dozen and thirty parishes, formed a readily defined district whose leading priest was called the 'dean of Christianity' (equivalent to the English 'rural dean'). To administer the large landed estates which formed the endowment of most sees the bishops normally had stewards chosen from among the more substantial knightly or freeholding families within the diocese, often themselves tenants of the bishopric concerned.

Ecclesiastical government operated in the following way. The parish priest, either a rector ('parson') or (after 1216) a vicar, would attend a chapter composed of fellow-clergy of his own deanery of Christianity (decanal chapter). Senior clergy, including all the deans, would attend the larger archidiaconal synod (Scots, senzie), while every parish was liable to be 'visited' (i.e., inspected) once a year by the archdeacon. In Lothian synods and chapters were well established by the 1180s. Once or twice a year there might be an assembly of the principal clergy of the entire diocese, including the senior dignitaries of cathedrals and heads of religious houses (diocesan synod). A representative council of the whole *ecclesia Scoticana* met at one or other of the chief church centres, in theory annually but in practice rather less often. In 1225 Pope Honorius III, in providing for annual church councils, had ruled that the Scots bishops, lacking a metropolitan, must elect one of their number as 'conservator of privileges'. It was usual for this office to be held by the bishop of either St Andrews or Glasgow, who would thus become the effective spokesman of the Scottish church during his term of office.

We may surely say that the greatest work of transformation for the Scottish church and people accomplished between the time of Saint Margaret and the middle of the thirteenth century was the creation of a national system of parishes, the outward expression of which was the construction of scores, indeed hundreds, of parish kirks. Church statutes of the thirteenth century declared that in every parish there ought to be a stone-built church, the nave, or public part, of which should be built and maintained at the cost of the parishioners, while the chancel at the east end, whose use was confined to the clergy, should be paid for by the rector. Parish kirks were also to be duly consecrated by the bishop, whether or not they were newly built. We have the record of extensive tours made in his diocese by David Bernham as bishop of St Andrews (1239–53) for the purpose of consecrating churches, many of which must have been small and remote. All over Scotland at the present day we can still see many of these modest structures, the parish kirks of medieval Scotland. Some, like the delightful old church of Saint Adamnan at Insh in Badenoch, which preserves its even more ancient bronze bell, are still intact and in use; many others are no more than forlorn ruins, like the little church of Saint Serf at

Creich in north Fife. A rectangular plan, often without any tower, thick walls of rubble masonry, and a few small windows are the standard features of these starkly simple churches. It is worth a moment's reflection that such were the places of worship of the majority of Catholic ancestors of those many Scots of later ages who have been justifiably proud of the austere simplicity of the presbyterian form of prayer and praise.

It is hard to be sure how far parish churches in any recognizable sense existed in Scotland before *c*.1120, except in the south and southeast. There were countless shrines, chapels, hermitages, possibly even small churches, bearing ancient dedications to an enormous variety of saints, the overwhelming majority of whom were of Celtic origin – Breton, Cornish, Welsh, and Irish as well as native Cumbrian, Pictish, and Scots. Only a small proportion of these sacred sites were selected for permanent parish kirks and we hardly ever know why one site was preferred to another. A large number of surviving Scots parishes bear names different from those of the biggest villages or towns within them (e.g., Moulin/Pitlochry, Auchtergaven/Bankfoot, Panbride/Carnoustie), and the roots of this curious anomaly often go back to medieval times and perhaps even earlier.

The essential prerequisite for a parish system was the provision of a big enough financial endowment to meet the stipend of a resident priest and some other necessary expenses, for buildings and charity and assistant clergy. Most parish kirks were endowed by their founders, or by conscientious bishops or lay patrons, with a glebe that often amounted to a whole or at least a half ploughgate of arable. This would hardly secure an adequate living for an incumbent who had to pay for the services of chaplains and clerks, maintain part of the fabric, and buy bread and wine for the mass and oil for the altar lights. The main source of parish revenue was in fact the teind (English, tithe), that is the tenth part of the annual production of all ordinary sources of livelihood which ought to show yearly increase – corn, hay, and other crops, livestock of all kinds, and animal products such as butter and cheese; and in towns even the profits of merchants and craftsmen. Although based on Old Testament authority, teind would have been a dead letter unless enforced by royal power. The credit therefore for being the founder of the parochial system must be given to David I, for he was the first king of Scots to enact a law compelling payment of teind in at least some, if not all, of the dioceses of his realm.

Parishes varied greatly in size and wealth. Older and larger parishes often contained chapels in which mass could be celebrated but no services of baptism or burial could be held, for these were the fundamental purposes of the true parish church. If such chapels did secure the right to baptize and bury they were in effect being promoted into new parish churches, and this is how many parishes came into existence in the period. There was also a tendency from the later twelfth century for great lords to obtain episcopal permission to provide their castles and manor houses with private chapels for the convenience of themselves and their families and households. Such a chapel survives, in ruin, at the great castle of the earls of Mar at Kildrummy on Donside; more commonly we have only documentary evidence, which proves that at one time they must have been fairly numerous. As for variations in parish wealth, we gain an insight into these from the taxation records, e.g. from those of 'Pope Nicholas's Taxation' of 1290. In the deanery of Linlithgow the parish kirk of the burgh of Linlithgow, St Michael's, was assessed for tax at 110 merks, and the Haly Rude kirk in the burgh of Stirling at 50 (both churches, incidentally, are well preserved). The rural kirks of Auldcathie and Slamannan, by contrast, were rated at only four merks each. Similarly in the deanery of Fife the four big parish kirks of Dunfermline (£100), Leuchars (120 merks), St Andrews Holy Trinity (100 merks), and Crail (90 merks) were vastly richer than Arngask at six, Methil at five, and Kirkforthar at only four merks apiece. The southern and eastern lowlands, as would be expected, were better provided with parishes than the northern highlands. For example, Fife and Dumfriesshire had about 70 parishes each, while the barren country of north-west Sutherland and Wester Ross had only eight altogether.

The parish system created in the twelfth century has survived to the present day. It was continued largely unaltered by the reformed church of the sixteenth century, which discovered that whereas the dioceses and archdeaconries were mostly irrelevant to its purposes the medieval parish could comfortably be adapted to presbyterian organization. The collapse of Christianity in our own time has meant the practical disappearance of the parish from the life of most people. It is therefore worth recalling that in addition to serving local government purposes the parish system was successfully adapted to the needs of Christian congregations as various as the Free Church of 1843, the Roman Catholic Church after the restoration of the hierarchy, and the Episcopal Church of Scotland — though not all these bodies used the actual historic parishes of medieval times. The system was the basis of the great *Statistical Account* of 1791 and is still the starting-point of most local history. Few institutions in Scotland have served the needs of so many men, women, and children so well for such a lengthy period of time.

There were nevertheless defects in the parochial system if we take its purpose to have been to maintain the people within the bosom of holy mother church, to bring the gospel to them, and to help to save their immortal souls from eternal damnation. An ill-educated clergy was at once too independent of its bishops and too dependent on lay patrons. These often used parish livings in their gift as a means of finding employment for younger sons and nephews. Such perfunctory 'rectors' did not always bother to take priest's orders; instead, they would pocket the revenues of their churches and pay a pittance to some poor chaplain who would serve the cure of souls. Even when the incumbent was a priest he was unlikely to be a frequent or regular preacher, and not every parson set a good example to his flock. John, parson of Inverkeithing in the 1280s, had enough classical learning to be tempted to revive the fertility rites associated with Priapus, and had the village maidens dancing round him naked before he was eventually stabbed to death in his own kirkyard. The poor parson of Slamannan in 1306 was simpleton enough to be conned by a wily Englishman into handing over six stones of cheese, ostensibly to help the pope out of his financial difficulties. On the other hand, we are told that the parson of Bothans near Haddington fitted up the chancel of his small church from floor to ceiling with carved woodwork. Ceres parish church in Fife was given a glass lamp and two gallons of oil to keep it burning throughout the year. The church at Dalmeny in West Lothian, which still preserves a good deal of its twelfth-century structure, was well enough endowed for its vicar to have a hall and garden, both described as 'old' in 1323.

The bishops did their best to serve their flocks and to ensure that their parish clergy were properly qualified. Ralph Lambley, who had been a Tironensian monk at Arbroath before becoming bishop of Aberdeen in 1239, continued to live very simply and visited the churches of his diocese on foot. After the Fourth Lateran Council of 1216 most bishops strove to implement the decree of that council which provided for the institution of a permanently resident priest, called a 'perpetual vicar', in every parish where for whatever reason the rector was an absentee. In 1293 William Fraser bishop of St Andrews refused to accept Master John of Bamburgh as vicar of Berwick upon Tweed, although he had been duly presented by the cathedral priory of Durham, patron of the living. The bishop's objection was that Master John was not even in deacon's orders, whereas councils presided over by the papal legates Otto (Holyrood, 1239) and Ottobono (London, 1269) had laid down that vicars must be priests on appointment or at least deacons. Instead, the bishop admitted William Procter to the vicarage, but said that John of Bamburgh might be vicar of Fishwick (a much smaller living than Berwick) as long as he got himself made deacon quickly.

It is not easy to gauge the strength of popular religious devotion. We hear of pilgrimages and the Whitsuntide visits of the faithful to the mother churches of their dioceses. Cathedral and parish churches were furnished with numerous altars which reflected more than the private devotion of the rich. Burgesses were obviously proud of the well-endowed parish churches of their towns and public processions of gild brethren and other groups on notable saints' days were a feature of urban life. On the negative side, we have no evidence of heresy, only of sacrilege, blasphemy, and careless indifference. Kirkyards were used for sports and pastimes, sometimes as unsuitable as bull-baiting and prize fighting; no doubt this was a custom that went back to very early times. As for irreverence, it is deeply rooted in human nature and far from proving the absence of reverence may often go hand in hand with it. A story told by Walter Bower of his own days (the 1430s) might well have had its counterpart a century and half earlier. One summer during a severe famine some starving girls of Dunfermline walked down to the seashore at Gellet near Rosyth to scavenge for food among the shellfish and seaweed. On their way home they were caught unawares by a sudden thunder plump and were soaked to the skin. At a flash of lightning all the girls save one crossed themselves, but the sauciest of them merely shouted 'Christ's cross upon my hinder end!' Even if the story — in which, of course, the blasphemer was instantly incinerated — happens to be fiction, it would not prove that Abbot Bower was not a Christian because he related such absurd nonsense, nor demonstrate the genuine faith of the survivors and lack of it on the part of the girl who perished. The story does no more than show us that ordinary life was lived in a consciously Christian mould.

With the help of able and zealous clergy, the twelfth-century kings succeeded in bringing the *ecclesia Scoticana* into line with the Catholic church of western Christendom. They established a fairly clearcut diocesan and parochial system governed by an orderly hierarchy. They defended the church they had thus brought up to date by preventing it from being absorbed into any of the three provinces whose metropolitan archbishops might have had designs upon it, York, Canterbury, and Trondheim. In effect, they threw it into the not unwilling arms of the papacy which gave it a distinctive, if not quite unique, place in the organization of the western church. But the ruling house of Scotland went further than this, for almost single-handed they introduced into their realm the monastic and quasi-monastic orders that were widely regarded as the shock troops of the Christian revival that swept Europe between *c*.1050 and *c*.1230. The reformed church of Pope Gregory VII and his successors was not at all averse to monasticism provided that it remained the faithful servant of the papacy and of the centralized church over which the papacy had been exalted.

Scotland had not been touched by the earliest forms of monachism associated with Benedict of Nursia, nor by the experiments at reforming Benedictine monachism which were carried out in the ninth and tenth centuries. When Margaret of Hungary became the queen of Malcolm III *c*.1070 the only forms of monastic life in Scotland, apart from ascetic hermits and solitaries, of whom there were probably a considerable number, were the old-fashioned communities of Irish type to be found in certain famous churches such as St Andrews, Abernethy, Brechin, and Iona and the surviving colleges of *Céli Dé*. Some of these communities inspired Queen Margaret's admiration (no easy matter, one would guess), but in general she seems to have been shocked at the spiritual backwardness of her adopted country. The English and continental models available to her were few and it is hardly surprising that she chose the Benedictine foundation of Christ Church or Holy Trinity at Canterbury. This great cathedral monastery was reformed under the direction of Lanfranc, formerly abbot of St Stephen's, Caen, whom William the Conqueror had made arch-bishop of Canterbury in 1070. From Canterbury a few monks were dispatched to Scotland to form the nucleus of a Benedictine priory founded by the queen at Dunfermline, the royal residence where she and King Malcolm had been married. A small romanesque church was built there, dedicated like its mother house to Christ or the Holy Trinity. In the 1120s this church was greatly enlarged by David I, who emphasized the independence of Dunfermline by having it raised to the status of an abbey. Nevertheless, the first abbot, Geoffrey, was brought from Canterbury, and links with the mother house remained close until the thirteenth century.

Margaret's encouragement of the disciplined religious life was eclectic, inasmuch as she restored the church of Iona and was a benefactress of St Andrews and other ancient shrines where there were *Céli Dé*. Even her introduction of the first Benedictine monks, important though this was psychologically, proved to be something of a dead end. It was overtaken by momentous events in the development of monastic life which were already taking place in Burgundy, the western Alps, and northern France before Queen Margaret died. The two conventional Benedictine houses in Scotland, Dunfermline Abbey and Coldingham Priory in Berwickshire, owed their existence to the fact that Malcolm III's marriage coincided with Lanfranc's dominant influence in the Anglo-Norman church. The future of continental types of monasticism in Scotland was to lie with the reformed orders of Benedictine or quasi-Benedictine pattern established at Cîteaux in the 1090s and at Thiron-le-Gardais north of Chartres early in the twelfth century. An equally important rôle, relatively greater than was the case in England, was played by the order of Augustinian canons-regular, which was only partly monastic and claimed to follow a rule for a community of celibate priests composed by the great Saint Augustine of Hippo (Bone) in the fifth century.

These Augustinian communities proliferated rapidly in England from *c*.1100, benefiting from the patronage of Maud, Henry I's queen and sister of the Scots kings Edgar, Alexander I, and David I. Their first Scottish house was founded by King Alexander at Scone in the heart of the Scoto-Pictish kingdom, whither canons were brought from Nostell in the West Riding of Yorkshire *c*.1115. It was a canon of Scone, Robert, whom the same king made bishop of St Andrews in 1124. His episcopate lasted 35 years and had a formative effect on Scottish ecclesiastical development. Bishop Robert cut the Gordian knot of intertwined and deeply secularized vested interests within the ancient church foundation at St Andrews by converting the cathedral church into an Augustinian priory (1144), as had been done at Carlisle. Earlier than this, David I had founded a church for Augustinians (from Merton in Surrey and from Huntingdonshire) at a completely fresh site a mile east of Edinburgh Castle. The canons of this church were influenced by the great wave of reverence for the True Cross of Christ that swept across Europe in the later eleventh century, and dedicated their house to the Holy Rood, hence the name of Holyroodhouse by which the abbey has been familiarly known since the later Middle Ages. At about the same time another colony of Augustinians, perhaps from Beauvais in northern France, took over an old church at Jedburgh close to the English Border. Cambuskenneth, opposite Stirling, was also a royal Augustinian foundation, its first canons coming from Arrouaise near Amiens. The Augustinians (sometimes called 'black canons' from the colour of their habit) seemed especially suitable for taking over and reforming the old *Céli Dé* communities as well as other eremitical churches strongly Celtic in character. Thus, in addition to St Andrews, Inchcolm in the Firth of Forth, St Serf's Inch in Loch Leven, Inchmahome in Menteith, Inchaffray in Strathearn, Restenneth near Forfar, and Monymusk on Donside all obtained convents of canons-regular by the first half of the thirteenth century. The Augustinians were specifically priests and did not form an enclosed order. Their mission was to go out into the world and exercise a pastoral and teaching office. It would not be anachronistic to see their houses, at least in the twelfth century, as group ministries, and it was normal for founders and benefactors to bestow upon Augustinian houses parish churches which could be served directly by the canons.

Of the various types of 'reformed Benedictinism' that emerged at the turn of the twelfth century by far the most renowned and popular was the order of Cîteaux. The Cistercians, as they are usually known, originated in a group of austere congregations in Burgundy of which, as far as the British Isles were concerned, Clairvaux was to wield the greatest influence. The order was brought into Scotland almost simultaneously by David I and Fergus, lord (self-styled 'king') of Galloway. Their respective foundations at Melrose (1136) and Dundrennan (1142) were both daughter houses of Rievaulx in the North Riding of Yorkshire, which was in turn a daughter of Clairvaux. The order had some 11 houses in Scotland and enjoyed much prestige, but it never seems to have struck such deep roots of popularity as it did in northern England. Nevertheless, Scottish monastic life would have been immeasurably poorer without such abbeys as Melrose, Newbattle, or Coupar Angus on the east side of the country, or in Galloway Dundrennan, Glenluce, and Sweetheart. Almost certainly to a greater extent than other orders, the Cistercians maintained regular contacts with their sister houses in England and on the continent through compulsory attendance at the 'general chapters' of the entire order, when abbots from all over Europe met at Cîteaux. Closely comparable to both Augustinians and Cistercians, in effect 'cistercianized' canons-regular, were the white canons of Prémontré, otherwise Premonstratensians. They were brought to Dryburgh near Melrose in 1150 by the king's constable Hugh de Morville and his wife Beatrice de Beauchamp, and to Saulseat in Wigtownshire by Fergus of Galloway, perhaps a little later. The six churches of white canons included, most unusually, the small cathedral foundation at Whithorn.

Of the remaining orders of Benedictine type, or strongly influenced by the Benedictines, a brief mention should be made of the Cluniacs at Paisley (easily the richest abbey of middle-western Scotland) and Crossraguel in Carrick, and the extremely uncommon Burgundian order of Val-des-choux which in the early thirteenth century set up colonies at Pluscarden near Elgin, Beauly west of Inverness, and Ardchattan on Loch Etive in Argyll. It may seem surprising to find monks of Cluny in Scotland at all, for the order reached England only after the Norman Conquest and was rapidly superseded in esteem by Cîteaux, Savigny, and Chartreuse. Paisley is to be explained by the deep attachment of its first feudal lord, Walter son of Alan, the king's steward, to the Cluniac house of St Milburga of Wenlock in Shropshire. Significantly, and contrary to the normal Cluniac practice, Paisley was an independent abbey almost from the time of foundation, *c.*1163. As for the Valliscaulians (*Val-des-choux, vallis caulium,* 'vale of cabbages'), their arrival seems to have been due to Alexander II, perhaps acting on the advice of well-informed bishops. They proved peculiarly well-adapted to the highlands, a region conspicuously neglected by most of the monastic orders whose growth we have looked at.

A strong Cistercian influence is apparent in the impulse to establish religious houses for women. Whether or not David I was once again the instigator here, by founding the house for nuns at Berwick upon Tweed whose inception is often attributed to him, there was a markedly royal and aristocratic flavour about the foundation of the early Scottish nunneries. Malcolm IV gave the first endowment for a nunnery at Manuel near Linlithgow, his mother the Countess Ada founded the house of nuns at Haddington, while the earls and countesses of Dunbar and Fife were responsible for founding nunneries at Coldstream, Eccles, and North Berwick. Almost all the medieval nunneries of Scotland were convents of Cistercian nuns, that is women who observed the Benedictine rule as reformed by the order of Cîteaux even though they were not admitted to membership of the order. Nunneries were certainly in need of more protection than houses for men, and in addition to depending more heavily upon a patron the Cistercian nunneries were each provided with a priest called a 'Master' who could doubtless deal more easily with inescapable secular business than all but the toughest abbesses or prioresses. Despite an ancient Celtic tradition of women saints and anchorites, nunneries were extremely rare in the highlands, but before *c.*1200 the lord of Argyll had founded a house for Augustinian canonesses on the island of Iona.

The most successful and popular order of reformed Benedictines in

Scotland was that originating as a remote eremitical community in the forests of Le Perche near Chartres early in the twelfth century. Some 10 years before becoming king, David I was attracted to this group of hermits at Tiron (now Thiron), whence, in 1113, he took a small band of pioneering monks under an abbot, William, to serve a church at Selkirk in the heart of the royal forest of Tweeddale. The community flourished and expanded, and 15 years after its arrival it was transferred to more spacious quarters at Kelso on the Tweed. Kelso Abbey (1128) was almost certainly the richest and in many ways the most influential of medieval Scots religious houses. Maintaining for many years its links with Tiron (which like Citeaux held general chapters for the Tironensian order), Kelso became the mother house of abbeys at Kilwinning in Ayrshire, Arbroath in Angus, and Lindores in Fife. It also took over the ancient church of Lesmahagow in Lanarkshire, which became a Tironensian priory under the impetus of the remarkable Bishop John of Glasgow, who had himself spent some time as a monk at Tiron. We are so accustomed to the cultural time-lag in Scottish history as far as southern or continental influences are concerned that it is worth emphasizing that the Tironensian colony at Selkirk represents the earliest appearance anywhere in Britain of the 'new wave' of reformed Benedictine monachism, antedating Cistercians, Savigniacs, Premonstratensians, and (in Scotland by three centuries) Carthusians.

It scarcely seems credible that David I, almost single-handed, was responsible for introducing such a wide variety of monastic orders between 1124 and 1153 and for endowing them so prodigally with large estates in land and revenues, estates that, as we have seen, often cut across ancient boundaries and overrode entrenched rights. But the king not only founded houses for monks and nuns but also welcomed the first representatives of the crusading orders of the Temple of Solomon ('Knights Templars') and of the Hospital of Saint John of Jerusalem ('Knights Hospitallers'), as well as endowing the brethren of 'Saint' Lazarus of Jerusalem with the parish kirk of Edinburgh, St Giles. Another order associated with the Holy Land, that of the canons of Bethlehem, was brought to St Germains in East Lothian by *c.*1180. In the reign of Alexander II, encouraged especially by the energetic and far-sighted bishop of St Andrews, William Malvoisin (1202–38), the orders of mendicant friars, Franciscans or followers of Saint Francis of Assisi (1231) and Dominicans, disciples of the Spanish missionary preacher Dominic Guzman (before 1240), began to move into the chief burghs, Berwick, Edinburgh, Haddington etc. Their mission in Scotland as elsewhere was one of preaching, teaching, and charitable work among the very poorest for which the existing parochial system was already recognized to be inadequate.

The transformation of the Scottish church in the century and a half that followed the marriage of Malcolm III and Margaret of Hungary was compounded of many elements, spiritual, intellectual, organizational, and architectural. It was largely informed by a feeling of supranationalism and corresponding opposition, at times vehement, to isolationism or the stubborn desire to cling to regional customs and peculiarities. It may seem paradoxical that by the end of the thirteenth century this transformed *ecclesia Scoticana* was once again turning unmistakably to nationalistic ways of thought, as were its sister churches in England and France. That this should have been so is in fact a measure of how deeply the church had taken root within society, despite the preponderance of external influences. Even in those churches, such as the Cistercian abbeys, where we might have expected external influences to have been paramount, we can find evidence of a mingling of older tradition with the newer ideas of the 'romanizing' reformers at a surprisingly early date. For example, the abbey of Coupar Angus in Perthshire, founded about 1164, possessed — evidently for use and not as a mere collector's item — a psaltery or collection of the psalms written in twelfth-century handwriting of 'Irish' style, probably produced in a monastery or other centre of learning within Scotland which nevertheless still adhered to the Celtic Christian tradition.[4]

The architectural aspect of church transformation is probably the one we are most liable to underestimate. New ideas in worship and liturgy called for settings of dignity and even splendour in which music could play an effective part and the eye be caught by carvings of wood and stone enriched by bright colours in paint and fabric. There can hardly be any art to which the Scots have made a more distinguished contribution than that of architecture and town-planning. It is one of the most startling paradoxes of the historical Scottish character that a sense of rightness and taste in respect of buildings and where to place them has, from early times to the present day, been forced to struggle against a profound and sometimes aggressively philistine indifference to what it is now fashionable to call the 'built environment'. The period from *c.*1130 to 1286 was a great age for the stonemason and

[4]H.M.Bannister, *Specimen pages of two MSS. of the abbey of Coupar Angus in Scotland* (Rome, 1910).

architect in Scotland. Much of their most conspicuous, beautiful, and enduring work was carried out on behalf of the church, notably in the construction of cathedrals and monasteries. Before 1100 it is doubtful if the Scots set much store by large-scale building and dressed stone-work would have been a comparatively rare sight. The period covered by this book saw the birth of a tradition of building in stone for both ecclesiastical and secular purposes, powerful enough to survive the material impoverishment of fourteenth-century wars and the aesthetic impoverishment of sixteenth-century iconoclasm. In this respect, as in others, it would be foolish to judge Scottish achievement of the earlier Middle Ages, a time of confidence and nation-building, by the sterility of our own day. It is now so widely assumed that all Scots with taste or talent will emigrate permanently as soon as opportunity offers that the built environment of Scotland has been allowed to settle down into an austere squalor against whose inhumanity our medieval ancestors would have instinctively revolted.

5

Burghs and Burgesses

Every nation has its stereotypes which are usually true to begin with but grow further from the truth the longer they survive. Among familiar Scots stereotypes, the laird and the highland chief are extinct or on the verge of extinction, the village dominie has vanished altogether, while the parish minister is a much altered figure and a great deal less kenspeckle than he used to be. One stereotype that has had an extraordinarily long life has been the burgh, typically a small or medium-sized urban community, conservative, tightly-knit, having a good conceit of itself, not greatly given to a broad and cosmopolitan world view. The Scots burgh was formally abolished by the Local Government (Scotland) Act of 1973 (21 & 22 Elizabeth, cap. 65), having played a part in national history for eight and a half centuries. Long before the burgh's abolition, however, it had become difficult to pinpoint the typical example of the species because the range of variation had grown so extended. At one extreme, a large number of very small burghs (mostly old 'burghs of barony') had been deprived of burghal status and had become mere villages or suburbs, while at the other extreme a handful of burghs had developed into industrial and commercial cities not easily distinguishable from their counterparts in other countries. The burghs and burgesses to be examined in this chapter had their origin in our period but preserved as a class an astonishingly unaltered, homogeneous character from the twelfth or thirteenth century to the eighteenth.

Where and why did burghs come into existence? These questions have been asked by urban historians of every European country where the phenomenon of the self-conscious, individually identifiable, organized town community is to be found. The first question, concerning geographical location and distribution, should not present too many difficulties and may be left until we have attempted an answer to the second. To this a number of different answers have been put forward. They are not necessarily incompatible but they do at least suggest differences of emphasis and usually reflect the different regional and other specialist standpoints of the historians concerned.

Wherever in the course of human settlement two or three are gathered together trading is likely to take place. This is as true of school children bargaining for 'swaps' in the playground as of diamond merchants in Hatton Garden. Although direct contemporary evidence is hard to come by, it is inconceivable that trade was not being carried on during the eleventh century in every inhabited part of Scotland and between Scotland and neighbouring countries. Continuity of trade at however primitive a level must in fact be supposed, as a matter of mere common sense, from prehistoric times right through to the earlier medieval period. Since there were no 'burghs' as such in Scotland before *c.*1100 it is obvious that trade in itself was not a sufficient cause of burghal origin. On the other hand, it is undeniable that trade was a necessary cause. Markets could exist without burghs, but a burgh without a market is almost a contradiction in terms.

Yet the word 'burgh' (equivalent to 'borough' in English usage and Latinized as *burgus*) does not in itself carry any implication of trade. It is a word found generally in the Germanic languages to indicate a place of strength. *Ein' feste Burg ist unser Gott* wrote Martin Luther, who had no thoughts of comparing the Almighty to a shopping centre. Until modern times, the word in Scots was pronounced 'broch', in which form it survives today as the affectionate nickname of Fraserburgh, a town founded by Fraser of Philorth in 1546 and long thought of as an exotic novelty in north-east Buchan. It is identical with the word 'broch' used to denote the mysterious apertureless drystone towers whose ruins are so thick on the ground in Caithness and the Northern Isles. Any theory formulated to account for the rise of the medieval burgh must explain why a term for 'fortress' or 'place of strength' was adopted as the generic term for what was typically a small mercantile community.

One of the older theories of burgh origins, not widely held nowadays, states that the burgh was essentially a defensible strongpoint which required a sizeable number of able-bodied men to form its permanent garrison. Its trading activity was merely incidental. Such an origin would, it was argued, explain the remarkable degree of equality to be found among twelfth-century burgesses and provided for in early burgh laws. It would be natural for any body of soldiers to serve on a roughly equal footing and expect equal rewards. Attractive though this theory might be in respect of (say) midland England, where King Alfred and his tenth-century successors, as part of their defence of Wessex against the Danes, undoubtedly set up earthwork encampments at existing towns or at sites that subsequently became urban, it can have no relevance for Scotland. The earliest known Scottish burghs did not form part of any general scheme of defence, even if it can be argued that a few individual towns in the twelfth century (e.g., Inverness, Dumfries, and Ayr) probably played a defensive role. It is true that the word 'burgh' is embedded in the names of some Scots towns, such as Roxburgh and Edinburgh,[1] and these did occupy old fortified sites. But in these cases the suffix is identical with that found in Bamburgh and Dunstanburgh in Northumberland, and refers to ancient fortifications dating from long before the days of commercial town life. It is almost accidental that a few early burghs have names of this type.

Moreover, this 'garrison theory' should not be connected with the fact that many Scots burghs were adjacent to medieval castles. A close study of both the physical layout and the tenurial record of such early towns as Berwick upon Tweed, Roxburgh, Edinburgh, Perth, and Elgin proves that at these places the castles stood outwith the burgh and formed no part of it. Even today, indeed, the old royal castles of Edinburgh and Stirling remain Crown property and occupy high rocky sites unsuitable for urban development. No castle could have functioned effectively if a town had been allowed to grow up around it. As long as castles were in active use they stood in clear areas either at one end or on the edge of any burgh with which they happened to be associated.

A solution to the problem of why the 'burgh' should have been given this particular name is not to be sought in a Scottish context. We are in fact dealing with a story closely comparable to that of feudalism and the knight's feu or fee. Concept and technical term alike must have been introduced ready-made by the twelfth-century kings and those whom they patronized. The Germanic word *burg* in the simple sense of 'fortification' can be traced back at least to the second century A.D., probably to the first. At a later period (fourth century onward, and clearly discernible from the eighth) the word was also used to denote an urban or quasi-urban community bigger than a village but smaller or at least of less consequence than a city. This usage was general in the

---

[1] Jedburgh is not another example for it was known as Jedworth (Jeddart) until the later Middle Ages.

territories where the population spoke one of the Romance languages which were the successors of vulgar Latin. In what are now north-east France and western Belgium this secondary meaning of *burg* or *bourg* was evidently known even to Flemish-speakers, although their own term for a town of less than civic status tended to be *poort*.[2] In Scotland, English- and Scandinavian-speakers simply continued to use their Germanic words *burh* and *borg* to denote fortresses and other strong places. But they also learned, more readily among the English-speakers than the Norse, to use the Roman-derived word to denote a new phenomenon, the settlement and community of privileged merchants and craftsmen established, very much as monasteries were being established, by kings and great magnates. The monasteries' purpose was to save sinful souls from eternal damnation. The burghs' purpose was to expand and regulate trade, thereby increasing royal and lordly revenues.

Most of the earliest burghs of Scotland, those in existence before *c*.1200, were on land belonging to the Crown, enjoyed royal protection, and had certainly or probably been founded by kings. That this was clearly understood by contemporaries is shown by a papal letter of 1186 which recalls that David I 'had constructed the burgh of Renfrew on land that was his own property (i.e. royal demesne)'. Without insisting on the technical sense of the phrase which became fixed from *c*.1450, towns such as Renfrew were 'royal burghs'. Although Renfrew happened to be given away by King David to his Stewart, Walter son of Alan, most towns on royal demesne were retained by the Crown. With few exceptions, they were founded at ancient centres of kingly power, shire capitals such as Edinburgh, Haddington, Stirling, Perth, and Aberdeen. These were, of course, the places most frequented by the rulers as they toured their realm. They tended to be on the eastern side of Scotland, in line with the markedly eastward orientation of the country from 1100 to 1300. Of the 40 or so burghs existing by 1210 no fewer than 30 were in the eastern half of Scotland. Most of the places at which burghs developed have very old names, demonstrating continuity of habitation and perhaps suggesting some continuity of trading activity. There were a few exceptions. Canongate beside Edinburgh, for instance, was a small burgh created by the Augustinian canons of Holyrood Abbey

[2]H. van Werveke, *'Burgus': versterking of nederzetting?*, *Transactions of the Royal Flemish Academy of Sciences* (Brussels, 1965), no.59, especially pp. 91–8.

with the king's permission. The Newburghs in Fife and Aberdeenshire were literally 'new burghs' on fresh sites developed in the mid thirteenth century and comparable with contemporary Newbrough near Hexham in Northumberland.

Physical and geographical advantages obviously determined the choice and growth of such sites. Ease of communication, the junction of much-used routes, seaports, river mouths, bridgeheads, and reliable fords across difficult streams and rivers — examples of all these can be found singly or in combination at the locations of our earliest burghs. Roxburgh controlled crossings of Tweed and Teviot close to their confluence; Ayr and Dumfries stood at the lowest point at which the rivers Ayr and Nith respectively could be bridged; Inverness, Aberdeen, and Berwick were at or near bridging points and river mouths; Arbroath, Montrose, Dundee, and St Andrews have useful harbours. But not all major towns were founded at sites offering advantages to traders. Edinburgh owed its existence to the immemorially strategic dominance of the royal fortress upon the rock and to the kings' need to have a community of merchants and skilled artisans close at hand, to whom they were willing to grant privileges. Had trading considerations been paramount no burgh would ever have been created upon the steep, narrow tail stretching eastward from the volcanic crag on which Edinburgh castle is built. Leith or Musselburgh (Inveresk) would easily have outdistanced Edinburgh; even as it was Edinburgh had to spend wealth and energy to suppress these rivals. Glasgow also had a site originally enjoying few advantages for trade. It was in essence an obscure village servicing the shrine and church of Saint Mungo, too far from the Clyde to control the river crossing and less favoured than the king's burgh of Rutherglen or the Stewart's burgh of Renfrew to exploit waterborne trade. Not until William the Lion came to the aid of Bishop Jocelin in the period 1170–90 did Glasgow's history as an urban community truly begin. The king confirmed the new burgh founded by the bishop at the Glasgow Cross site a little north of the Clyde and granted to the burgesses a weekly market and an annual fair in July. Even so, the episcopal burgh of Glasgow grew slowly and although pushed forward by the outstanding enterprise of its citizens it is doubtful whether it had overtaken Rutherglen before Robert I's reign.

It is not only in Glasgow's case that the evidence suggests experimentation with different sites before the burgesses or their patron were satisfied that they had the best position for long-term prosperity. At Peebles the earliest burgh (twelfth-century) lay north of the Eddleston

Water while the king's castle was just to the south of it, near its confluence with Tweed. Later (thirteenth century?) a new site was
developed to the east of the castle and the old town fell into some
decay. At Perth the original burgh axis was probably north—south on
the line of Kirkgate and Skinnergate, with the castle at the north end
and the parish church of St John Baptist at the south. The axis was
radically altered to an east—west line apparently before the close of the
twelfth century, allowing for a much more generous layout on an
alignment indicated by South Street and 'North Gait' (now High
Street), the latter leading across the Watergait, where were the
merchants' wharves, to an important crossing of the Tay. King
William seems to have abandoned a castle at Auldearn, with an atten-
dant burgh growing beside it, in favour of a site at the mouth of the
River Nairn, though the new burgh of Nairn must have occupied a
location inhabited since early times. Earl Cospatric of Dunbar, who
died in 1166, may have intended to have a burgh at Belhaven in East
Lothian, where the little Biel Water flows into the North Sea beside
the mouth of the River Tyne. If so, it looks as though the pull of the
earl's castle which needed to occupy the commanding hilltop site of
Dunbar led to the new burgh being shifted a mile to the east. The
Benedictine monks of Coldingham Priory north of Berwick may have
tried, unsuccessfully, to found a burgh based on their *villa* or toun of
Coldingham for the king gave the prior leave to bring his rural tenants
into the toun to increase its population. Dunfermline Abbey, on the
other hand, was able to create the burgh of Musselburgh on its land of
'Lesser Inveresk'. Its success was doubtless due to the convenient
harbour which is already referred to as dependent on the burgh in the
1180s.

In plan, the early Scots burgh showed remarkably few variations on
a simple theme, composed of a handful of more or less essential
elements. Of these the most primitive and important was the market
place, indicated and protected by the market cross (Scots, mercat
croce), close to which would be sited the tolbooth or *pretorium*, fore-
runner of the later Town House. No examples of tolbooths from our
period survive, but it is unlikely that none would have been built
before 1300. It was at the tolbooth, originally at least, that the market
tolls would have been payable to the lord of the burgh or his representative; and in course of time it was the tolbooth that became the
meeting place of the town council and often (in a convenient cellar or
ground-floor room) the town jail. In the majority of older burghs the
parish kirk was situated in or just off the main thoroughfare, often in a

commanding position. It is noteworthy that the dedications of the earliest burghal parishes show a much higher proportion of biblical and continental saints than the average for Scottish church dedications as a whole. Saint Mary is found very commonly (Berwick, Haddington, Dundee, Glasgow, Inverness), and there are dedications to Saint John the Evangelist (Montrose) and Saint John the Baptist (Perth). We may note also Saint Andrew (Peebles), Saint Giles (Edinburgh, Elgin), Saint Nicholas (Berwick, Leith, Lanark, Aberdeen), while Peebles and Stirling both had churches under the invocation of the Holy Cross or Haly Rude. These dedications give strong support to the belief that the earliest burghs were deliberate creations of the twelfth and thirteenth centuries.

A typical plan (such as may be found surviving at Forres and Elgin) would give the market a central position in a specially widened part of the main street (often the 'hie gait' or High Street, but at Roxburgh the 'king's street'), with the cross in the centre of the market and (found before the end of our period) a public weighbeam or 'tron'. Since many towns were communication centres the roads that met and crossed at their sites became the principal streets. They entered and left the town at gates usually called ports which would have been constructed at least partly of stone from an early period, and in larger burghs may have been embellished with towers or turrets. Heavy timber doors would close the ports securely by night and also by day in times of trouble. Perth was almost alone among Scottish towns in having true walls for its outer boundary, but all the old king's burghs would have been defended at least by earthwork banks called 'back dykes' running between the ports and forming the outer boundary of the rigs or tofts, the plots of land held by the burgesses. On these plots the dwelling-houses would normally be built at the end abutting on the principal street. To judge from later medieval practice, which has survived to the present in a few north-east fishing villages, houses were built with their gables rather than sides to the street. Between each house a lane — in later times often covered over to form a 'pend' — gave access to the toft or yard where a burgess might construct warehouses or workshops. Stone was not generally used for domestic buildings, the vast majority of which were of timber. A stone house, obviously a rarity, in the burgh of Perth was given to the Cistercians of Coupar Angus before 1198. In 1970 the remains of what was probably a two-storey house of stone dating from the thirteenth century were discovered at the corner of South Street and Abbey Street in St Andrews. Stone or timber, medieval houses were not necessarily mean affairs. Abbot Matthew of Melrose, although deposed in 1261, was remembered fondly by his fellow-monks, one of whom recorded his building achievements which included 'our great houses at Berwick'.

Timber construction and thatched roofs gave rise to a severe fire hazard, graphically illustrated by the laconic entry for 1207 in the Melrose chronicle: 'a large part of Roxburgh was accidentally burned'. Walter Bower, using thirteenth-century materials for his chronicle of Scotland written 200 years later, says that 'nearly all the burghs of Scotland' were burned to cinders in 1244, an exaggeration of course, but he lists Aberdeen, Forfar, Haddington, Lanark, Montrose, Perth, and Stirling. In wartime it was common for whole towns to be deliberately destroyed by fire, as happened in 1216 when King John of England burned Berwick, Roxburgh, and Haddington in revenge for Alexander II's alliance with the Magna Carta barons and the French. That conflagration was remembered for half a century.

The old town of Forres in Moray still preserves today, in a remarkably complete manner, the plan of a twelfth-century king's burgh. At the west end, occupying a typical position overlooking the Mosset Burn, stood the royal castle, of motte type, with, to the north of it, Bridge Street carrying the line of the king's highway westward to Inverness. The High Street runs east from the castle on two slightly different alignments to the point where the East Port formerly stood, beyond which the highway continued to Elgin and Aberdeen. A site was provided for the parish kirk of Saint Laurence (note the Mediterranean dedication) just east of the castle and north of the High Street. Where the High Street widened to form the market place there were the mercat croce and tolbooth, and at this point a north–south cross road runs through the town. The old 'back dykes' which formed the burgh's outer defences are represented by the line of North Road, Orchard Road, and South Street.

It was neither location, however, nor physical layout that converted a town or village into a burgh, but rather the peculiar status of the indwellers, the burgesses. The king created a burgh by granting a bundle of privileges, tenurial, legal, and commercial, to a group of men whose skills and capacity as craftsmen and merchants he valued and depended upon. In course of time, certainly before the end of William the Lion's reign, it became usual for the Crown to record its grants of privileges by charter. The fact that a community of burgesses could not only be treated collectively in being made the recipient of such a grant, but could also be given a formal written record to be preserved as its title to these privileges for the future, is clear evidence that by the end of the twelfth century a burgh was seen to be a corporate entity or institution even though it was actually composed of an ever-changing collection of individual burgesses. But corporateness may in reality have been recognized from a much earlier period. It is doubtful whether charters were ever issued to mark the formal foundation of Berwick upon Tweed, Edinburgh, Roxburgh, or Stirling, but there was no question of their status as fully-privileged king's burghs.

The men and women who formed the population of the early burghs would have included a proportion of native Scots, Lothian Northumbrians, Scandinavians, and Cumbrians. For the most part, however, they seem to have come into Scotland from Flanders, the Rhineland, northern France, and England, especially eastern England. The oldest charter for the burgh of St Andrews was issued *c*.1145–50 by the burgh's founder, Bishop Robert, who obviously saw advantages for the newly created cathedral priory and for his diocese in having a privileged market town and seaport established beside the already flourishing clerical community. The bishop's charter tells us that David I 'gave' to Bishop Robert an experienced Flemish burgess of Berwick, one Mainard, whose task was to supervise the building up of the new town. As his reward, Mainard was appointed first alderman and was given land on favourable terms. Of the next two aldermen to appear in record, Simon and Peter, the latter may be identified with a burgess called Peter the Fleming, perhaps a son of Mainard. In this same mid-twelfth-century period we have a story of one William son of Malger, an immigrant burgess of Berwick who traded with Friesland. William had two brothers, Thorald, described as 'a prudent man from Holy Island', and Thor who became the first archdeacon of Lothian. It is interesting to note that the St Andrews charter already mentioned was witnessed by 'William Torreld', an apparently singular name which may in reality represent the two immigrant brothers of Archdeacon Thor. A north-country English historian who knew Scotland well, William of Newburgh, says that English immigrants were very numerous in the Scottish towns, while Bishop Robert's second successor at St Andrews, Bishop Richard (1165–78) refers to Scots, French, English, and Flemish burgesses in the episcopal burgh.

We ought not to underestimate the importance of internal migration in the process of getting new burghs started and expanding existing ones. In this connexion it is worth noting that the first recorded burgess of Glasgow was Ranulf 'of Haddington', and among the burgesses of towns in south-eastern Scotland recorded in the twelfth and thirteenth centuries were men taking their names from Aberdeen and Stirling as well as towns only a few miles from those in which they appear as indwellers. Moreover, it would be wrong to suppose that because there were no burghs as such before 1100 men and women of Celtic stock did not become burgesses. When in 1294 we have the first two recorded names of burgesses of Cupar in Fife, one, John 'called Gilbuy' ('yellow lad'), had a Gaelic by-name, the other, Michael 'called Redhode', had an English by-name. A list of the town council of Roxburgh in 1296 shows a mixture of names indicating either occupation or place of origin or in a few cases a by-name which had hardened into a surname. The alderman or chief burgess was Walter the Goldsmith, which fits in well with Roxburgh's traditional rôle as a centre for minting the king's coinage. The remaining members of the 'dozen' who composed the council were: Richard 'le Furbour' (metal polisher), Richard Vigrus, Michael the Saddler (Sellar), William de Boseville, Alan of Mindrum, Adam Knout, Geoffrey of Berwick, Adam of York, Adam Corbaud, Austin 'le Mercer' (dealer in quality textiles), and John Knout. We know from other evidence that Vigrus, Sellar, Boseville (Boswell), Mindrum, and Knout were well-established Roxburgh or local families, and a contemporary burgess, Thomas 'le Pestour' (baxter or baker), though omitted from the 1296 list, also belonged to a well-known Roxburgh family. Geoffrey of Berwick was a wine merchant, from whom in 1291 the prior of St Andrews had bought wine worth £20 16s. 8d., 'with which he declared himself well content'. Knout is a form of the Scandinavian name Cnut or Knut, and it is interesting to recall that the *Orkneyinga Saga* tells a story of the robbing of Knut 'the wealthy', a merchant who 'spent much of his time at Berwick' in the mid twelfth century. In the earlier thirteenth century Hugh 'Cnot' (the same name) was a man of means who had some interests in the burgh of Haddington. East coast Scottish towns drew settlers from such places in eastern England as Orford, Barton on Humber, Filey, Whitby, Beverley, Selby, and York. A Berwick burgess who apparently became bankrupt in 1290 had the name Thomas of Ravenser. His place of origin, Ravenser, was a seaport at the mouth of the Humber long since submerged. It was the only non-Scottish town to enjoy the privilege of trading at Berwick free of tolls.

Burghs were small communities, scarcely more than villages by modern standards. Throughout our period, and beyond, most of them still retained a strong agricultural character, the burgesses owning small farms and the burghs as a whole controlling large open fields, corn mills, and common grazing. The population even of Berwick upon Tweed, the largest town in Scotland, or of Perth and Aberdeen, which may have ranked next in order of size, would have been numbered in hundreds rather than thousands. Eighty-four burgesses of Berwick and 70 of Perth recorded their fealty to Edward I in 1291, and these may have been close to the full count in each case. Unfortunately we have no reliable formula to convert a figure for burgesses into one for total population. The typical burgess was a family man whose wife and children (not forgetting a widowed mother or unmarried sisters) might well give us a multiplier of three or four. Below the rank of burgess proper there seem to have been in many Scots burghs 'stallagers', market-stall holders, who enjoyed fewer privileges and paid fewer dues than the full burgesses. In addition to this upper stratum of burgh society there would obviously have been considerable numbers of craftsmen not of burgess status, journeymen, apprentices, labourers and servants of all kinds, many no doubt having families of their own. Moreover, every prosperous town attracted a more or less permanent population of poor people, some only fitfully employed, some living by begging, and to their number we should add the chronically sick and disabled. Like the king's court, a town offered opportunities for skilled men and women who might have been hard put to it to earn a living in the country, and it is perhaps no coincidence that in the 1220s one Thomas the leech appears as holding property in the burgh of Haddington.

Town life also encouraged, indeed necessitated, a strong community spirit. The sick and infirm and the very old were cared for in almshouses or hospitals (a word to which we should not give any marked medical connotation in our period). Leprosy was the great endemic scourge of western Europe before the return of large-scale bubonic and pneumonic plague in·the mid fourteenth century. Although leprosy was no doubt widespread throughout Scotland it was only in the burghs that any serious attempt was made to alleviate the lepers' lot or to segregate lepers from the unaffected majority. Leper hospitals were founded and endowed during the twelfth and thirteenth centuries often by kings and wealthy magnates. They were usually sited on the outskirts of a town, for example the Maisondieu at Maxwellheugh (for Roxburgh), St Ninian's or Bridgend in Gorbals (for Glasgow), and St Nicholas by the East Sands (for St Andrews). Poor Cresseid, in Robert Henryson's poem *The Testament of Cresseid*, contracts leprosy and tells her father that she wishes to become an outcast or recluse: 'I would not be kend, thairfor in secret wyse ye let me gang into yone Hospital at the tounis end'.

The market was the focus of attraction for indwellers and outsiders alike, the very raison d'être for the burgh as an institution. The market cross, despite its name, was a pre-Christian symbol of the very ancient sanctity attaching to the market place, giving protection and the guarantee of fair dealing to all who came there in good faith. Not only was the market itself defended against casual trading, bargains made in the market were sacred and binding. 'No one', declared the burgesses of Berwick in their mid-thirteenth-century gild statutes, 'shall buy any merchandise brought for sale to the burgh upon the bridge of Tweed or in the Briggate or outwith the ports of the town before that merchandise has reached the burgh market. Anyone convicted of so doing shall forfeit the goods he has brought'. And again, 'anyone who has bought herring or other merchandise and given arles — i.e. an earnest or 'God's penny' — shall pay for the goods at the price agreed in the market bargain, without deduction or breaking of arles. Anyone convicted of doing otherwise shall give a tun of wine to the gild or leave the burgh for a year and a day'.

Markets were usually held weekly, the day varying from burgh to burgh. Glasgow and Kirkintilloch had a Thursday market, Ayr, Haddington, and Arbroath observed Saturday, Newburgh in Fife Tuesday, Crail Wednesday, while Brechin (a rare instance of a chartered market without burghal status) had a market every Sunday despite being a bishop's city. Privileged burghs could not only insist on their markets enjoying a monopoly of sales and transactions within the burgh limits but could extend this monopoly on the market day itself to include outlying areas. Thus although King William the Lion would no doubt have liked to favour the royal abbey of Kelso, across the river from Roxburgh, and allow the monks to turn Kelso into something like a town with trading rights, even he was forced to restrict the freedom of the men of Kelso to sell their bread, ale, and meat 'at their windows' (i.e. houses being used as shops) to those days when Roxburgh market was not being held.

In general, markets catered for local trade, both among the townspeople themselves and between the townspeople and the inhabitants of the local region. For longer-distance trade the market was reinforced by the fair, held at any particular spot perhaps no more than once, twice, or at most four times a year. Fairs probably go back further in Scottish history than markets, even though the majority of recorded fairs were held in burghs and towns rather than out in the country. It is relevant to note in this connexion that the Gaelic language has no special word for market, and that its word for fair, *féill*, is derived from Latin *vigilia*, which referred originally to a saint's day or other church festival. The link between fairs and religious festivals is very ancient, and it would be rash to state positively that trade came before worship or *vice versa*. The great fairs of the west European continent and of England attracted a truly international *clientèle* of wool and cloth merchants, dealers in spices, jewels, and precious metals. Some at least of the fairs of Scotland, e.g. Roxburgh Fair which began on the feast-day of Saint James the Great (25 July) and Glasgow Fair beginning three weeks earlier, would certainly have been the occasion for international and long-distance trade. The same may have been true of fairs held at seaports such as Dundee, or at Crail in the 'East Neuk' of Fife, a famous fishing port which had an annual fair lasting a fortnight, beginning on the second Monday after Easter.

Scots merchants for their part resorted to fairs beyond the borders of Scotland, especially the great fair of Boston in Lincolnshire, held on 17 June. At least one notable Scottish exporter, the Cistercian abbey of Melrose, maintained permanent warehouses at Boston to facilitate its wool sales to Flanders. The majority of fairs in Scotland were really no more than markets held at much longer intervals, usually lasting for more than one day, and dealing in a wider range of goods, including a proportion brought from afar. Some might specialize in horse- or cattle-dealing, forerunners of the famous 'trysts' at Crieff and Falkirk in the later cattle-droving days. We might easily underestimate the volume of trading in the Highlands if we considered only the conspicuous rarity of burghs west of a line drawn from Dumbarton to Inverurie and thence to Inverness. We may rather infer from the large number of fairs throughout the Highlands named after early saints and their feast-days, many of which survived until quite modern times and one or two of which still survive today, that this region was not ill provided with outlets both for local and for long-distance trade.

Some idea of the range of goods and commodities typical of thirteenth-century trade can be obtained from a statement of 1303 listing the traditional (i.e. pre-1286) customs levied at Berwick upon Tweed. Imports included wheat and other grains, beans, peas, salt, wine, oil, honey, garlic, onions, pepper, and cumin. For the textile industry came alum, woad, and teasels. Metal pots, pans, basins, and ovenware were imported, and also, somewhat surprisingly, tallow. In return Berwick merchants exported wool, woolfells, hides, and the skins of young calves, deer, lambs, kids, hares, and squirrels. Besides herring and bacon, the port also shipped live animals, horses, oxen, sheep, and pigs. This general picture is particularized by a report showing that in 1275 a partnership of two Berwick merchants exported through Hull 10½ lasts[3] of hides, 180 woolfells, and half a sack[4] of wool. By the end of the century such partnerships, 'companies' or 'firms' (*societates*), of merchants were not uncommon in the larger towns.

The importance of markets and fairs points to a familiarity with the use of coined money, although some bargains may have been transacted in kind. A standard royal coinage, as we have seen, was established for the Scottish kingdom by David I and maintained on very much the same lines by his successors until the death of Alexander III in 1286. The connexion between trade and markets on the one hand and coinage on the other is clearly shown by the siting of mints at the chief burghs, especially Berwick, Roxburgh, Edinburgh, Stirling, and Perth. Although we do not know in detail how a fresh issue of coin was put into circulation, it is overwhelmingly probable that the process began with the merchants of the leading mint burghs. This is confirmed by the fact that when the Scots coinage had to be renewed in haste in 1250–1 mints were specially activated for the occasion in no fewer than 16 royal burghs, from Ayr and Berwick in the south to Inverness and Aberdeen in the north. At the turn of the eleventh and twelfth centuries coined money was probably unfamiliar in most parts of Scotland save for Lothian and the areas under strong Scandinavian influence. Within a hundred years the situation had changed drastically. The use of coin had become normal in all but the most remote rural districts. It seems reasonable to attribute to the burghs most of the credit for this important change.

*   *   *

Burghs, especially the king's burghs, were regulated by a special constitution and by special laws and quasi-laws called 'customs'. Although there were elements in the earliest burgh laws which represented continuity with pre-burghal urban, or semi-urban, communities, the most important part of the 'Laws of the Four Burghs' which governed Scots town life in the Middle Ages was the result of deliberate innovation dating from the reign of King David I. The

---

[3] A last weighed roughly 4,000 lb.
[4] A sack of wool weighed 364 lb (English), 360 lb Scots.

oldest section of the laws is taken almost *verbatim* from the customs of Newcastle upon Tyne. These are believed to date from the reign of Henry I of England (1100–35) and in any case can hardly go back before 1080. It was in that year that King Henry's elder brother Robert built his 'new castle' at the northern bridgehead of the Tyne crossing. Had there then existed a community on the site large enough to possess a body of customs it seems most unlikely that its name would already have been superseded by the name 'Newcastle' in the early twelfth century. We may assume that the customs of Newcastle were established by the crown between 1080 and 1135 specifically to encourage a trading settlement to grow up beside the royal fortress overlooking the Tyne. And it is not rash to guess that between 1136 and 1157, when they held Newcastle and its hinterland, the Scottish kings transferred the customs of that comparatively young English borough to their own towns of Berwick upon Tweed, Roxburgh, Edinburgh, and Stirling, the original 'Four Burghs' of the Scots laws. In practice, the transfer may have taken place a good deal earlier, for the burghs named, together with several others, were in existence by c.1127, and would have required regulations of some kind.

Most of the early burgh laws may be classified as either jurisdictional or mercantile privileges. The distinction must not be pressed too hard, for a mercantile purpose can be argued for many of the jurisdictional privileges. The burgess was a free man, a free tenant of the king who could defend himself in the burgh court before his 'peers' or fellow-burgesses. There, by a privilege that may have been imported into Scotland direct from Flemish towns such as Bruges or St Omer, he could employ the defensive proof of compurgation — getting reputable friends to swear collectively to his innocence — instead of the armed combat or duel normally used in feudal courts. Lawsuits in burgh courts were also settled more cheaply and a great deal quicker than in other courts to which a free man might have recourse. The burgess held his land within the burgh, his 'burgage', as a free tenant. Unlike the typical feudal tenant, however, the burgess could treat his tenure almost as though it were outright ownership for he could sell freely to anyone or pledge his property as surety for a debt. A burgage, however, always remained a burgage and could not be treated as outwith the burgh save with the consent of the burgh lord and the community of burgesses. At the same time, it was not unusual for land on the edge of a burgh to be attracted into burgage, and this tendency must have facilitated the physical growth of many towns. Although subject to certain forms of taxation, including the 10 per cent demanded by the church on each year's business profits, burgesses could accumulate private fortunes in coin, jewels, gold, and silver more easily than country dwellers. They were, moreover, free of the burdensome dues that fell on many rural free tenants, such as heriot and merchet (respectively, payments for leave to inherit and to arrange the marriage of sons and daughters). The much-prized status of burgess could be inherited by sons from their fathers. If a man born and bred as the dependent vassal—even the merest serf—of a rural barony or other lordship would dwell within a burgh without challenge from his lord for a whole year ('year and day') he was then permanently free of his former lord and could qualify for burgess's rank. All these privileges were jealously defended by the court of the burgh which was already becoming the organ of burgh government, and to some extent self-government, by c.1200. The corporate identity of a burgh was given expression by the possession of a permanent burgh seal, of which we begin to have evidence from the early decades of the thirteenth century.

The mercantile privileges were designed to encourage a rapid build-up of population together with commercial and industrial activity. They began with 'kirset' (the word is Scandinavian), that is the period of grace during which a newly settled burgess was permitted to hold his burgage rent-free. This period might be two or three years or even longer in burghs on the edge of the highlands which might be thought unattractive to settlers from foreign parts. Only burgesses and stall-agers might buy and sell wool, hides, and cloth within their burgh or within a much wider trading zone defined by royal edict, and only the burgesses of royal burghs gained the right to trade freely throughout the realm without having to pay the king's tolls. Although some foreign and other merchants might obtain exemption from these severe rules (which were meant in origin to protect and stimulate trade), it is likely that well before the end of our period they were having a decidedly restrictive effect, in the usual manner of any monopolistic privilege.

If the burgh were a seaport (and medieval Perth and Stirling counted as such) its burghers had the first option of buying goods from whatever ships might put into port, and the right to insist that the cargoes of any such ships, even if their masters had not intended to visit that particular port, must be landed and exposed for sale. Disputes between burgesses and visiting merchants must, in the latter's interest, be settled by the third tide. Fish was allowed to be sold on board, and some Scots burghs, notably those along the southern shore of Fife from

Crail westward to Inverkeithing, seem to have been primarily markets for the fishing industry, which already in the early twelfth century was carried on as much by boats from the Low Countries as from Scotland.

Problems might arise when a single estuary gave access to more than one burgh. Perth, an old royal burgh of David I's time, became jealous of the growing prosperity of Dundee, a baronial burgh founded *c*.1190 by King William's brother David earl of Huntingdon. Since Dundee was located close to the mouth of the Firth of Tay while Perth was at the tidal limit on a river too fast to be navigable above it, the former attracted overseas merchants more readily. King Robert I (despite his personal links with Dundee) provided that no ship sailing past the great sandbank at the mouth of the Tay known as Drumley, or the Abertay Sands, should be allowed to break bulk until it reached Perth, unless it came in the period of Dundee's annual fair or was laden with goods explicitly destined for Dundee merchants. By this date Dundee had become a royal burgh, and in the later Middle Ages it tended to outstrip its three nearest rivals, Perth, Montrose, and St Andrews. Its harbour just west of the castle, roughly on the site of the present Tayside House, was larger or better sheltered than those of the other three towns.

Inter-burghal rivalry was already well marked before the end of the thirteenth century. Aberdeen and the Moray Firth burghs, which seem for some purposes to have worked together, complained in 1289 that although King Alexander III had confirmed an annual fair at Aberdeen to serve that town and all the burgesses north of the Mounth the burgh of Montrose had each year interfered with the fair (we are not told how), resulting in serious loss to those whom the fair was intended to benefit.

The special advantage of being a royal burgh lay in freedom from tolls throughout Scotland and in the right to enjoy one of the trading zones into which the whole of eastern and south-western Scotland was divided. Such zones might consist of entire sheriffdoms, or of large parts of sheriffdoms bounded by rivers and well-known landmarks. Only the king could create a trading zone and enforce one burgh's monopoly of trade within it. Burghs founded by subject-superiors such as earls and bishops had to be content with trading rights confined to their founders' estates, unless (like St Andrews) they could wangle honorary royal burgh status from the crown.

In many respects burghs presented a striking contrast with the feudal lordships of which they might form a part or at least be neigh-bours. We ought not to conclude from this contrast that burghal government was particularly free, still less democratic. Self-government came slowly and never involved control of a burgh's affairs by all its adult male inhabitants through some system of majority voting. The kings, when they referred to royal burghs, habitually used the possessive pronouns 'my' and 'our'. That this was no mere form of words is clear from abundant evidence. The crown kept a tight grip on its burghs and they in turn looked to the crown for protection and favour. The king's chamberlain visited the burghs annually on the 'chalmerlane ayre' to oversee their affairs, especially financial affairs. The chief officer of a burgh was called in English alderman or burgh grieve, in Latin *prepositus*, in French *prévost*. The *prepositus* or alderman, even if elècted by the burgesses and not appointed (as he must often have been) by the crown, was treated by the king as a royal official, answerable to him for the good order of his burgh. Only at Berwick upon Tweed, perhaps because of its close links with continental towns, was the chief magistrate called the mayor. This might conceivably imply that the burgesses of Berwick formed more of a self-governing community than other Scots townsmen and had the privilege of electing their leader. Yet in 1249 the mayor was a knight and brother of the bishop of St Andrews who had formerly been royal chamberlain, pointing unmistakably to royal influence. At Berwick, quite exceptionally, there were four aldermen under the mayor.

The word *ballivus* or bailie[5] was also used in early documents to describe an officer who seems identical with the alderman. In course of time it became usual to reserve the latter word, or the word provost which eventually succeeded it during the sixteenth century, for the single chief magistrate. 'Bailie' was then used for the next senior officer in the burghal hierarchy, and it became normal for two or more bailies to serve each year and take special responsibility for law and order within the burgh. Apart from the unique mayor at Berwick, aldermen and bailies are the only permanent burgh officials for whom there is record before *c*.1300, unless one includes the *brocarii*, 'brokers' or wine-testers, who appear rather fleetingly in the Berwick gild statutes. It would be unwise to infer from this silence of the records that other offices had not already come into existence. Some of those mentioned in the fourteenth century have a somewhat archaic appearance, and it is hard to believe that any large burgh could have been ruled, even in the twelfth century, merely by a pair of aldermen or bailies, aided by the general body of burgesses who formed the *curia*

[5]From Montrose northward the customary spelling is baillie.

burgensium or burgh court. During the thirteenth century it became the practice to commit town government to a council which, to judge by evidence from the following century, was chosen by the whole body of burgesses. The normal council of a king's burgh was composed of 12 senior burgesses, and even when this total was exceeded, as was usual in the later Middle Ages, the council was still called 'lie doussane', the dozen. At Berwick, again exceptionally, there was a council of 24 by 1249.

It might be thought that burghal administration was adequately cared for by the system just outlined. A roughly pyramidal town population was dominated by the community of burgesses or freemen, among whom a handful of the most substantial families tended to monopolize the offices of alderman and bailie, whether or not these were elective (as was certainly the case later) or filled by long-term appointment. But it is clear that well before the end of the twelfth century a number of important towns, including Perth, Roxburgh, Aberdeen, and the royal burghs along the southern edge of the Moray Firth, had acquired those special associations of burgesses to which the name gild was given. It is easiest to account for the existence of gilds by adapting the immortal phrase from George Orwell's *Animal Farm* and saying that all burgesses were equal but some were more equal than others. The 'more equal' burgesses may be assumed to have been the longest-established, the wealthiest, or at all events the most respected and substantial. They were fully paid-up members, as it were, of the burgh community, containing no doubt a preponderance of merchants though membership was certainly open to craftsmen. In the earliest days of gilds only the walkers (waulkers) or fullers and the websters or weavers appear to have been excluded, possibly because they tended to be strangers who flooded into certain towns in alarmingly large numbers, threatening to swamp the old-established families.

Thus we may see the larger burghs beginning to grow in two parallel and to some extent overlapping channels. On the one hand there was the full community of burgesses and stallagers, most if not all tenants and vassals of the crown, with which they dealt through their chief officer the alderman or burgh-grieve. It was taken for granted that this body of burgesses spoke and acted for the town as a whole. As long as laws were observed, good order maintained, and the annual ferme, or sum for which the king's rents and dues were compounded, was promptly and fully paid, the crown would have been, in theory at least, content for this to be the whole story. But in reality the organic mercantile life of the town was falling into the hands of a privileged inner community, the merchant gild, and the town's trade was so vital a part of its life that for many practical purposes the gild formed the effective town government. The alderman who answered to the king for the good order of his burgh was also the chief officer of the gild merchant, and conversely some of the officers elected by the gild brethren, for example the 'feryngmen' or treasurers, became officials of the town. Moreover in some of the larger towns the most powerful crafts may have been forming associations of their own, closely comparable to the earliest trades unions of modern times.

It was the mercantile and craft gilds rather than the town council or burgh court that gave expression to the social aspirations and communal feeling of the majority of townspeople. The gilds were a mixture of friendly society, burial club, trade union, drinking club, and religious brotherhood. A gild would normally have a patron saint and organize a solemn procession, accompanied or followed by notably less solemn junketings and merry-making, on the patronal feast-day. If there was only one gild, its saint would commonly be the patron saint of the burgh and its parish church, where in any case the gild would probably maintain a subordinate altar. An essential element in the ordinary activity of any gild was the care of widows and orphans of gild brethren, of elderly and infirm brethren, and of members of the gild who had become ill or disabled.

The gild regulations of Berwick upon Tweed drawn up in 1249 have luckily survived. The preamble to these *Statuta Gildae* (as they are called) shows the leading men of the town anxious to stamp out factions and sectionalism. 'In order that a single will and a single firm and sincere love of everyone for every other should result from many individuals gathered together in one place, lest any of our burgesses associated sectionally should be able to damage in any detail the liberty or statutes of the general gild, or might in future be able to think up new ideas against this gild', the members have agreed to put into force a long list of ordinances. The sentiments of the preamble seem unexceptionable to the point of being quite anodyne, but what the leading gildsmen may really have been attacking was a tendency for the Berwick crafts to gild together against the richer merchants. Certainly one of the first provisions declares that all lesser gilds shall henceforth be wound up and dissolved. The remaining provisions show a remarkable mixture of regulations to ensure fair trading within a jealously guarded monopoly and concern for the personal condition and behaviour of gild brethren and their families. Although it is not possible to discover in day-by-day detail how Berwick, the largest town of thirteenth-century Scotland, was governed, we may at least be grateful that the *Statuta Gildae* give us some picture of burgess life which, however imperfect, is nonetheless true and vivid.

6

The Winning of the West

No period in the history — or, for that matter, in the pre-history — of Scotland has been unaffected by the fact, already emphasized in this book, that the country faces east and west rather than north and south. However irresistibly the kings of our period might be drawn towards Norman and Angevin England or Capetian France it was only at their peril that they ignored the basic facts of geography. The feudal kingdom of David I and his descendants turned away from the western modes of thought and action which linked the country to Ireland and also, by the sea-route of the Minch and the Northern Isles, to Norway. A consequence of this re-orientation was that the north and the west highlands were reduced to a remote fringe area which became at once a refuge and a base for dynastic and other rebels. The 'Highland Line' so much beloved of modern writers was not in any sense a defensive boundary which the kings could seal off while they concentrated their attention on England and the continent. On the contrary, the long valleys of eastern Scotland north of Forth run far up into the highlands. Some, such as Tay and Spey, lead westward to passes that ultimately give access to the Atlantic coast. The Great Glen itself has always provided a direct and relatively easy route between the southern Hebrides and the Moray Firth.

For the Scottish monarchy it was not merely a matter of geography. Its historical roots, as the kings were well aware, lay in Argyll and northern Ireland as much as in the Tay valley and the country between Stirling and Inverness. The very name of Scotland was owed to the western connexion. In English as well as Latin and French (Scotia, Ecosse) this name, which emphasized the dominance of the Gaels of Dalriada, was coming to be preferred to Albania or Albany which would have perpetuated the traditions of the Pictish kingdom. As far as we know, even the most Normanizing of the kings, for example Malcolm IV and his brother William I, made no attempt to obliterate the Scottish antecedents of the monarchy. By the time Alexander III was raised to the throne as a boy of seven those antecedents were being deliberately paraded. It could not be long before the crown was compelled to devote less of its energies to southern affairs and turn its attention once again to the western approaches. Had the kings simply abandoned the west highlands their monarchy would have ceased to be Scottish. It does not seem that Alexander I or David I were content to be merely kings of Scone rather than kings of Scots. To concentrate on the east at the expense of the west would have cost them the cohesion and unity of the realm that they strove laboriously to build.

In any case long-term changes were taking place on the western seaboard which called imperatively for the intervention of Scottish kings. In the first place, Norse political power in the western isles[1] and Man weakened steadily from the earlier decades of the twelfth century. This happened in spite of the treaty said to have been made *c.*1098 between the king of Norway, Magnus 'Bareleg', and Edgar king of Scotland. The treaty confirmed Norwegian suzerainty over Man and all the islands of Scotland west of Kintyre and thence northward to Lewis. It may even be the case that the Norwegians regarded the islands of the Firth of Clyde, Arran, Bute, and the Cumbraes as theirs also, a view that would not have been shared by the Scots. The treaty, if it was really made, could be important only if the Norwegian crown had been able to enforce its authority. For much of the period from 1161 to 1208 Norway was torn by civil war and distracted by revolts (involving the northern isles) against the extraordinary Faroese usurper Sverre or Sverrir Sigurdsson, founder of what was virtually a new dynasty. Not till the 1230s was the Norwegian king, Sverre's grandson Haakon IV Haakonsson, able to intervene again in the affairs of the Scottish west. Instead of earls exercising strong rule in the name of the king of Norway, a turbulence verging on anarchy prevailed in the Hebrides and affected the adjacent mainland. A warrior aristocracy quarrelled for ascendancy not simply over the islands but also over broad tracts of territory that even the 1098 treaty would have allowed to be Scottish. In short, the distinction between 'shore' and 'offshore' was quite unworkable.

Despite a fondness for certain Scandinavian personal names (e.g., Thorkell, whence Torquil; Thorketill, whence Maccorquodale; Olaf, whence Macaulay; Liotr, whence Macleod; Sumarlidi, whence

---

[1]To the Norwegians the western isles were known as Sudreyiar or 'southern isles'. whence the name Sodor in the diocesan title Sodor and Man.

Somhairle, MacSorley), the Gaelic strain preponderated among these Hebridean rulers. The evidence suggests that Gaelic influence upon the Norse was at least as strong as Norse influence upon the Gael, as indeed the name 'bare-legged' for King Magnus, one of whose wives was Gaelic, would seem to indicate. There seems to have been a resurgence of Gaelic culture and an intensification of the old links with Ireland, a process contrasting sharply with what was happening in the east and in lowland Scotland. An attempt, for example, was made to restore and revive the greatest Christian shrine of the west, Iona, whose church (despite Saint Margaret's intervention) had become secularized and decayed. Significantly, this attempt was negotiated between Somerled of Argyll and the formerly Columban church of Derry in Ireland. It so much alarmed King William that he took away from Iona the churches it possessed in Galloway, transferring them to Holyrood. When a foreign-seeming Benedictine abbey was introduced into Iona early in the thirteenth century the conservative northern Irish clergy, guardians of the older Celtic order, solemnly denounced the innovation as a breach of the law and tried to prevent its establishment by force. Literary tradition suggests that the Gaelic language flourished in the isles during this period, encouraged by an active school of bards, seannachies (story-tellers), and other 'learned men'. Among the ruling families the custom of fosterage formed an integral part of the Gaelic system of education. We hear of Gillocrist, foster-brother of King Godfrey of Man (*c*.1160) and Gillechatfar, foster-brother of Uhtred, lord (in his own estimation doubtless 'king') of Galloway (*c*.1170). In 1258 the heir of Domnall Ua Domhnuill (O'Donnell) king of Tír Conaill returned to Ireland having been fostered with the king of the isles, apparently Dubhgall Macruaidhri (Dougal MacRory) of Garmoran, whose relations with western Ireland were very close. Twenty years earlier, Lachlan the warden of Man had died in a storm while trying in vain to save his young foster-son from drowning.

A notably non-Scandinavian feature of the hybrid ruling class in the Hebrides was the regular use of the title 'king' for the principal lords. This was not simply the usage of Irish chroniclers who tended to hibernicize features of a society that had close affinities with their own. 'Kings' were recognized by west highlanders themselves, from Man to Lewis, and also in Galloway, whose ruling class of mixed Norse and Hebridean freebooters had overrun south-west Scotland as the *Gallghaidhil*, 'foreign Gael', a nickname transferred to the province. The Norwegian kings also recognized royal titles within the western isles, but significantly not within the northern isles of Orkney and Shetland. At different times, or simultaneously, there might be kings of Man, kings of the northern Hebrides (Skye and Lewis), kings of the southern Hebrides, or simply kings of the isles. It was not only in Irish eyes that the 'isles of the foreigners', *Innsegall* as they were known throughout the Gaedhealtachd because of their Scandinavian invaders, were seen as forming a kingdom or even a network of kingdoms of Celtic type.

The second long-term change resulted from the protracted attempt by the English crown to annex Ireland to its already wide dominions. The English invasion of Ireland began on a private footing in 1167–9 and became 'official' in 1171 with the arrival of Henry II in Waterford harbour. The English seemed well on the way to complete conquest by the opening decades of the thirteenth century. Of the five historic provinces of Ireland, Meath, Leinster, and a large part of Munster were by then under the effective control of the royal government established at Dublin. Even eastern Ulster seemed securely in English hands as a result of John de Courcy's swashbuckling conquest of the 1180s. But Ireland is a large island, and the provinces least affected by English invasion, Connacht and western Ulster, were precisely those with which Manx, Hebridean, and other Scottish contacts were closest. On the one hand, therefore, our period witnessed the waning of Norwegian royal authority. On the other, it saw the arrival of English knights and men at arms on the cliffs of Antrim, only a few miles from Galloway and Kintyre, and aggressive English pressure which unsettled the rulers of Tír Eoghain (Tyrone), Tír Conaill (Donegal), and Connacht. These developments could not fail to affect the security of the Scottish kingdom. Direct relations with England were of course of the first importance for the Scots monarchy throughout the thirteenth century, but hardly of less moment (and, until 1266, actually more urgent) was the dispute with Norway over sovereignty throughout the Hebrides. The settlement of that dispute in Scotland's favour immediately raised the question of Scoto-Irish relations.

The history of the west from the mid twelfth century to the first war of independence is largely the history of the House of Somerled. As we have already seen, Somerled Macgillebrigte,[2] lord or 'king' of Argyll, was killed in 1164 while leading a formidable invasion of Scotland by way of the Firth of Clyde. Somerled belonged to a family that claimed

---

[2] Sometimes given the lineage name, from his grandfather, of Macgilleadhamhnain, 'son of Saint Adamnan's servant'.

descent from an ancient royal lineage of northern Ireland. His ancestors had somehow acquired, then lost, and then, in his grandfather's generation, regained a far-flung lordship of islands and mountainous mainland. It comprised, at its greatest extent, Lorn and Benderloch in central Argyll, Lismore, Mull, Coll and Tiree, the peninsula of Morvern and Ardnamurchan, Moidart and Knoydart, the Small Isles, Uist, and Barra, as well as Kintyre and the southernmost Hebrides, Islay and Jura with their dependencies. It is by no means certain, however, that Somerled held all this wide territory unconditionally, as the unfettered vassal of the king of Norway for whatever was insular and of the king of Scots for the rest. David I undoubtedly believed that he possessed royal demesne rights over Argyll and Kintyre and, as we have seen, brought men from that region to fight for him in England. Malcolm IV forced Somerled to come to his peace at Christmas 1160. In the isles Somerled profited from Norwegian weakness but found himself at loggerheads with the rival royal line of Man.

Somerled was the last head of his house to rule such a wide lordship. On his death his four surviving sons divided the estate between them. Dubhgall (Dougal), who may have been the eldest, inherited Lorn, Benderloch, Lismore, and Mull. It is from him that the Macdougalls are descended. He had at least five sons, and the senior line — Duncan, Ewen, Alexander, and John — were each in turn lords of Argyll or Lorn, Duncan and Ewen certainly being recognized as 'kings'. Their headquarters were the castles of Dunstaffnage, north of Oban, Dunchonnell, a remarkable sea-girt fastness in the Garvelloch Islands at the mouth of the Firth of Lorn, and the scarcely less astonishing fortress of Cairnburghmore in the Treshnish group off the west coast of Mull. Somerled's second son was probably Raonall (Ranald, Ragnvald, Reginald), founder with his father of the Cistercian abbey of Saddell in Kintyre and benefactor of the Cluniacs of Paisley. Raonall styled himself 'king of the isles', ruling Kintyre and Islay in the south and (probably) what was known as Garmoran in the north, that is the mainland territories of Moidart and Knoydart, Morvern, Ardnamurchan, the Small Isles, Coll, Tiree, Uist, and Barra. Raonall's elder son Ruaidhri (Rory, Roderick) took Garmoran. His sons, Dubhgall and Alan Macruaidhri (MacRory), were recognized as either kings or at least lords of the isles and their descendants carried that title until the extinction of the male line in the fourteenth century. Domnall (Donald), the younger son of Raonall, although an obscure individual, must hold an undisputed place in Scottish hearts and in the story of Scots the world over, for almost all Macdonalds,

Macdonnells, and MacConnells are named after him and descended from him. When John Macdonald married Amy Macruaidhri in the fourteenth century he acquired through her the claim to be lord of the isles. This Macdonald lordship of the isles, abolished in 1493, played an outstanding part in Scottish history in the later Middle Ages and its rôle in Irish history also was by no means insignificant.

The house of Somerled of Argyll, for all its vast domains, did not enjoy a monopoly of power. Theoretically above its various chiefs though in practice on a more equal footing was the more definitely Scandinavian dynasty of Godfrey Crovan based upon the Isle of Man in the extreme south but also controlling Skye and Lewis in the extreme north where the Manx kings also held Glenelg. In close touch with at least some of the kings of Norway, this Manx dynasty intermarried with Irish and Anglo-Irish potentates and with the ruling family of Galloway. Somerled himself took care to marry a daughter of one of the Manx kings, Olaf the Red (died 1153), but this did not stop him waging war on his wife's brother King Godfrey II (1153–87). Despite time-consuming journeys to visit the kings of Norway, Scotland, and England in search of help, Godfrey never fully recovered from the defeats that Somerled, at the head of a large fleet, inflicted on the Manxmen in 1156 and 1158. Somerled had become an over-mighty subject of two crowns simultaneously. Norway and Scotland were both challenged by the rise of the house of Argyll and the decline of the house of Godfrey Crovan.

As a rule, the Norwegian kings continued to support the Manx line from which it received tribute from time to time in acknowledgement of suzerainty. In the thirteenth century, Haakon IV's patience was sorely tried by the Manx rulers' tendency to be either too ineffectual or else too defiant, and invariably quarrelsome. Godfrey II's sons Ragnvald and Olaf the Black took Man and Lewis respectively. Ragnvald made light of the Norwegian connexion and, aping King John of England (from whom he had received a fief), solemnly declared that he held Man as a vassal of the papacy (1219). In 1226 Olaf ejected his brother and ruled alone for 11 years. His neglect of the Hebrides led King Haakon to promote the kingship there of one of Somerled's grandsons whom the Norwegians called Uspak son of Owmund – probably his native Gaelic name was Gilleasbuig Macgilleadhamhnain.[3] Uspak or Gilleasbuig was given a fleet and sent west

[3]See above, p. 108, footnote.

over sea from Bergen to establish himself as ruler not only over the Scottish isles but probably over Argyll and Kintyre as well.[4] He died of wounds in 1230 and eventually Haakon was forced to recognize simultaneously the royalty of Uspak's nephew Ewen Duncanson Macdougall lord of Argyll and of Ewen's cousin Dubhgall Macruaidhri lord of Garmoran, both of whom duly took the Norwegian side against the Scots king. On Olaf's death in 1237 his son Harald refused to go to Bergen to perform homage. Haakon promptly had him ejected from Man by two emissaries, Cospatric and Gillecrist Macmuircherthach, the latter most probably a son of the king of Tír Eoghain in Ireland and therefore King Harald's cousin. The two were merely caretakers who collected the royal revenues but did not govern as kings. The recalcitrant Harald made his peace at the Norwegian court in 1240 and ruled effectively for nearly a decade. He and his father Olaf were both knighted by the English king, part of a policy of playing one court off against the other, for Harald accepted King Haakon's daughter as his wife in 1248. English interest in Man ran parallel with the English conquest of Ulster and it is clearly no coincidence that the Manx kings were granted lands in Ulster which made them explicitly English vassals. The fate of Harald perfectly illustrates Norwegian difficulties in controlling an overseas colony, for he and his newly wedded bride were drowned in 1249 on their way home when their ship was caught by a gale in Sumburgh Roost, the tiderace south of Shetland. Their death precipitated a political crisis in the west which led to a major campaign by the king of Scots.

Contemporary with the House of Somerled there were in Argyll and the isles a number of lesser families greedy for power and lands in a fiercely competitive environment. The districts of Glassary and Knapdale, lying between Lorn and Kintyre, the country on the east side of Loch Fyne including Cowal, and the islands of Arran and Bute were divided among a number of families that may truly be said to have originated in the thirteenth century, even when their ancestry can be traced to an earlier period. Three of them were interrelated and claimed descent from Flaithbertach, an eleventh-century king of Ailech (i.e. Tír Eoghain): the Macsweens of Castle Sween on Loch Sween who married into the royal family of Connacht, the O'Connors; the Lamonts of Ardlamont; and the Maclachlans of Castle Lachlan in

---

[4]A.A.M. Duncan and A.L. Brown, 'Argyll and the Isles in the Early Middle Ages', *Proceedings of the Society of Antiquaries of Scotland* XC (1956–7), p. 202.

Strath Lachlan. Of these, the Macsweens who held the lordship of Knapdale and (it seems) Arran also were the most powerful. Other families to emerge in this region included the Campbells (probably from the Lennox and of Brittonic origin), with lands in Craignish and Kilmartin south of Oban and at the south end of Loch Awe; the Macgilchrists who also held land in Glassary and Cowal and were mysteriously displaced by a favoured clerk of Alexander III, Master Ralph of Dundee; and the Macnaughtons, lords of Inishail in Loch Awe and Kilmorich at the head of Loch Fyne. The extraordinary rise of the Campbells to dominance in the south-west highlands belongs to the fifteenth and sixteenth centuries, while their proliferation across the world (they are especially numerous in North America) is a phenomenon of comparatively modern times. But the foundations of Campbell power were already being laid while they were still only one of a dozen baronial families of equal standing in Argyll, before the end of the thirteenth century.

As far as the Firth of Clyde is concerned, the most remarkable development of our period was the spread of Stewart power and possessions across the water from their original lordship of Renfrew. By *c*.1200 the second of the Stewarts, Alan son of Walter, had acquired Bute and within the next 50 years his successors had become either the lords or at least the 'protectors' of Cowal. In the 1260s a junior branch of the Stewart family, already ensconced in the earldom of Menteith, gained a foothold in Arran and Knapdale. By the end of Alexander III's reign the Stewarts must be counted among the greatest lords of the entire south-west highland region. To them must go the credit for building, at Rothesay in Bute, one of the very earliest stone castles of the west, and their example was rapidly followed, if indeed it had not already been anticipated. The building of stone fortresses, often on seagirt rocks, islands in lochs, and on bold promontories, is not the least remarkable characteristic of the 'barons of Argyll and the isles' whose rise has just been sketched. These strongholds, in situation and construction alike, presented a notable contrast to the earthwork and timber castles of motte-and-bailey type scattered across eastern and lowland Scotland by feudal lords and knights of the period 1100 to *c*.1250. The most important of them, listed according to the lordships for which they served as military and naval headquarters, were, for Garmoran, Kisimul in Barra and Castle Tioram in Moidart; for Lorn, Dunstaffnage, Dunchonnell, Cairnburghmore, and Duart in Mull; for Islay and Kintyre, Loch Finlaggan and Dunaverty at the south end of Kintyre; and for Knapdale, Castle Sween on Loch Sween and

Skipness on the east coast of what is now north Kintyre. To these we should add Inverlochy, probably built in the later thirteenth century by the Comyn lords of Lochaber, Tarbert on the narrow neck that nearly makes Kintyre an island, possibly built by Alexander II, Innis Chonnell in Loch Awe, and Mingary in Ardnamurchan. Together they constitute a unique monument of private fortification, indisputably the most remarkable collection of thirteenth-century lords' strongholds to be found in any single region of Britain.

William the Lion, who had generally bad relations with England, paid little attention to the west highlands and islands. His son Alexander II, enjoying much better relations with England, was able to devote a good deal of time and energy to highland affairs. When on 8 July 1249 he died of a sudden illness on the island of Kerrera at the entrance to Oban Bay he may have been on the point of securing for the Scottish crown control not just over the west highland mainland but also over the island kingdom of Somerled and his descendants. The contrast between King William's seeming inaction and the aggressive success of his son and grandson may be partly due to the simple fact that the Alexanders had discovered how to build or at least commandeer for royal use the galleys and other ships that were indispensable for Hebridean conquest.

For Alexander II the problem of Galloway was inextricably linked to the general problem of the west. The lord of Galloway, Alan son of Roland (1200–34) -- incidentally hereditary constable of Scotland – and his neighbour as lord of Carrick, Duncan son of Gilbert, were much too independent for Alexander's liking and, what was worse, inclined to look to the English kings for favour and support. Both were deeply involved in the English settlement of eastern Ulster which not only gave them larger resources but also a feudal foothold beyond the political reach of the Scots crown. In addition, Alan of Galloway had designs upon the Isle of Man whose king, Ragnvald, had given his daughter to be wife of Thomas, Alan's only son but born out of wedlock. The link between Man and Ulster transcended any racial differences, for Ragnvald's sister had married John de Courcy, the Anglo-Norman conqueror of Ulster. Alan and his brother Thomas (earl of Atholl *c.*1210–31, in right of his wife Isabel) backed King Ragnvald against his brother Olaf. They were thoroughly accustomed to the naval warfare of the islands and commanded a formidable fleet which was clearly not yet under the king of Scotland's orders. Moreover, Alan, who had already been the husband of one lady of the

great Anglo-Norman family of de Lacy[5] and of a daughter of Earl
David, William the Lion's brother, married as his third wife a
daughter of Hugh de Lacy first earl of Ulster, who supplanted John de
Courcy in 1205.

Until Galloway was held by lords of more certain loyalty than
Duncan of Carrick and Alan son of Roland it behoved King Alexander
to move with caution. His father had built a new castle at the mouth of
the River Ayr in 1197, no doubt to keep Duncan of Carrick in check
even though Duncan was allowed the rank of earl. About this time the
hereditary Stewart was established west of the Clyde in the isle of Bute.
By the 1220s the young king, now of full age, decided to assert royal
authority in Argyll. Raising the common army of Lothian and,
perhaps significantly, of Galloway, Alexander embarked with a fleet
and sailed from the Clyde to Argyll, presumably by way of Loch Fyne
and Tarbert rather than round the Mull of Kintyre and into the Firth
of Lorn. We have only the barest accounts of this expedition and do
not even know whether the year was 1221 or 1222. Many Argyllsmen
are said to have come to the king's peace and yielded hostages. One
result may have been the granting of Cowal to Walter the Stewart,
recently come of age, and the building of a castle for him at Dunoon.
Another may have been the construction of the first phase of Tarbert
castle as a royal stronghold, although as yet without any sheriff or
sheriffdom to go with it.

Duncan of Carrick did not die until 1250, apparently long deprived
of his earl's title which was revived in favour of his son Neil, grandfather of King Robert the Bruce. Alan of Galloway died in 1234,
leaving three married daughters but no legitimate son. The petty
nobles of Galloway were determined that the province should be preserved intact and treated as the kingdom they felt it to be. They therefore offered the lordship to the king, but Alexander was no less determined to uphold feudal law. This meant that the lands would be
divided equally among Alan's sons-in-law, though by right of seniority
the lordship itself would pass to Roger de Quincy because he was
married to Helen, Alan's only child by his first wife. Rather than
accept that, the men of Galloway rose in revolt, attempting to ambush
the king's army but without success. Neatly reversing the part played
by Roland of Galloway who routed Donald Macwilliam in Ross in

[5]K.J. Stringer, 'A New Wife for Alan of Galloway', *Dumfries and Galloway
Nat. Hist. and Antiquarian Soc. Transactions*, 3rd ser., XLIX (1972),
pp. 49–55.

1187, Farquhar Mactaggart earl of Ross took a crucial part in routing the Gallovidian rebels. The bastard Thomas, whom they had wished to make their lord, was imprisoned first of all at Edinburgh and then in Barnard Castle, guarded by John Balliol. Balliol's wife Derbforgaill (Dervorguilla), elder of Alan's two daughters by his second wife, eventually acquired the entire lordship of Galloway because of her sisters' childlessness, thus fulfilling the native wish to preserve the integrity of the province. For a few years Walter Comyn earl of Menteith, one of the king's most prominent barons, was put in charge of Galloway to enforce royal authority. It seems likely that Earl Walter's headquarters were at the well-sited castle of Cruggleton on the western shore of Wigtown Bay.

The pacification of Galloway, harshly enforced, opened the way for Alexander II to press ahead with a final solution to the west highland problem, namely the acquisition of the isles. Ambassadors were repeatedly sent to Haakon IV during the 1240s to complain of the injustice of the treaty said to have been secured by Magnus the Bareleg and to offer to buy the islands for much refined silver. Haakon adamantly refused to sell his rights in this way. Instead, as we have seen, he first of all confirmed Harald Olafsson in the kingship of Man and then, on Harald's untimely death, offered protection to Ewen of Argyll and Dubhgall of Garmoran. We know that as early as 1240 the Scottish king had been building up a following in Argyll, for there survives a royal grant of crown lands in Glassary and Cowal for feudal knight-service to a local man, Gilleasbuig Macgilchrist, kinsman of the amenable Lamonts and the less amenable Macsweens, and this infeudation must surely have had parallels. The castle and burgh of Dumbarton on the Clyde were strengthened as a useful base for operations in the western approaches. In this decade too a forceful Dominican friar, Clement bishop of Dunblane, was administering the vacant and inadequately endowed diocese of Argyll. He evidently found much amiss and urged the king to undertake reforms and transfer the bishop's see from Lismore to the mainland. This displeased Ewen Macdougall who looked on the diocese as being under his family's special patronage.

Alexander II's answer to Haakon's refusal was to gather a large fleet and army, in which Argyllsmen may well have served, and sail round Kintyre into the Firth of Lorn. His immediate intention was to overawe the house of Somerled, especially Ewen Macdougall, into submission. It is equally clear that he was bent on annexing the western isles as a whole and making them part of the Scottish realm. His unexpected death brought the greater plan to a halt but not to nought. The leading men of the west must now have realized that it would only be a matter of time before the Scottish monarchy exerted its full strength and annexed the Hebrides in spite of Norwegian opposition.

Ewen Macdougall was in fact the first to trim his sails to the wind of change. In 1250 he failed to persuade the Manxmen to accept him as king of the isles and although he dutifully attended Haakon IV's winter court at Bergen in 1252–3 it was only to see the Norwegian king set him aside in favour of Magnus Olafsson, brother of the late King Harald. These rebuffs threw Ewen into the Scottish camp and he used the good offices of Henry III of England to be reconciled with the council of lords ruling Scotland on behalf of the boy king Alexander III (1255). By them he was accepted as lord – no longer as king – of Argyll in return for an annual ferme of 60 merks.[6] This forbearance was sensible, for Ewen and his son Alexander proved thereafter to be staunch lieges of the Scots crown. It was quite otherwise with Ewen's cousin and rival, Dubhgall Macruaidhri, who had also wintered at the Norwegian court in 1252–3. He had no intention of becoming a Scot, politically speaking, and instead led plundering raids to the west of Ireland, where he slew an English sheriff in old-fashioned Viking style and also married his daughter to the king of Connacht.

Alexander III took personal control of royal government in 1261 on reaching the age of 20. He showed at once that he was determined to extinguish not only what was left of Norwegian power over the isles but also the anarchy that prevailed whenever that power was ineffectual. Applying, in vain, to the now ageing King Haakon for an agreement to buy the isles, Alexander undertook a series of measures, some peaceful enough but others aggressive, which may be seen as preliminaries to outright annexation. By 1262, for example, Walter Stewart earl of Menteith had ousted the Macsweens from Knapdale and Arran. The earl of Ross, William son of Farquhar, laid waste the isle of Skye, an act of provocation that could not have been perpetrated without the king's leave even if he did not directly order it. This happened in 1262 and by the following year energetic steps were being taken to defend Scotland against the full-scale Norwegian attack that the Scots rightly judged inevitable. That soldiers were even stationed at the extremely remote post of Inverie on the north shore of Loch Nevis is proof not only of the urgency with which the king's government acted but also of

[6] A.A.M. Duncan, *Scotland: the making of the kingdom* (1975), p. 581, n. 31.

the existence of a Scottish naval force, for Inverie is virtually inaccessible from the landward side and could serve only as a base for naval operations.

King Haakon had taken the precaution of having his son Magnus crowned in 1261, thus leaving himself free to lead an expedition from which he might not return alive. The campaign, when it came, was left too late in the year from a Norwegian point of view. The army and fleet were of unprecedented size, led by the king's own splendid ship built at Bergen entirely of oak and embellished with a gilded dragon prow. The Norwegians reached Lerwick in Shetland in mid July. Much time was wasted in the northern isles, partly because the local men proved reluctant to join the expedition. The fleet rounded Cape Wrath on 10 August and rendezvoused with King Magnus of Man at Kyleakin ('Haakon's narrows'), where Skye is within a mile or so of the mainland and Loch Alsh forms a fine natural harbour. From there it sailed through the Sound of Mull to Kerrera, where Alexander II had died, and was met by Dubhgall Macruaidhri lord of Garmoran whose followers brought the combined fleet up to a strength of between one and two hundred ships, representing a force of perhaps three or four thousand men. The outlook was hardly auspicious, for Ewen of Lorn refused to desert his new-found Scottish allegiance and had to be honourably detained, while the Macdonalds under Angus Mór, lord of Islay, and the Macsweens under Murchadh, dispossessed lord of Knapdale and Arran, seemed of such doubtful loyalty that although they joined Haakon they had to surrender hostages.

The invaders now sailed south for the Firth of Clyde, seizing *en route* the castle of Dunaverty at the south end of Kintyre, issuing a protection for the Cistercian monks of Saddell Abbey and overrunning the island of Bute. In the usual way many of the inhabited localities were laid waste or burned. While Haakon sheltered in Lamlash Bay on the east side of Arran peace negotiations were begun at Ayr with King Alexander. They made little progress, for the Scots knew that time was on their side. Impatient and running short of victuals, the Norwegians sent a raiding party up Loch Long. Its ships were portaged across the isthmus between Arrochar and Tarbert so that the shores and islands of Loch Lomond could be thoroughly plundered. On the evening of Sunday 30 September, before this party had returned, King Haakon and his fleet moved to the east side of the Great Cumbrae, very close to the Scottish shore at Largs. A westerly gale arose and blew with great fury through the night and for much of the Monday. Ships, including the king's, dragged their anchors and a few were blown across to the mainland, where their crews were at once shot at by Scots bowmen. We have no evidence for the size of the defending force mustered by the Scots, but there is no reason to dismiss it as inconsiderable. When the safety of the realm was in peril it was normal for a royal decree to be proclaimed calling out every able-bodied man without exemption. From a contemporary account we may deduce that the Norwegians were confronted by the common army of Cunningham, Strathgryfe, and Kyle which with maximum turn-out should have amounted to many hundreds if not thousands of men. Alexander of Dundonald, fourth hereditary Stewart, was locally in command and augmented the foot levies with a respectable force of knights and men at arms, the quality of whose horses and equipment impressed the invaders. One of his young esquires, Piers de Currie, fought so valiantly before being felled by a sword blow on the thigh that his name found its way into the *Saga of Haakon*.

As Monday wore on the storm slackened enough for Haakon to order a rescue party to relieve the stranded crews. Night brought a lull in both storm and fighting, but on the Tuesday (2 October) the Norwegian king himself came ashore with a much larger force and something approaching a true battle was joined. In this a big part was played by the Scots infantry armed with spears, Lochaber axes, and slings. The saga account, much fuller and more vivid than anything preserved on the Scots side, obviously exaggerates Norwegian prowess and Scottish ineptitude, but it admits that the invaders were forced to give ground. The saga may not overstate Scottish numbers but its estimated ratio of ten Scots to one Norwegian must be viewed with scepticism. Largs, it is true, was no set-piece battle of which any experienced general might have been proud, but assuredly it was not a minor skirmish.

At the end of the day the Norwegians, who had earlier got their king to safety, withdrew to their ships. Badly bruised, they had not been utterly shattered or ignominiously put to flight. Nevertheless, the only course now open was to pull out. The wisest decision they now made was to reject, against King Haakon's own wishes, an Irish invitation to cross to Ulster and help to rid Ireland of its English settlers. Slowly the fleet sailed northward, and whenever it sent parties ashore for food and water they were attacked by the Scots. Neither the old king's formal allotment of the Hebrides among his loyal supporters nor his saga-writer's impudent assertion that 'in this expedition King Haakon won back all the dominions that King Magnus Bareleg had acquired' could hide the fact that this full-scale Norwegian campaign had been a failure. It failed not merely because the Scottish realm had shown that it could defend itself; more serious from the Norwegian point of view was the realization that the men of Shetland, Orkney, and much of the Hebrides were unwilling or reluctant to fight for continued Norse supremacy. There were even deserters from Haakon's own fleet. Only the king of Man and King Dubhgall of the Isles with his brother and heir Alan had come out decisively in support. Haakon reached Orkney at the end of October and fell ill at Kirkwall, where he lay in the bishop's palace. Stories were read to him from the bible and, probably nearer to his heart, the sagas of all the kings of Norway from the days of Halfdan the Black. He died in the early hours of 16 December. Although he was advanced in years it is hardly fanciful to suggest that frustration and disappointment hastened his end.

The news that King Haakon had died reached the Scottish king at about the same time as he heard of his first son's birth. The doubly propitious omen spurred Alexander to a final effort. An expedition was fitted out for the Isle of Man which Magnus Olafsson anticipated by coming to Dumfries to surrender his kingdom. Henceforth he would hold it of the king of Scots by the service of 10 galleys of 24 oars and 5 of 12. But he too soon died and the island was put in charge of royal bailies, Godfrey Macmares, Alan bastard son of Thomas of Galloway earl of Atholl, and Maurice O'Carson. Though the first and last may have been Manxmen their administration was not popular and in 1275 the whole island broke into revolt. Alexander III suppressed it severely and probably as a result two parties emerged, one adhering to the Scots king, the other chafing for independence. No doubt it was the latter that asked Edward I for his protection after the death of Alexander III, but there were to be several long periods of Scottish rule in the Island before Edward III's conquest brought suzerainty to the English crown permanently. It says much for the new position of authority that Alexander III enjoyed in the isles from 1264 that his expedition to suppress the Manx revolt was led by Alexander Ewenson Macdougall lord of Lorn and Alan Macruaidhri (brother of Dubhgall) lord of Garmoran. These two, along with Angus Mór Macdonald lord of Islay, the remaining chief of the house of Somerled, were among the barons of Scotland who swore to uphold the right of Margaret of Norway in 1284 as heir to the Scottish throne. The king, however, was not prepared to leave Argyll and Kintyre as a 'no go area' where Macdougalls and Macdonalds held a monopoly of control. By 1267 the king had built a castle on Fraoch Eilean, the little island at the 'bend' of Loch Awe, and committed its custody to

Gillecrist Macnaughton. Alexander III also seems to have taken over the strategically sited castle of Dunaverty, which Haakon IV had 'given' to Dubhgall Macruaidhri, and to have made sure that the Comyn family as well as the Stewarts acquired a stake in Kintyre.

As for the Scottish isles, they too were the object of a major campaign in 1264, under the command of the earls of Buchan and Mar and Alan the Doorward (Durward). Islesmen who resisted were slain or put to flight, prisoners and hostages taken, and lands devastated. Dubhgall Macruaidhri would not submit, but in 1268 he died, and his son Eric Dugaldsson became completely Norwegian. Murchadh Macsween, to whom King Haakon had 'given' the isle of Arran, was betrayed in 1267 by one of his O'Connor kinsmen and died in the earl of Ulster's prison. The new king of Norway, Magnus the Law mender, realized that he would have to come to terms. Plenipotentiaries were therefore sent to Scotland and concluded the Treaty of Perth on 2 July 1266. It was an honourable settlement, never seriously challenged and reflecting credit on both countries. The Scots paid a lump sum of 4,000 merks, spread over four instalments, 'for the sake of peace'. They also promised to pay 100 merks annually in perpetuity (though payment ceased in the course of the fourteenth century). In return the Norwegians gave up all claim to the western isles, though explicitly reserving the northern isles of Orkney and Shetland. The inhabitants were to become lieges of the Scottish crown and must accept the approved laws and customs of Scotland. Any who were unwilling to do so might freely take their goods and leave in peace.

The Treaty of Perth ushered in a long period during which Scoto-Norwegian relations became very much better than they had been between the eleventh century and 1263. Alexander III's only daughter, Margaret, was married to Magnus VI's successor King Eric in 1281, a wedding that inspired the first hymn in which both countries, Norway and Scotland, were personified:

> Sweet Scotia! from thee a light emerges
> In which we know that Norway will shine.

The only child of this marriage was Margaret, commonly known as 'the Maid of Norway', who through the early death of her two uncles became heir to the throne and briefly, but in absence, queen of Scotland from 1286 to 1290. Trade and other connexions with Norway increased after the middle of the thirteenth century and this undoubtedly helped to re-open the western seaways as customary Scottish routes. The west highlands and islands became more subject to influences from the east and these included feudalism and the English language. But equally Scotland received a powerful fresh instalment of Gaelic influence. The west had been in certain important respects the cradle of the Scots nation. In 1266 it was won back by the feudal kingdom of Scotland, but it would be fair to say that this was not the whole story, for the west did some of the winning too.

7

Communities of the Realm

In the thirteenth century men and women were familiar with the notion of community, even though it was only gradually that they learned to use any general words with which to give expression to the idea. From birth, and normally by birth, everyone belonged to a particular group, membership of which automatically allocated a person to a network of other groups. The immediate family of parents and children was part of a lineage and kindred. It was usual for several kindreds to be concentrated within a particular district or province whose inhabitants would tend to acquire an identity of their own. Every unfree family was thirled to some saint's church or secular lord and would expect protection from the superior. It was also normal for a free person to be a lord's vassal and his tenant for land and office within the lordship, which might be one of the earldoms or bishoprics or, more typically, a barony held in chief of the crown for military service. Families, kindreds, provinces, lordships, and baronies all formed communities marked by more or less social cohesion. Medieval Scottish society, in short, was socially and geographically immobile and preponderantly vertical in its structure. It was not occupation or loyalties that determined a man's community; it was his community that determined his occupation and loyalties.

It is surely no accident that the notion of community was first articulated among clergymen and townspeople. The groups already mentioned formed what may be called unconscious communities, whose members acted communally by habit, almost by instinct. When, for example, the men of Wedale (the valley of the Gala Water) maintained their bitter quarrel in the 1180s with the Cistercian monks of Melrose over grazing rights they did not need to call themselves a community or swear any oath of confederacy. They and their fathers and their fathers' fathers had been pasturing beasts on the moors above Stow long before the intrusion of Melrose Abbey and they would naturally be fierce in defence of their rights. But the group of clergy gathered in the service of a major church or the merchants and artisans settled in a newly-founded burgh might be drawn from anywhere and had every incentive to foster a truly communal spirit. In 1163, for instance, the prior and canons of St Andrews cathedral (themselves forming one clearly-defined 'community') were confirmed by Pope Alexander III in their right to hold a free election of whoever the whole chapter or its wiser part might agree to choose as head of their house, a right originally given by Bishop Robert. They also possessed, from 1147, the right to elect every new bishop of St Andrews. This constituted a truly national responsibility, involving the crown and at least senior prelates. Not surprisingly, in 1238, on the death of Bishop Malvoisin, the chapter were persuaded to enlarge their 'community' by sharing the election with the two archdeacons as representatives of the diocesan clergy at large.

Burgesses, like the clergy, were in close contact with the European continent, where the idea of a commune or community, a self-conscious and coherent body of people bound by common rules and often sharing a common purpose, was well established before the end of the twelfth century. The Berwick gild statutes of 1249 prescribed the framework of government for the 'commune' of the town, declaring that the mayor and aldermen shall be elected 'by the view and judgement of the entire community', by which can hardly have been meant anything less than the whole body of burgesses. Such concepts were not peculiar to a large southern town like Berwick, for already in 1289 the ruling body of a small burgh on the Moray Firth could be described as 'the aldermen and remaining burgesses of the commune of Banff'. It is easy to understand how a burgh, whose burgess inhabitants at least formed a definable membership and whose territory constituted a recognized locality within marches that were 'ridden' or defined once a year, could be thought of as a true community. But the notion could be extended to vaguer and more rural entities. By 1309 it was possible to refer officially to the 'community' of an earldom. To Robert I's St Andrews parliament in March of that year came representatives of the communities of all the Scottish earldoms save Lennox, Ross, and Sutherland whose earls attended personally and Dunbar which lay under English control. Parliamentary representation of an 'earldom' (*comitatus*) does not seem very far removed from parliamentary representation of a 'county' (*comitatus*), such as England had known since the 1220s. The comparison should not be pressed too far but the point is worth making since the English county was undoubtedly recognized as a community. It elected parliamentary representatives ('knights of the shire') precisely because it was a community.

Nearly all our words for political ideas and institutions, e.g. democracy, representation, parliament, patriotism, and liberty, are borrowed from foreign languages, normally Greek or Latin, and were introduced into English usage by academics and scholars. It would be wrong to draw the conclusion that such ideas were somehow unreal, airy-fairy abstractions impossible for ordinary people to grasp. The human mind refuses to be constricted by ideologists of right or left and is infinitely capable of receiving ideas. If a fresh idea turns out to be useful but can be expressed only by an exotic term then such a term will be duly adopted and absorbed. So it was with the idea of the community, a concept easy to express in Latin, so rich in abstract nouns, as *communitas* or *universitas*, the 'totality' or 'collectivity' of something. It was not too hard to convert into medieval French as *la communauté*, *la commune*, *le commun*, but it proved difficult to render into native English. In England, where in any case French was the language of the ruling class, the problem scarcely arose before the thirteenth century. But as soon as the crown granted the Great Charter of Liberties (Magna Carta) some phrase was needed by which to denote the body politic, the totality of the king's lieges or at least of his free subjects. King John made a permanent grant of liberties in 1215 to all the free men of his realm. Much earlier, his father had already referred to 'the whole commune (*communa*) of free men', but in that case we might best translate *communa* by 'class', for Henry II certainly never meant to imply that his free subjects were banded together into any kind of corporate institution. During the course of the thirteenth century the idea of a 'commune' or 'community', already applied by educated persons to the citizens of a town or the clergy of a religious foundation, came to be applied, at first cautiously but soon with confidence, to the kingdom itself. There was still no word for it in English. This we know because in 1258 Henry III and his council, deeply engaged in a thoroughgoing reform of English government, ordered a presumably well-educated royal clerk named Robert of Fulham to translate from French into English an important writ announcing the king's promise to abide by the reforms already proposed, or yet to be proposed, by his barons. The writ had to have the maximum publicity and so copies in English, obviously meant to be read aloud, were despatched to every shire. In its original French the writ said that the reforming council had been chosen 'by us [i.e. the king] and by the community of our realm [la commune/alternatively le commun/de nostre reaume]'. The best that Robert could make of this in his English version was that the council had been chosen 'by us and by the native inhabitants of our kingdom'.[1] The episode is instructive for two reasons. It proves that the phrase 'community of the realm' had no precise equivalent in English. It also shows that in the opinion of a trusted royal official the phrase indicated the totality of the king's subjects within the realm, in other words what we should call 'the nation'.

There was a strong reason why such an abstract idea as 'community of the realm' should be given wide publicity in England during the 1250s and 1260s, for the constitutional upheavals of the baronial reform movement accelerated the development of political ideas and brought academics and churchmen, for whom a term such as *communitas regni* came readily to mind, into close contact with the king and his major barons. What is interesting for the Scottish historian is to see how in the next quarter-century the same idea became familiar north of the border, not just to university-trained clerks who could have learned it much earlier but to men who customarily counselled the king and administered royal government. One might have expected the idea to surface during the minority of Alexander III, between 1249 and about 1260, especially as in that period there was so much contact with England and English politics. In fact it does not seem to have left any trace in surviving documents. In November 1260 careful provisions were made to cover all contingencies when the young queen, Margaret, was allowed to travel to her mother's court in England to have her first child. The committee of four bishops, five earls, and four barons appointed to supervise the newly-born child's return to Scotland was clearly acting on behalf of the Scottish nation. The same is true of the five bishops, five earls, and five barons who acted as sponsors and sureties on behalf of the Scottish realm in 1282 when Alexander III's son and heir Alexander married the daughter of the Count of Flanders. These symmetrically arranged groups look very like the committee of two bishops, two earls, and two barons elected explicitly by the community of the realm of Scotland in 1286 on King Alexander's death. As we should expect, the idea came in advance of the actual phrase required to express it.

In English history it is impossible to keep the idea of the community

---

[1] 'ure raedesmen alle . . . thaet beoth ichosen thurgh us and thurgh thaet loandes folk on ure kuneriche' (W. Stubbs, *Select Charters*, 9th edn, pp. 387–8; T. Rymer, *Foedera*, I, pp. 377–8; *Annales Monastici*, ed. H.R. Luard (1864), I, pp. 445–6).

of the realm distinct from the growth of parliament. As the king's council, in its most solemn and omnicompetent aspect, develops into parliament after c.1230 it is seen more and more positively as representing, indeed in some sense as actually being, the community of the realm. Such a connexion of ideas was inevitable, for thirteenth-century feudal kingdoms were not primitive Greek democracies where all the citizens could assemble in the agora to debate and legislate. Consequently, in the community of the realm, just as in that of burgh, barony, or village, it was the *prodes hommes*, *probi homines*, the older or richer or more experienced or more highly-born members who took the lead, who spoke first or longest or were listened to most attentively. Government was democratic only in being public, otherwise it was aristocratic and oligarchic. Not surprisingly, there was a tendency for the great men to consider that they formed the essence of a community and possessed the right to speak and act for all its members. Yet even in England, where the feudal aristocracy was much richer and more powerful than its counterpart in Scotland, it is doubtful whether the 'community of the earls and magnates' — predecessors of the House of Lords — was ever totally identical with the 'community of the realm'. In Scotland the phrase 'community of the realm', from the moment it emerges in 1286 until it begins to fade in the middle of the fourteenth century, seems to have been used more conservatively and consistently to denote the totality of lawful subjects who composed the realm, the body politic, the nation.

Parliament, in Scotland as in England, long antedates the emergence of the community of the realm as an articulate idea. The king's power and authority were never absolute, however fond contemporaries might be of quoting the Roman Law tag 'whatever pleases the ruler has the force of law'. In the broadest sense the king must rule by consent, obtained first of all at a meeting of his council. Parliament, *parlement* in French, was simply a nickname for the debates and consultations (counsel) which took place between the king and his magnates, lay and ecclesiastical, and thus for the actual institution (council) where the talking was done. In his lively account of the war waged unsuccessfully by William the Lion against Henry II in 1173–4, Jordan Fantosme describes two sessions of the Scottish king's solemn council which he calls 'his full parliament' (*sun plenier parlement*). These were summoned so that the king might consult his baronage. In one Duncan earl of Fife spoke first and 'spoke like a baron' (i.e. wisely). In the next we are told that the king was openly opposed by the majority of the substantial magnates; in particular, the bishop of Glasgow and the earl of Dunbar spoke out against the king's plan to recover Northumberland by armed invasion.

We know extraordinarily little about how the king's council operated in normal circumstances. It seems certain that there were frequent sessions of a lesser council for day-to-day business, presumably composed of the chief household officials and such barons and knights as the king chose to have in attendance. But from time to time each year, in most cases at major feasts in the calendar, this lesser council would be reinforced by a much larger gathering of bishops, earls, and other important magnates. These sessions, 'full parliaments' or, as they were usually called in Latin documents until the 1290s, *colloquia*, colloquies, were omnicompetent in the sense that they could and did look at all aspects of domestic government and foreign relations. Law making, an important but not very frequent activity of the crown and royal government during the thirteenth century, was normally associated with large and solemn sessions of this kind. It was in parliament that treaties were ratified and replies approved from the king to foreign rulers, including the pope, on matters of the greatest moment. By far the most commonly recorded activity at sessions of parliament was deciding legal disputes, some of which had probably been appealed, or at least adjourned, from the lower courts of justiciary and sheriffdom. It was also normal, and was to remain a common feature of the Scots parliament for the rest of its history, to promulgate royal charters and even private legal deeds at great councils and colloquies. Many of the magnates present could conveniently be named as witnesses; sometimes they appended their seals to the non-royal documents, possibly for a consideration. Grave crimes might be tried in parliament and 'dooms' (judgements) pronounced upon convicted wrongdoers through the mouth of the king's chief *judex* or dempster, predecessor of the dempster of parliament.

Although colloquies or parliaments were by definition solemn occasions where final judgements were given and the most momentous decisions taken, we ought not to envisage a typical colloquy as a numerically very large assembly attended by a great crowd of lords and others. It seems that colloquies summoned by the king were in the habit of meeting in the shelter of some building long before the 'popular' courts of justiciar and sheriff had ceased to meet in the open air. We know that a 'full colloquy' was held at Holyrood Abbey in January 1256; that the king and the magnates of the realm assembled in Roxburgh Castle on 20 May 1266; and that in 1285 a colloquy of the lord king met at Holyrood Abbey on 25 January and adjourned next day to the great hall of Edinburgh Castle. These facts make it probable that major council sessions recorded at Stirling on 30–1 March 1226, at Roxburgh on 30–1 March 1231, and at Scone in September 1227 and February 1284 met under the roof of a royal castle or a monastery. Some of the chambers or monastic refectories involved may have been big enough to house a fairly large assembly, but one to be numbered in dozens or scores rather than in hundreds.

It is also clear that the colloquy or parliament of thirteenth-century Scotland was not simply the king's council, if by that is meant an instrument of the royal will, composed only of royal servants and other men chosen by the king for their loyalty or pliability. The inner council may have been at the heart of any colloquy, but this was nonetheless a genuine meeting place where the needs of king and government could be expounded and at the same time confronted by the needs, objections, and petitions of the king's subjects. Parliament did not even depend on the initiative of the king, although it is inconceivable that any authentic parliament could assemble during the reign of an adult sovereign personally present within the realm which lacked his formal consent. Assemblies that had all the character of a full colloquy, or that were actually called parliaments, met during the minorities of 1249–58 and 1286–90. In this last period the treaty of Birgham (itself made in the very fully attended parliament of March and July 1290) shows that parliament was regarded as the guarantee of the integrity of the Scottish realm, the sole body capable of giving political expression to the community of that realm. During the brief reign of the ill-fated Queen Margaret we can see that parliament and community were complementary. The six guardians, among whom the two bishops, Fraser of St Andrews and Wishart of Glasgow, were university-trained, were well aware that the authority of the queen, a child in Norway not yet inaugurated as monarch, was fictitious. They had to base their government upon something less tenuous, namely the authority of the Scottish nation. Hence their use of the expression 'community of the realm' which denoted the nation in formal terms. When in 1290 they made their cautious treaty of Birgham with the English king, providing for the queen's marriage to his son and heir Edward of Caernarvon, they were careful to ensure that papal confirmation of the treaty (involving spiritual penalties against Edward I if he failed to fulfil his obligations) should be obtained at Edward's expense within a year of the marriage and handed for safe keeping to the community of the realm of Scotland. More symbolically, the seal that the guardians caused to be made for their use, with the royal arms on one side and on the other an image of Saint Andrew on his cross with the legend 'Andrew be leader of the Scots, your fellow countrymen!', represented for all to see the concept of the community of the realm. On the other hand, for the purposes of royal government there needed to be regular sessions of parliament to give practical effect to the idea of the community.

The community of the realm has been discussed at some length because, next only to that much larger community of the faithful or *respublica Christiana* to which all Scots of our period belonged, it constituted the highest application of the idea of community and possessed the greatest constitutional significance. It is also worth emphasizing because some present-day historians, anxious that modern Scotland should not be considered a nation in any sense, have insinuated that Scotland was never a nation. They have dismissed the 'community of the realm' as either meaningless or a figment of university intellectuals out of touch with reality. These historians have been perfectly happy to accept that the villagers of Great Peatling in rural Leicestershire had grasped the notion of the community of the realm of England as early as 1265[2] while denying that even the politically conscious class in Scotland 20 years later could have comprehended anything of the kind. But of course it would be absurd to claim that the community of the realm was what mattered most to the majority of Scots in the thirteenth century. Getting and spending, incurring poverty and debt, making profits, cultivating the soil in spite of winter frost and rains at harvest time, seeking pleasure and amusement, all these things were as much matters for the individual in Scotland as anywhere else. They hardly involved even the humble communities of barony or burgh, let alone the exalted community of the realm. In the remainder of this chapter we shall be considering some of these activities, all too conscious of the fact that our evidence is tilted disproportionately in favour of the richer classes and of the male sex.

Many of the higher nobility were chronically, even carelessly, in debt. If their carelessness was over-optimistic, theirs was not the optimism of Mr Micawber. Unlike him they possessed substantial security in land which could be pledged, recovered, and pledged again almost *ad infinitum*. Theoretically wealthy, they seem often to have been short of cash and borrowed from religious houses and Jewish moneylenders in England. Robert de Quinci lord of Tranent owed £80 to a Jew named Abraham in 1170 and persuaded Holyrood Abbey to

[2]F.M. Powicke, *King Henry III and the Lord Edward* (1947), p. 510.

pay off the debt in return for a lucrative lease. Malise earl of Strathearn had debts of £62 in 1268, perhaps in connexion with his marriage to Mary Macdougall of Argyll, widow of Magnus last king of Man. In 1304 Robert Bruce, earl of Carrick and newly lord of large English estates (two years before becoming king of Scots as Robert I), ran up a bill of nearly £100 in London for clothes and other goods which was still unpaid 10 years later.

A bad example in indebtedness was notoriously set by the crown. At the time of his sudden death Alexander III owed large sums for wine to a Bordeaux shipper named John Mason. In the 1250s King Alexander was owed a large amount of money by his father-in-law King Henry III of England, who was even more habitually insolvent than the Scottish kings. Explaining apologetically that his treasury was empty, Henry promised to pay when times were better, which they were not likely to be as long as he diverted every spare penny he had to the building of Westminster Abbey. Alexander II, who had to provide a dowry of land worth £1,000 annually for his first wife Joan of England, was much occupied in the 1220s trying to find 4,000 merks (a large sum by Scottish standards) to pay for the wardship of lands in Norfolk due to be inherited by Roger Bigod who had married the king's sister Isabel. At home Alexander II, like other kings, may have lived on credit, if we may trust a vivid story told about the elderly widow of an Edinburgh burgess. As the king, soon after the birth of his only son, was riding out from Edinburgh Castle, the widow grasped the reins of his horse, holding up a handful of exchequer tallies.[3] 'My lord king', she exclaimed, 'I was once rich but am now poor. All I have to show for the fruits of my labours devoted to your feasting are these tallies which your servants gave me and which I now surrender to you. I only beg you to pay me for one hen which yesterday morning was all my wealth but which your servants seized from me. I shall not bother about the rest of my losses'. The king blushed for shame and replied 'Madam, all shall be paid for. Meanwhile, take this'. But she followed him as he put spurs to his horse, uttering a solemn curse: 'May the God of heaven give you as much joy of your only son as I had yesterday in my hen when its neck was wrung'.

Already, it seems, the Scots bourgeoisie had learned to address the sovereign in tones of familiarity, as happened on the night of

---

[3]Notched slips of wood used for receipts, one interlocking portion being kept by the debtor, the other by the creditor. The widow's tallies would have been equivalent to I.O.Us. from the crown.

Alexander III's death when his namesake Alexander, master of the royal sauce-kitchen but speaking as alderman of Inverkeithing, openly rebuked the king for travelling after dark. But if the old widow's outspokenness was characteristic her poverty was not. Among many fascinating household objects dating from the thirteenth century discovered in the centre of Perth during an archaeological 'rescue dig' in 1976–8 is a lady's hairnet made of fine silk, an expensive luxury probably imported from Italy. Trade in quality goods, however, was not invariably one-way. Scotland could evidently export manufactured articles. In 1271 a burgess of Lincoln, Henry of Coleby, made a will in which he bequeathed to Thomas Makait, a witness to the document, 'a sword of Scotland'. 'Makait' looks suspiciously like the Scots surname Mac Aed, later Mackay, and Thomas may have been a Scottish merchant established at Lincoln.[4] Much valuable property was held by such burgess families as those of Serlo and Audoen of Edinburgh in the twelfth century, of Cristin Lyle and John Ailbot of Perth in the thirteenth, and of Sir Robert Bernham and Philip Riddell, mayors of Berwick upon Tweed in the 1240s and 1280s respectively. Merchant burgesses had close links not only with the crown but also with noble families. Walter Deacon, burgess of Perth and a member of the town council in 1291, was described as merchant of Joan de Clare, the young dowager countess of Fife, on whose behalf he engaged in trading down the English coast. The fact that in 1291 the English king forbade him to go to Flanders must mean that the Flemish ports were among his usual destinations.

Burgesses can be found owing money as well as being owed, but their indebtedness may have been in furtherance of trading ventures. Thus in 1287 John son of Henry Burnet engaged to repay to Jedburgh Abbey the sum of 70 merks over a period of 12 years, payable at the abbey's daughter house of Restenneth beside Forfar. When, 10 years later, William Wallace wrote to tell the German cities of Hamburg and Lübeck that Scotland was freed from English rule and open to Hanseatic traders, he added a postscript asking for help to be given to the Scots merchants John Burnet and John Frere. The Flemish town of St Omer had close links with Scotland and the St Omer merchants Denys and Jacques Dribrod ('Dry bread') are recorded between 1291 and 1306 as being owed much money by Scots and as involved in trading to Perth, Dundee, and the north of Scotland. During the thirteenth century Scots traders and craftsmen were busy not only across

[4]*Lincoln Wills*, I (ed. C.W. Foster, Lincoln Record Soc., 1914), p. 1.

the North Sea but also in Irish towns such as Drogheda, Dublin, and Cork. Most, naturally, came from the south-west (Glasgow, Greenock, Renfrew, Irvine, Dumfries, and Kirkcudbright), but they included men from Berwick, Edinburgh, and Lasswade.

For the community of merchants travel to foreign parts was an obvious necessity. It was no less necessary for the community of clergy and students. Elementary education in reading and writing and a grounding in the Latin language had been fairly widely available in Scotland since the earlier twelfth century. We hear of schools established in a few of the principal royal burghs in the reign of David I and some schooling must also have been offered at the major churches. At leading ecclesiastical centres such as St Andrews and Glasgow there may even have been facilities for some advanced study. At the former we may guess that there was a struggle between practitioners of the older Celtic learning, transmitted through the medium of Gaelic as well as Latin, and advocates of the teaching characteristic of twelfth-century Europe, closely associated with the French vernacular and also perhaps just beginning to be associated with the use of English. Before the close of our period Celtic learning was in full retreat and already confined to a few centres in the west highlands. For organized courses in higher study, especially those leading to the formal degree of Master of Arts which qualified its holders to teach anywhere in catholic Christendom, the Scotsman who wished to proceed beyond the rudiments had to make his way to English and continental centres which had already acquired or were acquiring the status of 'universities' — i.e. communities or gilds of masters and students specializing in advanced education. From the second half of the twelfth century we have record of 'masters' among the Scottish clergy. After *c*.1220 we begin to see the emergence of a real community of Scots university scholars and graduates, many of whom returned to their own country to fill responsible positions in the church or to take service in royal and noble households.

The Lanercost chronicler, writing in the 1290s, tells us about a vicar of Dalmeny in West Lothian who in his youth had studied at Cambridge, perhaps *c*.1240. In the 1240s the murder by townspeople of Gilbert of Dunfermline, a young Scots student at Oxford, led to Henry III's grant of Oxford university's first great charter of privileges. The Lanercost writer also refers casually to Scots travelling to Bologna for the start of a new session at that famous centre of legal studies. There seems in fact to have been a strong tradition, especially in the outward-looking town of Dundee, for Scots to obtain a law qualification at Bologna. Paris was also favoured, and there were enough Scots studying in France in 1293 to make it worthwhile for Philip IV to deport all Scottish students when he quarrelled with Edward I. The proctorial system at Oxford goes back to the mid-thirteenth-century custom whereby students were divided into two groups, 'northerners' and 'southerners'. The Scots were a prominent element among the northerners, and we may suspect that the often violent quarrels between the two groups (there was an especially outrageous riot in 1274) were in reality feuds between Scots and Irish (prominent among the southerners), fought out in the streets and taverns of an English midland borough. Among Scots who attained distinction in the academic world of our period Peter Ramsay was lecturer to the Franciscan school at Oxford in succession to the famous Robert Grosseteste. He later returned to Scotland and eventually became bishop of Aberdeen (1247–56). Master Matthew of Scotland, singled out by the pope as an especially able teacher at Paris in 1218, may have been the Master Matthew Scot who was appointed chancellor of Scotland in 1227. Adam of Gullane archdeacon of Lothian was a professor at Paris in the 1280s, where he may have briefly overlapped with the most famous – but unfortunately least well documented – Scots academic of the period, John Scot of Duns, 'Duns Scotus', one of the outstanding theologians and philosophers of medieval Europe. Mention must also be made of Master Baldred Bisset, trained in law at Bologna and active in the service of St Andrews diocese, who in the final stages of his career, evidently spent in Italy, became a jurist of European stature, entrusted with the defence of Pope Boniface VIII at his posthumous 'trial'.

If we turn from the hard, unnatural work of merchants' ledgers and Latin school books to the relaxation of sports and pastimes we find ourselves hampered severely by the nature of our evidence. The clerks who wrote most of our surviving documentary and chronicle sources often showed moral disapproval of what they considered frivolous games and sports. They were, moreover, snobbish in their discrimination between the 'respectable' pastimes of the aristocracy and the 'deplorable' entertainments of the peasantry. Apart from parchment evidence it is only a lucky chance – for example, the discovery in the Isle of Lewis last century of a superbly carved ivory chess set, now in the British Museum – that now and again throws light on society at play in twelfth- or thirteenth-century Scotland. The sport of which we have easily the most abundant evidence, undoubtedly because it was pursued with passion by royalty and nobility, was hunting the red deer by means of specially trained hounds, the actual killing being done by bow and arrow. Deer hunting has left physical traces on the landscape in the form of banks and dykes used either as park boundaries or for trapping the deer after they had been gathered and driven by fleet-footed men. The sport has also left many indications in place-names, especially those containing the Gaelic words *eileirg*, 'elrick' or deer-trap, and *saobhaidh*, 'lair of wild beasts'. Falconry, the pursuit of game birds by means of peregrine falcons and other teachable species of raptor, was second only to deer hunting as the sport beloved of the noble class. The men who served the kings as professional huntsmen and falconers were admitted at least to the knightly order and some-times enjoyed baronial status. Norman, the king's hunter at Polmood in upper Tweeddale in the time of David I and Malcolm IV, founded a laird's family which lasted for centuries; Ranulf, William the Lion's falconer, settled at Haulkerton (= hawker's toun) in the Mearns, was ancestor of a family that eventually gained a lordship of parliament. In 1212–13 we hear of the king of Scots' falconers, Michael Bibois, Simon of Ceres (or 'the southerner'?[5]), Hugh le Bret and Richard of Airth, who were well rewarded when they brought a gift of five ger-falcons to King John of England. In the next reign a valuable fishery in the Tweed at Berwick was given by the king to his falconer Ralph de Hauville, who may have been imported from Hauville in the great forest of Brotonne at the mouth of the Seine in Normandy.

Jousting or tournaments, a form of mock warfare which was often violent enough to cause death and injury as though it had been the real thing, was necessarily an aristocratic pastime. It called for the pos-session of trained horses and expensive weapons and body armour. Skill in jousting might offer an avenue of advancement to a relatively poor young man of the knightly class, who could win a rich ransom from a defeated opponent. It also allowed young men of good looks and promise to catch the attention of the marriageable young women of noble birth, or for that matter of married women too, if the some-times prurient tongue-wagging of clerical chroniclers can be trusted. The sexual affairs of the nobility are a perennial source of interest, and no opportunity was ever lost of openly stating or slyly implying that there might be improper relations between a noble lady and some squire or youthful knight in her own or her husband's retinue. When Walter Comyn earl of Menteith – one of the most powerful noblemen in the realm – died in 1258, his wife Isabel, in whose right he held the

[5] Alternatively 'de Sireis' or 'le Surreis'.

earldom, quickly married an Englishman named John Russell, a young protégé of Alexander III. At once there were accusations that she had poisoned her first husband. The other Scots nobles assumed that only infatuation could have made her spurn their eligible sons in favour of a mere English knight. Even queens were not immune from malicious gossip. A handsome young squire, recommended by Edward I of England to the service of his sister Margaret, first wife of Alexander III, was accidentally drowned in the River Tay at Kinclaven while entertaining the queen and her ladies one summer afternoon. We have the story from a misogynist Franciscan who had it from the queen's chaplain; one of them meanly thought the tragedy a just retribution for the secret passion which Queen Margaret was believed to be cherishing for the young man.

Tournaments might be enjoyed by noble ladies, for whom life must often have seemed excruciatingly boring, but they were frowned on by the church because of the needless shedding of blood. They were not always appreciated by the kings since although they were good training for war they often provided a pretext for lawlessness. In Scotland the concept of the blood feud was deeply engrained, and both hunting and jousting could give rise to damaging feuds. In the mid twelfth century Malcolm de Morville, a brother of the king's constable Richard de Morville, was accidentally killed by Adolf de Saint Martin while they were hunting. In order to avert a feud the head of the Saint Martin family had to make a gift to the white canons of Dryburgh of whose house the de Morvilles were patrons. A tragic episode in 1242 began with a tournament at Haddington and, as we shall see in the next chapter, had serious and long-lasting consequences, including the threat of a blood feud. Walter Bisset, member of an Anglo-Norman baronial family comparatively new to Scotland but much in favour with King Alexander II, is said to have been knocked from his horse by young Patrick of Atholl, son of Thomas of Galloway earl of Atholl and prospective heir to the earldom. In the following night the lodging occupied by Patrick was burned to the ground and he himself was found dead. At once the powerful Comyn clan, to whom Patrick was kin, accused the Bissets of murder. Walter and his nephew John fled, the former to England, the latter to the west where he may have found refuge in northern Ireland and may also have gained a foothold in Arran and Kintyre. When, some years later, Patrick's bastard half-brother Alan son of Thomas besieged the Bissets in Dunaverty castle at the south end of Kintyre he was probably pursuing a vendetta which arose from Patrick's death, although it is possible that rival claims to western and Ulster lordships were involved as well.

However surprising it may seem, the earls and barons did not constitute a well-defined or coherent community within Scottish society as a whole. In the fourteenth century they would be treated as one of the 'estates' (*status*) of the realm in recognition of their special position at the head of lay society. But in our period the nobility had less class cohesion than they were to acquire in the later Middle Ages. The earls, a dozen or so all told, retained much of their older character of provincial governors — aristocratic certainly, but at the same time royal officials. The barons were still a heterogeneous group united only in being tenants-in-chief of the crown. If the nobles could be said to show any class solidarity it was not a straightforward case of closing ranks whenever they felt themselves collectively threatened. Quite simply, there was no other class which could threaten them. A strong king might restrain them, but it was not in their interest to weaken the monarchy from whose patronage they all benefited. The crown exerted great moral authority, but it lacked the vast material resources that gave its English counterpart a power-base from which to overawe the baronage. Unassailable as a class, nobles and noble families could be individually vulnerable and there was little sympathy or mercy for those who fell by the wayside. Obeying the rules of a game that was broadly accepted, the earls and barons were competitive, acquisitive, quarrelsome, and liable to outbursts of violence.

During the reigns of Alexander II and his son we see some feudal families that had already come to prominence in the previous century, e.g. Comyns, Stewarts, Olifards (Oliphants), and Murrays, forging ahead in the race for landed wealth and power. In their wake came a number of other families only slightly less rich and influential, e.g. Lindsays, Grahams, Douglases, and Moubrays, all putting out new branches, gradually extending their estates, making advantageous marriages, winning offices of profit or power under the crown. As it happens, all the families named traced their ancestry in the male line to incoming settlers from Normandy, Flanders, and England, but it would be a mistake to suppose that success in the baronial stakes was confined to settler families. Not only were a majority of the earldoms still held by native dynasties in 1286; many old thanages, baronies, and other free estates, held either for military service or a money rent, were in the hands of descendants of the old gentry of Lothian, Cumbria, and the country north of Forth. In taking our leave of the nobility we may look briefly at the position enjoyed under Alexander

III by one of these magnates of native stock, Hugh son of Laurence, lord of Abernethy on the Tay, close kinsman of the earls of Fife, heir of the secularized 'abbots' of the old Celtic religious foundation of Abernethy. Hugh succeeded his father *c*.1245 and died *c*.1291. He held in chief of the crown estates that stretched along the south bank of the Firth of Tay from the mouth of the Earn to Flisk, broken only by the lands of Lindores Abbey. He had another lordship a few miles south of Forfar. For each block of estates there was a baronial court with jurisdiction of life and limb, that is the right to inflict the capital penalty or mutilation in case of grave crime. It is a striking illustration of how little we know about the life of the higher nobility in our period that the character of Hugh's chief residence at Carpow (on the site of a Roman fort) cannot be reconstructed with any certainty. Presumably it was a fortified manor house, if not actually a castle, but it has left no remains to compare with those of Ballinbreich east of Lindores, the fine castle built by Hugh's Leslie successors from the fourteenth century onwards. Hugh possessed other estates besides those in Fife, Perthshire, and Angus. From the 1230s he held Oxton at the north end of Lauderdale in Berwickshire. On Palm Sunday (6 April) 1259, at Edinburgh, Hugh put his seal to an elaborate marriage contract with William, lord of Douglas in Clydesdale. Hugh's sister Marjorie was to marry Hugh Douglas, William's son and heir, before 22 May next. The bride's tocher, provided by her brother, was to be 20 merks' worth of land either at Glencorse near Edinburgh or Newton north-east of Hawick. At this time Hugh was at the height of his power. He joined the Comyn faction when they made an alliance with Llywelyn of Wales in March 1258 — their last bid to form the government of Scotland before Alexander III's minority came to an end. Hugh served as the young king's ambassador to England in 1260, was appointed to the committee of estates responsible for bringing home Queen Margaret's first-born child, and is found often at court in the next decade, presumably as a member of the king's inner council. After 1270 his political influence may have waned, but he did not cease to acquire land or form important dynastic connexions. Between 1271 and 1275 he married Mary Macdougall (dowager queen of Man, dowager countess of Strathearn, an indefatigable snapper up of well-considered husbands). In 1277 he persuaded a lady name Ethena, widow of the Argyll baron Gilchrist Macnaughton, lord of Dundaraw on Loch Fyne, and herself heiress of land in Atholl, to give him the tenancy of all her estates during her lifetime, paying her the ancient customary fermes and performing the king's forinsec service on her behalf. After

Alexander III's death Hugh became involved in a bitter, though unexplained, feud with his kinsman, the youthful Earl Duncan III of Fife, one of the six guardians of the realm, whom a contemporary describes as 'more than averagely cruel and grasping'. In September 1289 Hugh incited some of his younger relations and Sir Walter de Percehay, a landowner between Ceres and Cupar, to ambush the earl as he rode westward from Brechin through the little farm of Pitpullox. Duncan was killed, but the government's pursuit of the criminals was dramatically successful. The lesser fry who had done the deed were summarily executed. Hugh of Abernethy, though confined in the lord of Douglas's jail, was too great a man to be prosecuted by the remaining guardians. Nevertheless he had to throw himself on the mercy of the pope and to beg for the intercession of Edward I of England at the papal court. The scandal seems to have been too much to bear, for he was evidently dead by 1291. Here was a wealthy man who controlled estates widely scattered across the country from Forfar to the English border, from Argyll to Fife. One of the great barons of the realm, he was nevertheless prepared to take the law into his own hands, even to the extreme of *lèse-majesté*, to settle personal or family scores. A strong kingship was needed to curb the violence of such an unruly lord as Hugh Abernethy.

If the nobles did not form a true community we can hardly expect to find any community of the peasantry. At the very end of our period, in 1305, a petition was sent to the king of England and his council (then the rulers of a conquered Scotland) on behalf of the king's husbandmen, that is the peasant tenants on Scottish royal demesne. It asked that they might have the same security of tenure as the villeins on royal demesne in England enjoyed, and in particular that they should not be liable to eviction each year at the expiry of their 12-month leases. We have no means of knowing how this petition was organized or who was responsible for it. Even if it was not the work of the peasants themselves it proves that an important section of their class might be treated as a distinct community whose common grievances could be formulated. The same thought may have been in Edward I's mind a year later when he rescinded the orders given to his troops in Scotland for fear that the 'poor commons' might be dealt with too harshly. In the Anglo-French treaty of Asnières (1301–2) which chiefly concerned the Scots, safeguards were written in for the lesser folk (*le menu peuple*) of south-western Scotland 'who work the land of which they are tenants either by inheritance or on fixed leases in accordance with the custom of the country'. The words suggest that these peasants had found a spokesman among the Scots at Philip IV's court who helped to draft the treaty. In 1297 we have a number of interesting references to the 'common people'. The revolt against English rule organized by the earl of Carrick, the Stewart, and the bishop of Glasgow pressed into service certain of the 'common folk' of south-western provinces. An English chronicler says that the *communitas terre* – by which he means the common people of the land – followed William Wallace as their leader and ruler. We also hear of the fears of the 'middling folk' of Scotland that they would be conscripted to fight for the English king overseas, but it is not clear whether middling folk were identical with common or ordinary folk.

In practice, however, the peasantry were rarely thought of as a class. Instead of constituting any sort of general community they were divided into innumerable local communities determined by lordship, district, or village. A court case of 1206 throws some light upon such a small agrarian community, at Arbuthnott in the Mearns, towards the close of the twelfth century. Much of the parish was royal demesne held as a thanage under the crown. Part belonged to the church of St Andrews and its bishops, who paid 'cain', i.e. rents in kind, to the king's thane but were otherwise independent. Under the bishop eight 'parsons' – presumably secularized quasi-clerical tenants surviving from the old Celtic order – enjoyed freehold tenure. Although they paid a rent in cows their holdings included arable land. Under them in turn were a large number of lesser, unfree tenants to whom the technical term *scoloc* is given in our record; to later generations they would have been 'gersemen'.[6] These poorer folk had little or no arable but got their living by pasturing cattle and sheep. Each family possessing a house had to pay the thane, in recognition of his lordship, 10 cheeses a year and must also find a man to work for one day at the harvest. Every Friday they might grind their corn at the thane's mill free of charge. A series of thanes, and their successors, lords of knight's rank put in by the crown, began to oppress these tenants of the church lands of Arbuthnott, demanding unaccustomed services and threatening to plough up their pasture land. The tenants found a leader called Gillanders the One-footed – whether one of the eight 'parsons' or one of the multitude of *scolocs* we do not know. When in the 1180s the thane tried to get rid of him by bribing Bishop Hugh with a valuable horse worth five merks, the bishop refused to oblige because Gillanders was his 'native man', his neyf, unfree to leave the estate of

[6]See above, pp. 17–18.

his birth but equally entitled not to be evicted from it. After the bishop and Gillanders had died a later thane evicted many of the *scolocs*. From the record we are left with an impression of an independent pastoral community of poor tenants who had only light labour services but suffered from severe insecurity of tenure. There is record of a comparable clash in the 1230s between the rights of an ancient episcopal estate and those of a bustling feudally-minded baron in the upper Spey valley. The baron, Walter Comyn, newly-made lord of Badenoch, bargained with the bishop of Moray to be freed from old annual payments of money, pigs, cheese, and oatmeal while in return the bishop secured the sites of three parish kirks, Laggan, Kingussie, and Insh, and also two davochs of land, one at Laggan and one at Invereshie by Loch Insh, with all the neyfs belonging to the clerical grade and two native laymen with their families, Walter being given a free hand with all the remaining neyfs formerly judged to belong to the bishopric. To this day one of the estates secured by the bishop of Moray is still called Balnespick, i.e. 'the bishop's toun'.

All our evidence from the country north of Forth reinforces this picture of an overwhelmingly pastoral population in the rural areas, paying rents in cheese, pigs, cattle, and an occasional 'dinmont' (two-year-old wether sheep). It is of course true that some corn was grown nearly everywhere. Rents in oats, malt, and bere (six-rowed barley) were by no means uncommon. But pastoral farming predominated and there is little trace of fixed and agreed peasant holdings of arable. The peasantry were poor and had little if any security. Equally, there seems to have been small scope for agricultural improvement by the great lords, even if they or their stewards had progressive ideas about extracting a greater income from the land. Nevertheless, some schemes of improvement were undertaken, especially by the religious houses which had adequate supplies of capital and labour and perhaps a greater farsightedness of outlook than the laity. Improvement might take the form of better drainage and the clearing of woodland and scrub to allow a bigger share for arable. It might also involve the colonization of estates thus improved with fresh settlements of agricultural tenants to open up their own small holdings and work on the lord's demesne. In the 1190s the earl of Strathearn had temporarily parted with the lands of Aldie in Kinross-shire to supplement a marriage portion for his daughter. At that time, Aldie may not have been much more than a small arable clearing within an essentially pastoral estate. Three-quarters of a century later, however, Sir John Murray granted Aldie to his brother William (ancestor of the Murrays of Tullibardine) in return for a merely nominal rent of a penny or a pair of gloves at Easter. But the new tenant was to pay to the earl of Strathearn, as superior, no less than 10 pounds of silver *per annum*, a substantial economic rent by Scottish standards. We can hardly fail to connect this with the visible presence today at Parks of Aldie of the cottage sites, tofts, and lengthy curved ploughed rigs of a long-vanished peasant settlement, undoubted evidence of deliberate agrarian colonization by a younger son of the knightly class anxious to increase the income from his lands.

South of Forth, arable played a more important rôle in the pattern of peasant farming. This undoubtedly enabled large landowners to impose greater uniformity and discipline, but even so we note that labour services remained comparatively light. There was hardly anything approaching the intensive manorialization typical of midland and southern England. Kelso Abbey's surveys made *c*.1290 may be taken to illustrate the resources of what by Scottish standards was a very large agricultural estate, of which we may single out Bowden in Roxburghshire as a typical separate 'toun' or agrarian unit, complete with its own village – as close an approximation to an English 'manor' as might be found in thirteenth-century Scotland. Bowden contained 22 'husbandlands' (units of two oxgangs, 26 acres of arable with commensurate grazing). The year's rent for each husbandland was half a merk, of which 3s. 4d. was payable at Whitsun, 3s. 4d. at Martinmas (11 November). Each husbandman's entire household had to give four days' labour at harvest and a further day's work with only two men. From Greenknowe Moss near Gordon every husbandman had to cart one load of peats annually to supply the abbey with fuel. Each husbandman must take a horseload of goods to Berwick once a year, his food being provided by the monks. There were also some not very burdensome ploughing and harrowing services. One man was to be found to help at the annual sheep washing and sheep shearing, and one day's carriage of wool from Bowden to the abbey's storehouses was demanded.

Beside the husbandlands Bowden contained six cottage holdings each of 12¾ acres, the cottars paying about nine shillings in rent and supplying nine days' labour in the autumn. There were also four brew-houses and a corn mill to which the men of Bowden would be thirled, so that the abbot was guaranteed a further useful income. The only service performed by the peasants of Bowden beyond the boundaries of their village which did not directly benefit Kelso Abbey was their contribution to the common army, for which we are told that 30 archers would be found from among the men of the village, organized by a man-at-arms provided by four husbandmen tenanting a particular ploughgate.

About 1285, Abbot Richard of Kelso commuted the husbandmen's labour services for a money payment. This may not have been a bad bargain for the peasantry at that period, when agricultural incomes, especially from wool, could be considerable. But we should remember that before commutation the peasant received stock ('stuht' or 'steel-bow') from his lord at the start of a tenancy. In the case of Kelso Abbey's estates that consisted of two plough oxen, a horse, three 'chalders' of oats (about 48 bolls), six bolls of barley, and three bolls of wheat. This provision of stock ceased when labour services were converted to an additional money rent. The transition was not invariably from labour services to cash, and presumably it was the lord, not the tenant, who had discretion as to which form of reward he required. About 1250 Alexander de Montfort received a farm from his brother John at Athelstaneford in East Lothian. Sixty acres of it were 'in hand', but there were six oxgangs, i.e. three husbandlands, each with a house and yard, held by three husbandmen whose labour, together with that of their families, was to be at Alexander's disposal. But we are told that formerly these same husbandmen had farmed their land from John de Montfort, that is, they had worked it independently, without being given stock, in return for a money rent.

An undated document surviving from the close of the thirteenth century gives us a picture of the terms on which a peasant — in this case a rural craftsman — might take a small agricultural holding from a landlord in upper Tweeddale. Bernard the soutar ('shoe-maker') got the tenancy of a house and two acres at Drumelzier from William Fraser lord of Oliver Castle. The rent was sixpence a year or a pair of silver-gilt spurs. The property included a house, brewhouse and garden (presumably for herbs and vegetables), an acre of arable and the same area of meadow. There was pasture for a fixed number of plough oxen, cows with calves, and ewes with lambs. Bernard might cut peats for his own use on the moor. He must contribute the same 'aid' towards the king's army, i.e. the common army of Scotland, as William Fraser's other husbandmen usually contributed, and he must attend three sessions each year of Fraser's baronial court at Drumelzier. The document shows that, as we should expect, a skilled village craftsman was also expected to be a small farmer. The mention of a garden is also of interest, for although we have a good deal of evidence of gardens belonging to the king, to religious houses, and to earls, nobles, and other gentry, the lack of such references at a lower social level might tempt us to suppose that a garden was an unheard-of luxury for a humble peasant.

8

Scotland in Europe

Every historian is occasionally tempted to speculate on what might have happened but did not. In the history of medieval Scotland an inescapable turning-point is the reign of Robert I and the restoration by him of an independent kingdom of Scotland after it had apparently been conquered by Edward I in the years 1303–5. It is natural to wonder what political and social pattern might have been established had Robert the Bruce failed and had Edward I and his son successfully achieved their aims. In view of what actually happened after 1333, it is not rash to guess that a large region of southern Scotland, perhaps as far up as the Tay, perhaps only to the Forth, would have been annexed to England, while the north, the west highlands including the isles, and possibly separatist Galloway, might have been allowed to become a regality or palatinate either for the Balliol dynasty or more probably for a younger son of the Plantagenet royal house. Alternatively, the whole of Alexander III's kingdom, with its 26 sheriffdoms and other organization more or less intact, might have been absorbed into the English realm, necessitating itinerant justices of English common law riding on circuit to Aberdeen and Inverness, while knights of the shire from Lewis, Argyll, and Galloway got used to making long, troublesome journeys, once a year or oftener, to attend the Westminster parliament.

It would be rash to state positively that neither alternative could have worked in practice, but the feasibility of these admittedly hypothetical developments in the long term seems highly doubtful. The addition to fourteenth-century England of English-speaking Scotland, however much it might have been welcomed by a handful of ambitious and greedy Scots eager to better themselves through the generous patronage of a wealthy king, would undoubtedly have affected the lopsided balance of England. Already in that century (as we know from a marital lawsuit heard at York in 1364[1]) there was a clear threefold distinction in speech between south-country Englishmen, north-country Englishmen, and English-speaking Scots. These well-established speech differences, so familiar in our own days, reflected a marked difference of culture and way of life within England itself between north and south which ran deep and was, in the fifteenth and sixteenth centuries, to prove politically divisive. They also reflected a difference between England on the one hand and Scotland on the other which can be traced to the thirteenth century and indeed earlier. The political stability and unity of a country ruled from London cannot be taken for granted if it was to include a vigorous and self-conscious, even though obviously not very wealthy, Scottish south and east, along with a comparable English north. As for the total annexation of Scotland by England, it is doubtful whether the technological level of fourteenth-century governments could in the long run have surmounted the difficulty that most of England is focused on the south-east while most of Scotland looks westward or north-eastward. It seems a reasonable surmise that without cannon, small arms, gunpowder, and much bigger ships (with which even Oliver Cromwell did not find the conquest and annexation of Scotland a walkover) an English government would have seen Norwegian or Danish rulers once again nibbling at the northern mainland and Irish potentates, both native and Anglo-Norman, exploiting the geographical and social proximity of the western isles and seaboard of Scotland.

These things, however, did not happen. The histories of England and Scotland in the later Middle Ages were sharply different in almost every important respect. To understand this superficially rather surprising fact we must look at the political and social development of Scotland between 1214 and 1286. At first sight there seems to have been less of a gulf between the kingdoms of Henry III and the two Alexanders than there was between those of (say) Richard II and Robert II or between those of Henry VI and James II. But the divergent courses taken by later medieval England and Scotland were already being mapped out long before the first war of independence. By far the most important single factor in this process was the unbroken development of the Scottish monarchy and royal government. Closely connected with this was the growth during the twelfth

---

[1]D.M. Owen, 'White Annays and others', in D. Baker (ed.), *Medieval Women* (Ecclesiastical History Society, 1978), pp. 332, 343–4.

and early thirteenth centuries of the concepts of 'Scotland' and 'Scot'. A further factor, by no means insignificant, was the relationship of Scotland to other powers and states in western Europe. Relations with England could hardly fail to be the most important of all, but they no longer counted for quite as much as they had in the twelfth century. What mattered most, certainly from 1266 onward, was the position of Scotland as a force to be reckoned with in the community of North Sea kingdoms and principalities, together with the special relationship that the Scots church enjoyed with the papacy.

In the remainder of this chapter we shall look at these three factors in turn, endeavouring finally to see how they combined during the crisis years after 1292 to provide the conditions in which Robert I could succeed and the most strenuous efforts of English kings were almost certain to fail.

Alexander II was 16 when he succeeded his father at the end of 1214. Although knighted by King John he adopted a much more independent stance in relation to England than William the Lion ever achieved. He seems to have resented the underhand manner in which the English king had tricked his father into surrendering his sisters, Margaret and Isabel, with the prospect of marriage into the English royal house. Instead, they were left on the shelf, a prey to the ambitions of Hubert de Burgh, a faithful servant of King John but an overmighty subject of his son Henry III. Alexander also hankered after the northern counties of England (Northumberland, Cumberland, and Westmorland) for whose recovery his father had made so many vain sacrifices. He allied with the disaffected English barons who in June 1215 extracted the Great Charter of liberties from King John. At Runnymede he won no more than the vague promise that his grievances would be listened to and justice done — in the English king's own court. The Scots doubtless shared the total distrust of John which prompted the diehard wing of the English baronage to reject the Runnymede agreement, attempt to drive John from the throne, and even accept the kingship of Louis, heir to Philip II of France. In the winter of 1215–16 John brought his hated *routiers*, mercenary troops hired from Brabant and elsewhere, north of the border, burning and harrying far and wide from Berwick to Haddington. He swore that he would smoke the little fox-cub, as he called the red-haired king of Scots, out of his lair. Alexander's answer to this devastation was to march south by the west-coast route, supported by many north-country English barons. They took Carlisle and committed many of the same dismal atrocities that John and his men had inflicted on

Lothian. The Scots were confident enough to ride all the way to Dover, easily the deepest penetration of south Britain ever recorded by any army from the north. Alexander met Louis of France and did homage to him, evidently for Northumberland. But after John's death in October 1216 the Scots received no more satisfaction from Louis and the disaffected barons than they had had from John. Alexander ought to have recalled the harsh lessons learned by Malcolm IV and William I, namely that in adversity English aspirants to the throne would always promise to give the Scots what they wanted but would forget their promises as soon as they came to power. The regency government set up to rule on behalf of the nine-year-old Henry would make no deal with an absurdly optimistic Scottish king. They persuaded Louis to go home, pacified all but the most recalcitrant barons, and left Alexander with not even the vaguely-worded chapter on Scotland from the original Magna Carta when they reissued the charter in 1216 and 1217.

Indeed, the Scots got all the kicks and few of the ha'pence from the general English settlement of 1217. In this a key rôle was played by the papacy and its agents in England. The inveterate opponents of John, including the Scots, were excommunicated, and the realm of Scotland was laid under an interdict, or suspension of services, from which Alexander II only obtained release early in 1218. It was perhaps some consolation that in 1219 the feudal superiority over the Honour of Huntingdon, held by Scottish kings for over a century, was restored to Alexander. There was undoubted satisfaction that in 1221 the king of Scots was given Henry III's sister Joan in marriage. Huntingdon was important not because of the earldom's rich resources, for these were actually in the hands of the king's uncle David until his death in 1219 and from then until 1237 held by David's son John of Scotland, on whose death they were divided equally among John's three sisters. Recognition of Alexander II's superiority meant that he could be the king of England's vassal explicitly and obviously for a great English fief, just as the king of England could be the vassal of the king of France for Normandy or Aquitaine. It made it easier for the Scots to deny that the homage and fealty of their king were given in respect of the Scottish realm. For this purpose the lordship or 'liberty' of Tynedale in Northumberland, of which the Scots kings had hardly ever been deprived since the mid twelfth century, was inadequate. Although it was large in area and attractive as a hunting preserve it was not, like Huntingdon, a first-class feudal barony held of the crown in chief. As for the marriage with Joan of England, it was of course important in terms of both prestige and goodwill. The prospect of children would give rise to longer-term hopes of better relations between the two countries.

For the next 16 years Alexander II was much occupied with domestic affairs. A pillar of the monarchy in this period was the rising Scoto-Norman family of Cumin or Comyn, by now fairly thoroughly naturalized. William Comyn, son of Richard, head of the clan from *c*.1180 till his death in 1233, was the first member of any of the incoming settler families to acquire a Scottish earldom. By marriage to the heiress he became earl of Buchan in 1212. Earl William took a leading part in northern campaigns against the Macwilliam rebels who still vainly sought the throne. For many years he served as justiciar of Scotia (Scotland north of Forth). William's son Alexander succeeded to the earldom of Buchan which he held for nearly 50 years. By an earlier marriage William had fathered a senior branch of the Comyn family which included another son, named Walter, who also married the heiress to an earldom, in his case that of Menteith, which he held from *c*.1234 to 1258. Another member of this branch was John Comyn 'the Red' whose descendants carried the senior line, the Red Comyns, down to the fourteenth century. An ambitious and widely-ramifying family marked by the clannishness of the Celtic society they had adopted, the Comyns dominated the political scene in Scotland for almost a century. Their position stemmed from a personal ascendancy acquired in the reign of Alexander II by the two earls, William of Buchan and his son Walter of Menteith.

Of their usefulness to the crown there can be no doubt. Alexander II spent more time in Moray and directed more of his energies towards solving the problems of royal government in the northern highlands than any of his twelfth-century predecessors. The Comyns, hitherto a south-country family with estates on both sides of the border, began to take a leading rôle in the north, not only as earls of Buchan but also, in the senior line, as lords of Badenoch, the district formed by the upper valley of the Spey. Control of this district seems to have been given to Walter Comyn by the king about 1230, and it passed after his death in 1258 to his next of kin John Comyn the Red who survived for a further 20 years and was probably the builder of Lochindorb Castle in Moray. John's son, of the same name, was knighted by Alexander III in 1270 and married Eleanor Balliol, whose brother became king of Scotland in 1292. This John Comyn served as Guardian of Scotland from 1286 to 1292 and died at Lochindorb in 1303.

Other northern earldoms such as Mar and Caithness provided

support for the crown in this period. King Alexander was never afraid of his earls and added to their number by reviving the earldom of Ross and creating a new earldom of Sutherland (the southern part of Caithness) for William Freskin, head of one branch of a settler family of Flemish origin only slightly less influential than the Comyns. In the course of the thirteenth century other branches of William Freskin's family, because of their power in the province, adopted the surname *de Moravia*, 'of Moray', or, as it is usually spelled nowadays, Murray. It is noticeable that under Alexander II the earls of Scotland were more often at court and more frequently consulted and employed by the king than had been the case under his father or great-grandfather. This was as true of the majority of the earls who were of native Scots or Northumbrian blood as of the growing minority who belonged to 'Anglo-Norman' families. At the same time, the king took care to ensure a balance of power among the higher nobility. In confirming the earldom of Lennox to its native heir he retained Dumbarton as a royal stronghold. He never revived the earldom of Moray, preferring to rule the province through non-hereditary sheriffs. Although the justiciarship of Scotland north of Forth was held by Earl William Comyn till 1232 he was not immediately succeeded by his son or any northern earl, but by the hereditary Stewart, Walter II son of Alan. On his death in 1241 the office was held jointly by men of lairds' rank with experience of sheriffships. About 1244 it passed to Alan the Durward (i.e. royal doorward or usher), who, though he aspired to the rank, was not in fact an earl by birth. The justiciarship of Lothian, covering southern Scotland, was never held by an earl under Alexander II or his son. In the former's reign it was at first shared by the sheriffs of Berwick and Stirling before being held for many years by Walter Olifard, lord of Bothwell on the lower Clyde. In the last decade of the reign it passed to David Lindsay, lord of Crawford in upper Clydesdale.

It was not possible for the crown, even if it had wished, to turn the justiciars into assize and common law judges on the English model. The latter were men of relatively humble background but possessed of legal training, and wholly devoted to the king's service. In Scotland feudal society lacked any cadre of trained lawyers. On the one hand there was the old and increasingly discredited caste of *breitheamhan* (*judices* or dempsters), skilled in the traditional law of Celtic society. On the other hand, the church courts gave increasing employment to clerical experts in canon law, most of whom would also have some knowledge of the Roman civil law. Neither group provided a suitable recruiting ground from which the king could obtain justices with the knowledge or authority to administer feudal law to a powerful and potentially unruly class of knights, barons and freeholders. Consequently, the kings had to steer a difficult middle course between allowing the justiciarship to degenerate into an aristocratic sinecure and appointing obscure royal servants who did not carry enough weight to be obeyed by the baronage at large. Alexander II and his son were in the main remarkably successful in finding justiciars of the right calibre, loyal to the crown but also respected by the feudal lords.

We have already seen something of Alexander II's vigorous policy with regard to the west highlands and Galloway. His successful assertion of royal authority in the north and west was made possible by peaceful relations with England. In the 1230s it was borne in upon him, however reluctantly, that he would never be given control over Northumberland and Cumberland and that English promises of 1209 and 1212 with regard to his sisters would never be honoured nor their repudiation adequately compensated. The outcome of this realization was the treaty of York (September 1237), sealed by Henry III and the king of Scots under the aegis of the papal legate in England, Cardinal Otto. Much credit is due to the two kings and the legate for an impressively statesmanlike agreement. Alexander II gave up all claims to the northern counties, thus in effect establishing the Anglo-Scottish frontier along the Solway—Tweed line. He also freed Henry III from any obligation in respect of the two Scottish princesses and waived his right to the huge sum of 15,000 merks which his father paid to King John as the price of the promised marriages that never took place. In return, Alexander was granted a large estate in Cumberland, the 'Honour of Penrith', which, when added to Tynedale and the superior lordship of the Honour of Huntingdon, gave him a dignified position as one of the greater feudal magnates within the English realm. A mere consideration of the substance of the treaty of York would suggest that the statesmanship, if measured by readiness to make sacrifices, was all on the side of the Scots. They had yielded much, the English almost nothing. But we ought to look at the treaty against the background of Falaise (1174) and Norham (1209), or even in the light of what would happen in 1291. Neither the crown nor the baronage of England (whose leaders are reported at this time to have declared they could wipe out Scotland without any help from abroad) saw any need or justification for the survival of Scotland as an independent realm. The point of lasting importance about the York treaty lies therefore in its implicit acceptance of the separate existence of Scotland, in its diplomatic format as a courteous agreement between equals, and in the absence of any hint of an Angevin claim to the overlordship of Scotland.

In 1238 Queen Joan died in the south of England, never having been happy as queen of Scots. There had been no children of the marriage and Alexander almost immediately chose a second wife, not from England but from among the great nobility of France, Marie daughter of Enguerrand de Coucy. Marie adapted more readily than Joan to life in Scotland and on 4 September 1241 gave birth to an heir at Roxburgh, named after his father. These events alarmed the suspicious Henry III who used a serious baronial quarrel which flared up north of the border in 1242 to interfere more actively than the treaty of York seemed to justify either in letter or in spirit. By 1244 a large Scottish army at Ponteland and a large English army at Newcastle upon Tyne eight miles to the south, each led by its king, were saved from what might have been a bloody and destructive battle only by the common sense of magnates on both sides. Once again, Henry pressed no overt claims to feudal suzerainty, but he obtained a confirmation of the York treaty along with specially sealed bonds for good behaviour from two separate Scottish baronial groups. He also secured the betrothal of the infant heir of Scotland to his own daughter Margaret, only slightly older.

The quarrel in Scotland which the English king had been able to exploit arose, as we have seen, through the jealousy of the native magnates, among them the Comyns, against a family of relative newcomers, the Bissets. Their representative in Scotland, John, had won royal favour early in Alexander II's reign and with it the lands of Lovat west of Inverness. He and his uncle Walter, who seems to have been a trouble-maker, were accused of murdering Patrick of Atholl after a tournament at Haddington in 1242 at which Walter Bisset was unhorsed. Patrick was found dead in a burned-out building the morning after the tournament, but we have no means of knowing whether the suspicion that fell on the Bissets had any foundation. Baronial indignation was widespread and the Bissets fled the realm, complained loudly to King Henry, and stirred up anti-Scottish feeling at the English court. The incident had long-lasting consequences. It gave the English king a pretext for intervention in Scottish politics of which he took advantage, on and off, for nearly 20 years. It showed Alexander II that he had allowed the Comyns to wield too much power, and until his death in 1249 he offset this by encouraging their chief opponent Alan the Durward. The episode also brought into sharp relief the potentially violent factiousness of the nobility, despite their acceptance of feudal obligations and underlying reverence for royal authority. It must have been very much in the minds of the more responsible magnates, including the leading bishops, when Alexander II died suddenly in July 1249. But we should not exaggerate the seriousness of the Bisset affair. The attention that King Alexander paid to west highland problems in the 1240s and the fact that he undertook a full-scale expedition in 1249 to assert the crown's authority in that region are evidence that the king was confident of the respect that he and his dynasty generally commanded.

Support for the crown was underlined in the years 1249–51 when the bishops, the earl of Menteith as chief of the Comyns and his allies, and Alan the Durward with his allies, shared the work of government, however uneasily, and successfully carried through two solemn public events, the inauguration at Scone of the boy king Alexander III and the reburial at Dunfermline of the remains of Queen Margaret, now officially recognized as a saint. The culminating achievement of this period of power-sharing was the wedding at York in December 1251 of the two royal children. It is clear that the young king of Scots was carefully schooled by his advisers, for when his father-in-law characteristically tried to take advantage of the happy occasion by raising the question of Scottish homage to the English crown for Scotland itself Alexander cut him short by saying that he had not come to York to discuss difficult matters on which he would require advice.

For the next nine years, however, it proved impossible to prevent faction, and consequently English interference, from dominating the political scene. Faction went to the extreme of a virtual kidnapping of the king and queen in 1255, in the interest of Henry III, who imposed upon Alexander a council of his own choice, and a counter-kidnapping in 1257 by the Comyns against the interest of Henry III, followed up by an anti-English treaty which the Comyns made in March 1258 with Llywelyn prince of Wales. Scotland was freed from faction partly by Henry III's political difficulties from 1258 onward but mainly by the king's coming of age, which seems to have been arranged for his eighteenth birthday in 1259 rather than his twenty-first birthday in 1262. Certainly by 1260 Alexander III had emerged in full command of government. Some years earlier he and his queen, Margaret of England, had thrown off the last traces of personal tutelage forced on them by Scottish regents and Henry III and were able to live together as man and wife. As for political faction, Earl Walter Comyn died in 1258. Menteith was held by Walter Stewart, brother of the hereditary

Stewart and a staunch upholder of the crown. The Comyns were now led by Alexander earl of Buchan, whose loyalty to the king never seems to have been in question. Alan the Durward virtually retired from politics. In his distribution of offices and power, the king successfully balanced actual and potential baronial rivalries. Conditions could hardly have been better for Scotland to face the challenge of King Haakon's expedition of 1263 and for the absorption of the western isles within the Scottish realm.

Under the two Alexanders the name *Scotia*, *Ecosse*, 'Scotland' ceased to refer only to the country north of Clyde and Forth and came finally and definitively to be synonymous with the kingdom of the Scots. Not surprisingly, it was foreigners who hastened this development. Just as nowadays, throughout the world, the United Kingdom and Great Britain are invariably though incorrectly called England and the Netherlands are often though incorrectly called Holland, so in the twelfth and thirteenth centuries the inhabitants of England, France, and other European lands gave the name Scotland, or its equivalent, to the whole kingdom ruled by the king of Scots. It was partly this foreign usage which accustomed the king's lieges to think of themselves as Scots and their country as Scotland. As late as 1216 the Cistercian writer of the chronicle compiled at Melrose Abbey referred to 'Scots' as barbaric outsiders who, having committed atrocities at a Cumberland daughter house of Melrose, were carefully excluded from the army which the king led south to Dover. By 1250, however, the word Scot had come to be applied to all liege subjects of the king, whatever their race or mother tongue. A steady stream of official documents emphasized the importance of the *regnum Scotiae* (kingdom of Scotland) as the political entity to which all Scots belonged and whose laws they obeyed.

The ceremonial inauguration of Alexander III and the canonization of Queen Margaret were both deliberate exercises in heightening national consciousness. The eight-year-old Alexander, solemnly placed on the Stone of Destiny by the Earl of Fife and blessed by the bishop of St Andrews, was hailed by an aged highland seannachie or historian who, using the Scottish – i.e. the Gaelic – language, traced the king's ancestry back through the generations until he reached the first Scotsman known to legend, Iber Scot. Whether they spoke Gaelic, English, or French, Scotsmen and Scotswomen of the mid thirteenth century could be persuaded to take a pride in the history of their country and in the great antiquity of its kingship. When Matthew Paris, the Benedictine monk of St Albans whose English patriotism was never in doubt, tells us that the Scots infantry whom Alexander II led to Ponteland in 1244 were not afraid to die for their native land because their priests had assured them of the righteousness of their cause, we need not discount the statement as the product of Matthew's zeal for whatever was native against whatever he saw as foreign. This after all was the very spirit in which the descendants of these men would fight at Stirling Bridge and Falkirk.

The great King David was the first Scottish ruler to occupy a position which can truly be called European. His younger grandson William the Lion also enjoyed a European reputation in the last decades of his life, partly because he reigned for so long, partly because as an old man he was widely believed to possess some personal sanctity. Although neither of the thirteenth-century Alexanders could boast the same prestige there is no doubt that their realm held a recognized place among the Christian states of western Europe, or that they themselves were accorded respect by contemporary rulers, the papacy, the kings of France and Norway, the dukes, counts, and burgomasters of the various principalities and cities around the North Sea with which Scotland was in regular contact, even by the kings of England.

We can see this in a variety of ways, but particularly in the matter of royal marriages. With the notable exception of Malcolm III, eleventh-century kings had married women of their own country. Alexander I had to be content with a bastard daughter of Henry I while his brother David married, richly it is true but not royally, into the Anglo-Norman nobility. The celibate Malcolm IV gave his sisters in marriage to the duke or count of Brittany, who was the feudal vassal (however reluctantly) of Henry II, and to the count of Holland, who was the somewhat independent vassal of the 'emperor' or king of Germany. The wife whom Henry II found for William the Lion in 1185, Ermengarde de Beaumont, belonged to a minor feudal family, but we need not attribute the choice to deliberate humiliation by the English king. The thirteenth century brought a change. It was intended that King William's eldest daughters would marry into the Angevin royal house. In 1219 Alexander II proposed that one of their younger sisters should marry the powerful count of Champagne and Brie. Although these schemes came to nought, Alexander himself married first an English princess and secondly the daughter of one of the greatest nobles of France, while his son exactly repeated the pattern, his wives being Margaret of England (daughter of Henry III), who died in 1275, and Yolande or Yoleta, daughter of the count of Dreux, who after her first husband's death became by a second marriage duchess of Brittany. Alexander III's elder son Alexander was married to Marguerite, daughter of Guy de Dampierre count of Flanders, in 1282, his daughter Margaret to Eric king of Norway in 1281. Nine years later, when her mother, her uncle, and her grandfather had tragically died, the little 'Maid of Norway', another Margaret, was betrothed to the son and heir of Edward I of England. Taking our period as a whole, it is possible to see in the pattern of these royal marriages the gradual emergence of the Scottish realm as one of the recognized powers of middle rank within the family of west European states.

Alexander III was at the height of his prosperity in 1272 when his father-in-law died and was succeeded by Edward I. Baronial faction had been put firmly behind him; the Hebrides and the Isle of Man had been added to his dominions; his marriage had produced one son and one daughter, and a second son would soon be born. If there was ever truly a 'golden age' in thirteenth-century Scotland it was in the '60s and '70s, between the treaty of Perth and the death of Queen Margaret. In 1274 her brother Edward returned from his crusade and within a few years he was reconsidering the relations between the English crown and the only remaining independent, or seemingly independent, potentates within the British Isles whose territories bordered his own — the prince of Wales and the king of Scots. As yet there seemed no urgent cause for concern over Anglo-Scottish relations. Alexander's first marriage had brought the two royal families close to one another in genuine affection. In 1268 Edward of England and his brother Edmund had spent a holiday in Scotland at the court of their sister and her husband. But Edward the king was a different proposition from Edward the prince, and his sister's death had removed a strong influence for friendship.

Of the two wars waged by King Edward against the prince of Wales, the first (1277) was fought to establish the English king's superior lordship over Llywelyn, who in English eyes had been behaving much too independently. The Welsh example must have been fresh in Edward's mind when in 1278 he proceeded to define relations with the king of Scots. Both sides were wary, mindful of many precedents and of the existence, by now, of several leading documents. On the English side there was recollection of a long series of acts of homage by Scottish kings going back into Anglo-Saxon times. There was the precedent of Falaise (1174), still stressed while its cancellation at Canterbury (1189) tended to be ignored. King John was remembered to have behaved as though he were overlord of Scotland. The papal practice of levying taxes for the crusade from Britain as a whole, through the English crown, seemed to support the English view of Scotland as subordinate. On the Scottish side Richard I's quitclaim of Canterbury was paramount. The Scots tended to ignore events prior to Falaise and Canterbury, not surprisingly since the series of Scottish homages to England were recorded almost exclusively in chronicles compiled in the south of England. They also found support in more recent precedents, for example the treaty of York apparently made between two sovereign independent rulers and the fact that throughout the long reign of Henry III (1216–72) there had been no successful – indeed, no public – assertion of English suzerainty. In the minority of Alexander III a lawsuit concerning the earldom of Menteith and thus touching the royal dignity was appealed to the papal court. The pope emphatically rejected a demand made on behalf of Henry III that the case be transferred to his court.

Against this background we can appreciate why the two Alexanders set so much store by their lordship over the English earldom or 'Honour' of Huntingdon. On Earl John's death in 1237 Alexander II had at once requested that his lordship be recognized by the English crown. In 1256 Alexander III visited the chief manors of the earldom to demonstrate his lordship. He was deprived of it, inexplicably, in the 1260s and in 1270 sent two highranking envoys, Simon abbot of Dunfermline and the earl of Mar, to regain the Honour. The mission may have been unsuccessful; if so the loss of Huntingdon would certainly have rankled. In the spring of 1278 arrangements were made for a visit by the Scots king to the English court. There was evidently mistrust of English intentions, for the Scots laid down conditions for the visit to safeguard their king's status. By October Alexander III was at Tewkesbury on the Severn, whither Edward I had invited him. Edward went far to confirm Scottish suspicions by refusing to accept Alexander's homage there and then. Instead he adjourned the ceremony to Westminster some weeks later, when it would take place in parliament.

We have two different minutes of the proceedings. The English minute, surviving in a contemporary copy, states that Alexander did homage to Edward using the accustomed formula 'I become the liege man of King Edward against all men'. Whereupon, we are told (and at this point something has surely been left out of the minute), the English king reserved his right to homage for the kingdom of Scotland if he should wish to raise the matter. Then through the mouth of

Robert Bruce earl of Carrick (father of the future King Robert I) Alexander's fealty was sworn in these words: 'I Alexander king of Scotland will bear faith to Edward king of England in life, limb, and earthly honour, and will faithfully perform the services due for the lands I hold of him'.

The Scottish minute may also be contemporary, but our only text is a copy made 40 years later in the cartulary (i.e. register of title deeds) of Dunfermline Abbey. The entry stands beside copies of documents belonging to the time of Abbot Ralph of Greenlaw, Abbot Simon's successor, who may well have been present at the 1278 homage ceremony. The wording of the Scottish minute is significantly and, at one place, vitally different from that of the English minute. The king's homage is related as above, but Alexander is reported to have added the words (which would explain the lacuna in the English minute) 'reserving my kingdom'. At this, the bishop of Norwich intervened to say 'let that also be reserved to the king of England if he has the right to homage for it', to which Alexander's firm reply was 'No one has the right to homage for my kingdom for I hold it of God alone'. And when the earl of Carrick took the oath of fealty on his king's behalf the Dunfermline version makes Alexander promise to perform the services due from the lands he holds *in the kingdom of England*, thus excluding fealty for Scotland itself.

Had Alexander III done homage and sworn fealty explicitly for his realm the English record would certainly have said so and Edward I and his successors would never have tired of telling the tale. The non-committal blandness of the English record, and the fact that the bishop of Norwich was despatched to the border early in 1279 to discuss the question of homage with the Scots in strict confidence, show that Edward I was foiled by his brother-in-law's firmness. Later in 1279 Alexander made a charitable gift to Canterbury Cathedral in honour of Saint Thomas Becket. It was a pointed reminder that the Scots admired Becket for resisting the tyranny of a Plantagenet king who had subjugated their country.

Within four years the bright prospects of the 1270s had faded. In 1283 the king of Scots, whose younger son had died a child, learned of the death in Norway of his daughter, probably in giving birth to her only child, Margaret the Maid of Norway, whose health and strength were always in doubt. In January, 1284 the king's elder son, newly married, died at 20 leaving no heir. At a parliament held in the following month the magnates agreed, however reluctantly, to accept the Maid as heir presumptive. The king lost no time in remarrying. It was because of his impatience to rejoin his bride of only six months, Yolande of Dreux, that Alexander III, always impetuous, rode from Edinburgh towards Kinghorn in Fife on a night of gathering storm (18–19 March 1286). Safely across the Queen's Ferry he and his small party turned eastward in the darkness but before reaching Kinghorn Alexander fell from his horse and was killed. He was not yet 45 and the young child in Norway was the last survivor of the ancient Scottish royal line. More than a dozen men believed that they had a claim to the throne. King Edward, far away though he was in Gascony, can hardly have seen as other than an act of divine providence an event which would make renewed English intervention in Scotland both possible and respectable.

It says much for the political cohesion of Scotland that the majority of magnates, laymen and churchmen alike, rallied in loyalty to the female child they had never seen. By insisting that, in the absence of a duly enthroned sovereign, political authority must stem from the nation as a whole, that is from the community of the realm, they were able to hold parliaments, enforce an oath of loyalty to Queen Margaret, send embassies to England and Gascony, and elect six Guardians to govern the country. The Guardians in turn appointed justiciars and sheriffs, mustered local forces to defend the realm and keep the peace, and approved (as a king would have insisted on doing) the choice of new bishops in vacant sees. The Guardians (two bishops, two earls, and two barons) were representative of the magnates and of the old twofold division of Scotland, for William Fraser bishop of St Andrews, Duncan III earl of Fife, and Alexander Comyn earl of Buchan were powerful in the north while Robert Wishart bishop of Glasgow, James the Stewart, and John Comyn of Badenoch held leading positions in the south.

Keeping the peace was largely a matter of quelling the ugly threat of a *coup d'état* by the earl of Carrick's father, old Robert Bruce lord of Annandale. As grandson of William the Lion's brother Earl David of Huntingdon by his second daughter Bruce was one of the two strongest claimants to the throne by hereditary succession, if the Maid should die before she could marry and have a child. The other strong claimant was John Balliol lord of Galloway, whose lands were awkwardly wedged between Bruce-held Carrick and Annandale. Balliol was great-grandson of Earl David, but by descent from the eldest daughter. His relatively peaceable behaviour before the Maid's death may reflect confidence that seniority would be preferred to nearness of descent. As for defending the realm, the Guardians did not see

Edward I, whose help they requested, as a military threat, but they realized that he might well press English claims by mere opportunism. The English king proposed marriage between the Maid and his own son and heir, Edward of Caernarvon. King Eric of Norway seems to have raised no objection. The Scots too were not unwilling provided there were safeguards for the independence and integrity of their kingdom. They obtained these safeguards in the treaty of Birgham (July 1290), which set out the terms on which Scotland would retain its own laws and liberties and also its own sovereign ruler, even though as wife of the king of England she would often be absent. Birgham contained no hint of English overlordship and Edward ratified it in his parliament at Northampton in August. So far his conduct had been correct, even punctilious. But he now tried to put his henchman Anthony Bek, newly promoted to be bishop of Durham, in control of Scotland, as 'lieutenant' of the betrothed pair. Edward's excuse was, characteristically, the need to keep Scotland in tranquillity (which the Guardians had managed to do with some success) and to 'reform the state of the country' (although the Scots had never said it was in need of reform). It was perhaps ominous that John Balliol tried to buy Bek's support by gifts of land which would be his to give only if he became king, but in general, Bek seems to have been largely ignored north of the border. The Scots were later to claim that his 'improper' appointment had given rise to 'certain unaccustomed novelties' affecting the ancient liberties of the realm.

In any case, the treaty of Birgham and Bek's appointment were overtaken by the news that on her way to Scotland the Maid had died at Kirkwall in Orkney (September 1290). It was now a matter of urgency to identify the man who had the best claim to the vacant throne. Apparently the Guardians invited King Edward to help, or at least did not refuse when he offered to help. Almost certainly, the Guardians intended that Edward should act as a friendly outside arbitrator, presiding over a form of legal action with which they were very familiar. But at some point during the winter of 1290–1, in the course of which he lost his first wife, the much-loved Eleanor of Castille, whom he mourned for many weeks, Edward took the fateful decision to act as the feudal suzerain of Scotland, exercising what his clerks henceforth called 'superior or direct dominion'.[2] Arriving at Norham

[2]The words 'superior' and 'direct' are here almost synonyms; 'direct' refers to overriding or supreme authority under which lesser powers might legitimately function.

on the English side of the Tweed early in May 1291, the English king and his council met the Scots leaders in what was seen as a joint parliament of both kingdoms. He confronted the Guardians and their fellow magnates with an oddly oblique statement that he had come from afar to keep the peace in a disturbed land (an echo of Bek's appointment in the previous August) and to do justice to all 'by virtue of the superior lordship which belongs to him'. He thus laid the onus of proof that he was *not* overlord of Scotland upon the Scots, who can hardly have been so completely surprised by the turn of events as they claimed. Bishop Wishart of Glasgow protested that the Scots should not be compelled to prove a negative, especially when their rights and laws manifestly supported their constitutional independence. Less academically he told King Edward that the Scottish realm was held directly of the Almighty and reminded him that the wizard Merlin had foretold the reign of the 'Covetous King' against whom the Scots and Welsh would rise as one to regain their ancestral territories. Edward's reply was that the Scots could defend their independence by force of arms if they did not accept his claim. Though under the vow of a crusader he would deflect his troops from their sacred mission to crush any Scottish rebellion. He gave the Scots leaders three weeks to reply formally to his demand for recognition as overlord. Their answer has luckily survived. It is evidence that the Scots did not wish to recognize Edward's claim, were nevertheless anxious not to have a showdown with him, and placed their trust in the lawful succession of a new king who could defend their rights.

Brushing aside protests and demurs, Edward pressed home his advantage in the face of a divided Scottish community and a group of claimants eager only to win the throne or at least reap some profit by way of bribe or compensation. By the middle of June 1291 he had obtained a full acknowledgement of his suzerainty from the claimants, the surrender, under protest, of the royal castles of Scotland and *de facto* recognition by Guardians and magnates, in return for a written undertaking to preserve Scottish laws and liberties and not to demand from the new king anything but homage and its incidental rights. The Guardians allowed themselves to be re-appointed by the English king with the addition of one English baron.

The process of finding the new king was long drawn out. The court of claims was composed of King Edward's council (24 members) with 80 Scottish 'assessors' elected with the assent of the community of the realm, 40 chosen by Balliol, 40 by Bruce, under the king as president. Floris V, count of Holland, whose legal claim through descent from a sister of William the Lion was shadowy, held up the proceedings with a request to search for a lost twelfth-century document which he alleged would vindicate his claim. More seriously, the court was occupied with two legal questions of the utmost importance on the first of which there was no clearcut ruling. First, was the realm of Scotland, in the absence of a direct heir, to be treated as indivisible, in other words, as a truly political entity, a 'state', to use modern terminology, and not merely as a feudal lordship? Had it been like a barony either in England or in Scotland, or like an earldom in England, it would have been divided equally among the female heirs, as the Honour of Huntingdon had been divided in 1237. In that case, Balliol and Bruce would each have received a third, the remainder going to John Hastings, grandson of Earl David by his youngest daughter. Since each of them already held one third of the Honour of Huntingdon the precedent would have been familiar to them. Balliol's sole advantage would have been to retain the title of king, though it would be little more than honorific. If, however, the Scottish realm was like the English, or for that matter like an earldom in Scotland, it must be preserved intact and pass to a single rightful heir. The second point was whether seniority of line, i.e. descent from the eldest in each generation (males preferred), was to have precedence of 'nearness of blood', i.e. the smallest number of generations between the claimant and the king from whom his claim derived. As far as Scotland was concerned, the rule of seniority with males preferred, failing whom females would be accepted, had been solemnly declared as recently as 1281, when Alexander III's son Alexander had married Marguerite of Flanders.[3] Balliol's line was undoubtedly senior, though it involved a double female descent (Earl David – Margaret – Dervorguilla – John). Bruce's line was junior, but he was a whole generation closer to King David I (Earl David – Isabel – Robert).

Towards the end of 1292 the court, after many and lengthy adjournments, declared that seniority was to be preferred and that Scotland, as a true kingdom, was not to be divided. John Balliol would therefore be awarded the throne and (aside from any bribes taken secretly) there would be no compensation for Bruce, Hastings, or the count of Holland.

King John was enthroned at Scone on St Andrew's Day, 30 November 1292. Edward I lost no time in making it clear that relations

[3]E.L.G. Stones and G.G. Simpson, *Edward I and the Throne of Scotland* (1978), II, pp. 188–90.

between the new king and the English crown would be radically different from those which had obtained in Alexander III's time. It was precisely as if the court of claims had in fact divided Scotland and awarded Balliol no more than the courtesy title of 'king'. Not only did John have to do homage and swear fealty and record these ceremonies several times over, he was made to repudiate the treaty of Birgham and all other safeguards of Scottish liberty and to allow a long-continued interference in Scotland by the English government on the pretext that it had the right to complete all business begun during the interregnum. Most ominously, King John was compelled to appear in person at the English parliament to answer for his own court's decisions, against which appeals were now to be allowed to go from Scotland to England. This was wholly contrary to the practice prevailing before 1286 and explicitly prohibited by the treaty of Birgham. If not designed deliberately to make the new king's position intolerable, there can be no doubt that the English measures were meant to demonstrate that a Scottish ruler was now no more than one of the king of England's feudal barons, perhaps possessing the trappings of a king but with none of the 'royal dignity' of his predecessors. The last straw was a demand that feudal military service overseas should be rendered by King John and many of his nobles in the war that broke out between Edward I and Philip IV of France in 1294.

Whatever John Balliol's personal feelings may have been, the Scottish magnates were not prepared to accept these accumulating burdens and humiliations. A representative council of 12 took the control of government out of John's hands in 1295 and made a treaty with Philip IV providing for mutual military assistance and a marriage between John's son Edward and Philip's niece Jeanne de Valois. These actions obviously implied nothing less than war between Scotland and England. In Edward I's eyes it was armed rebellion by a foolish, recalcitrant vassal. For the next eight years, Scotland was to be put to the test with which King Edward, contemptuously it seems, had challenged the country's leaders in 1291. An independent kingdom was no more and no less than a kingdom which could defend itself by arms.

In spite of the fact that his war with France was leading to severe difficulties with the tax-paying classes, magnates, clergy, merchants, and country gentry, King Edward was not unjustifiably confident at the prospect of war against the Scots. He knew without the aid of precise statistics that England was much richer and more populous than its northern neighbour. An English royal army was conspicuously strong in cavalry, mail-clad knights fighting on horses trained for battle. As far as we know, the king shared the widespread assumption that cavalry was superior to infantry and in any case he could recruit or hire more and better archers and crossbowmen than the Scots. In addition to arms and equipment the English possessed experience. Some had campaigned with crusading armies in the Mediterranean, some had fought in Gascony, many more had served in the victorious wars by which the Welsh had been reduced in 1277 and 1282–3. The gravest problems would arise from extended supply lines and sheer distance. Nevertheless, the English seaports were rich in shipping, though the fact that Scotland lies west of England meant that prevailing westerly winds often gave no help to mariners sailing to Scotland on the east side of Britain. Above all, Edward I and his baronage, even if they had serious political and constitutional quarrels, believed in the lawfulness of English claims to suzerainty. In this sense, England was united. A consequence of Edwardian doctrine was that any Scot appearing in arms against the English king was a rebel or traitor. The restraints that applied to some extent in the case of war between equals did not need to be observed in Scotland and, increasingly after 1297, were not observed.

By contrast, the prospect before the Scottish leaders in their endeavour to save the freedom of their country seemed bleak. They were separated from their ally France by 400 miles of hostile English coastline. Their king was relatively untried and his failure to withstand browbeating from Edward I or the English parliament inspired no confidence. Scottish knights were comparatively few, Scottish infantry of necessity amateur, inexperienced, and old fashioned. The Scots' claim to fight on a footing of legal equality meant that they could not treat their foes as criminals who ought to be punished. James the Stewart, for example, was deeply shocked to hear that when the English captured his nephew they executed him and stuck his head on a pole erected above the castle he had held against them. When the Scots recovered Stirling Castle from the English in 1299 they allowed the garrison to go safely to England; when Edward I recaptured Stirling in 1304 it was only with difficulty that he was persuaded not to hang every man found in the castle alive. If the worst obstacle for the English was vulnerable supply lines, for the Scots it was defectors or outright opponents within their own ranks. Under John Balliol the Bruces and their friends were disaffected. After John had left the scene there was deep-seated rivalry and even open feuding between different factions. Throughout the war there were a few magnates whose loyalty was given to the English king. Earl Patrick of Dunbar was one such, and we cannot know whether his motive was fear of losing his not very large English estates, sincere belief in the rightness of Edward I's claims, or a cynical judgement that the English were too strong to be resisted. Although their numbers have been much exaggerated, this pro-English element – in modern eyes anachronistically constituting a 'fifth column' – was not insignificant. The remarkable fact is not that Edward I was able to conquer Scotland twice, in 1296 and again in 1303–4, but that the Scots were able twice to recover their freedom, in 1297 and again in the years 1306–14. In remembering the earl of Dunbar's support for the English we should also remember that his wife the countess of Dunbar remained loyal to her own country.

The war began at the end of March 1296, with an ineffectual Scottish raid into Cumberland and Northumberland to which the English, led by their king in person, replied by capturing and sacking Berwick upon Tweed, Scotland's largest town, massacring many of its inhabitants. The Scots had simply failed to take the measure of their enemy. In late April their army was decisively defeated south of Dunbar, with heavy casualties among the infantry. In July King John and his closest supporters – more truthfully, his manipulators – the senior members of the Comyn family were taken prisoner at Montrose in Angus and placed in the Tower of London. The ancient insignia of Scottish royalty and nationhood – the Stone of Destiny upon which kings of Scots had been enthroned at Scone since time immemorial, the fragment of the True Cross venerated by Saint Margaret, the crown jewels and relics, the records and rolls of government preserved in Edinburgh Castle – all were seized as war booty by Edward I and carried off to London. Administration was entrusted to the earl of Surrey, who disdained to stay north of the border, and two royal justices, Hugh Cressingham and William Ormsby. The king felt confident enough to concentrate on domestic problems, increasingly serious in the winter of 1296–7, and in August 1297 he sailed for Flanders to engage in a leisurely autumn and winter campaign against the French. He took with him Scottish nobles and knights captured at Dunbar.

It was now the turn of the English to learn some lessons. Scotland had fallen more easily than Wales, but holding it permanently was another matter. Beyond a 60-mile radius from his headquarters at Berwick, in the south-east extremity of the country, Cressingham's writ hardly ran and the Scots began to restore their own local government. In the south-west, in the early summer of 1297, influential magnates who had not been *persona grata* at King John's court, among them Robert Wishart bishop of Glasgow, James the Stewart, and young Robert Bruce, grandson of the claimant and earl of Carrick by inheritance from his mother, rallied their forces to resist English occupation. Their movement soon collapsed through loss of nerve, but behind their aristocratic smokescreen a socially humbler revolt broke out under the brilliant and ruthless leadership of one of the Stewart's vassals, William Wallace from Elderslie near Paisley. If we ask ourselves from what sources Wallace could draw on support we might consider the stories of Thomas of Edinburgh and William of Bolhope. As the victorious English army advanced upon Edinburgh in the summer of 1296, an obscure priest of the town named Thomas, duly equipped with bell and candle, solemnly pronounced sentence of excommunication against King Edward and his men in a spirit of hostile defiance. He and his assistant Richard Gulle who had rung the bell were both sent for punishment to the appropriate church court, which may well have dealt with them very leniently. William of Bolhope was a Scotsman (evidently from the Borders) who at the time war broke out in 1296 had been long resident in England, probably in Northumberland. He had hurried home to enlist with the Scottish army, only to see King Edward 'gain the upper hand over his country', as the record has it. Whereupon, undaunted, he armed himself with two swords and set off southward on a one-man expedition against England which took him as far as Alnmouth. There he was challenged by two local men, refused to acknowledge fealty to King Edward, and was promptly put to death. We have no reason to suppose that this trio of Tom, Dick, and Willie, who happen to have found their way on to surviving record, were in any way untypical.

By August Wallace had joined forces with another youthful warrior, Andrew Murray, who had raised a similar revolt north of the Mounth. These young men were in no way inhibited by the gentlemanly considerations already mentioned, which restrained the Scots nobles from butchering Englishmen in cold blood. Together on 11 September Wallace and Murray and their infantry army – the 'common army of Scotland' – inflicted a startling defeat upon the largely cavalry force hastily brought against them by Surrey and Cressingham. The battle was fought at the bridge of Stirling, the Scots being stationed just to the north, along the slopes of the Abbey Craig, the English foolishly attempting to advance across the river using the narrow and inadequate timber bridge. Surrey was one of the few who escaped to England. Cressingham was killed and the English administration collapsed, although garrisons held out in Roxburgh and Berwick upon Tweed. The Scots raided deep into northern England causing much loss of life and destruction.

Tragically, Murray had been mortally wounded at Stirling. Wallace, the hero of the hour, whose victory had electrified western Europe, was made Guardian, still in the name of King John, but also of the community of the realm. An earl girded Wallace with the belt of knighthood, a promotion not only fitting but necessary for he was now 'captain of the Scottish people against King Edward of England', to use a contemporary description. He issued commands to earls and barons, appointed new bishops – most importantly, his friend William Lamberton, treasurer of Glasgow cathedral, to succeed William Fraser as bishop of St Andrews – and planned the defence of Scotland against the onslaught which King Edward was sure to launch. It would be misleading to picture Wallace as the common man leading an army solely composed of common men fighting to establish a proletarian republic. Wallace's army was national and he himself thought in national terms. Coming of a knightly family attached to one of the great feudal lords, Wallace was passionately seized of the ideal of a free and independent Scottish kingdom under its lawful king. He may not have had any admiration for Balliol personally but he fought in the name of King John and utterly denied the English king's right either to depose a Scottish ruler or to classify himself, Wallace, as an English subject and therefore a traitor. Some of the nobles may have been jealous of Wallace, but they fought under his command and a few even escaped from English custody in Flanders in order to give him their support.

Wallace's mistake was to offer a pitched battle instead of harassing the invading English army when eventually it came north in the dry summer of 1298. Gravely short of food, the English might well have fallen a prey to protracted guerrilla tactics. Whether from over-confidence or the psychological need to give his followers a victory, Wallace invited Edward I to attack him. The hillside site east of Falkirk compelled the Scottish infantry brigades or 'schiltroms' to remain stationary in a confined space, an easy target for English and Welsh slingers and bowmen. The latter were able to manoeuvre flexibly and were interspersed with the heavy cavalry. The knights charged only when the rain of arrows had caused much slaughter among the Scots spearmen. The day-long battle, fought on 22 July, the feast of Saint Mary Magdalene, destroyed Wallace's army but could not efface his glory.

Collective leadership, strictly aristocratic, replaced Wallace's single command. Yet the new leaders of the community of the realm held firmly to the same ideal that had inspired Wallace. Bishop Lamberton and John de Soules, the earls of Atholl, Buchan, and Lennox, even the timorous Stewart, all set before themselves the concept of the community of the Scottish realm working to recover its independence and restore its ancient monarchy. Lamberton told the king of France that his sufferings had come about because of his love for his native land, while Soules's record of selfless patriotism can stand beside that of Wallace. The two other chief leaders, John Comyn the Red of Badenoch (of which he was lord after his father's death in 1303) and Robert Bruce earl of Carrick, were the exception rather than the rule. Both served the community as Guardians, but whereas Comyn saw only his uncle John Balliol as rightful king of Scots and could not stomach the notion of a Bruce on the throne, Bruce on the other hand was convinced of his own family's right, and after his father died in 1304 was determined to take the throne himself. Comyn had been a consistent upholder of the national cause from 1296 to 1304, when, on terms which cannot be regarded as dishonourable, he and his followers submitted to Edward I. Thereafter, though his estates in England were negligible, he remained loyal to the English king, paying for his loyalty with his life. Bruce also upheld the national cause, but early in 1302, two years before the general Scottish surrender, he came into Edward I's peace, evidently because he feared a restoration of King John whose loyal subject he refused to be. His English lands were extensive but do not seem to have influenced his decisions in any way. There was an inevitability about the tragedy of 10 February 1306 in the Greyfriars' kirk at Dumfries, when Bruce, having resolved to make his bid for kingship, challenged Comyn to aid him and on meeting with refusal uttered the hot words which led to Comyn's murder. It is easy to see both these young men as selfish, concerned mainly with their own or their family's inherited rights. Both also believed firmly in the justice of the Scottish cause. We must bear in mind how comfortable it would have been for either of them to have abandoned that cause and taken the rewards in England and elsewhere which King Edward would have been only too glad to bestow on them.

The English were not able to follow up their victory at Falkirk. From 1299 to 1303 the Scots remained in control not only of the country north of Forth and Clyde but also, throughout lengthy periods, of most of the country to the south of that line and as far east as the middle of Tweeddale. Throughout this large area of Scotland a respectable government of regency was established and maintained, invoking the authority of King John and the community of the realm. Justiciars and sheriffs held their customary courts, parliaments met, and a chancellor, Nicholas Balmyle, upheld the traditions laid down by his predecessors in the more tranquil days of Alexander II and Alexander III. It must have been difficult to raise revenues and enforce the ancient obligations of military service, whether from the knights and barons or from the general body of freeholders and peasants. Nevertheless, it was done. Understandably reluctant after Falkirk to engage in any more full-scale battles, the Scots skirmished and raided with considerable effect.

They also kept open the difficult lines of communication with lands across the North Sea and with the French and papal courts. Under the direction of Bishop Lamberton, clergy with legal expertise and an aptitude for history were enlisted to prepare a massive propaganda campaign against Edward I's claims to overlordship. Baldred Bisset, the distinguished ecclesiastical lawyer, whose career has already been noticed, pleaded the Scottish case at the papal *curia* in 1301 and emerged with much credit. Admittedly, we have to remember that papal decisions to favour one side rather than another tended to spring from ulterior political motives and were not necessarily based on the intrinsic merits of the argument. Pope Boniface VIII pursued a markedly pro-Scottish policy from 1298 to 1302 and then, to the consternation of the Scots, turned against them and helped Edward I and the king of France to make peace without including Scotland in the peace terms. Boniface was deposed in 1303 and (after the brief reign of Benedict XI) the next two popes (especially Clement V, 1305–14) were to prove notably anti-Scottish, although John XXII at long last came to sympathize with their cause. The presentation of the Scottish case before the bar of European opinion was largely the work of a small band of university-trained clergy. We should not, however, imagine that the clergy formed a class apart, developing ideas of patriotism and national freedom that were incomprehensible to the laity. In the Scottish struggle against Edward I and his son the clergy took their instructions from the laity rather than the other way round, although in truth it would seem that often the two groups worked closely together. Leadership in the last resort had to come from the laymen, and in the very last resort of all had to come from a lawfully chosen king. Stirling Castle had surrendered in July 1304 after a long siege, its commander William Olifard (Oliphant) declaring defiantly that he held it 'of the Lion', that is of the crown of Scotland. Wallace, betrayed in Glasgow in the following summer, was taken to Westminster for a summary trial and then drawn on a hurdle to Smithfield for the revolting butchery of a traitor's death, denying to the last that he had ever been King Edward's liege man. The future of Scotland for more than 400 years lay with the spirit that animated these men and others like them. That was why, even after Edward I had provided, as he thought, a wise and conciliatory settlement of Scotland in the wake of his conquest of 1304, the way was open for Robert Bruce to have himself made king in a ceremony at Scone as close to the ancient and accustomed manner as possible (25 March 1306). It was through acceptance of a common kingship that the varied peoples of Scotland had gradually come to political unity. It was to be the task of Bruce, as King Robert I, to restore that common kingship and in doing so bring back the unity which had been shattered after the death of the Maid of Norway in 1290.

A Note on Further Reading

The period dealt with by this book has received full-scale treatment in the first two volumes of the Edinburgh History of Scotland, which divide approximately at 1286: A.A.M. Duncan, *Scotland: the Making of the Kingdom* (Edinburgh, 1975) and R. Nicholson, *Scotland: the Later Middle Ages* (Edinburgh, 1974). Useful shorter surveys may be found in W.C. Dickinson, *Scotland from the Earliest Times to 1603*, revised A.A.M. Duncan (Oxford, 1977), and in G.W.S. Barrow, *Feudal Britain* (London, 1956; revised paperback edn, 1971). None of the Scottish kings before Robert I (for whom see G.W.S. Barrow, *Robert Bruce and the Community of the Realm of Scotland*, 3rd edn, Edinburgh, 1988) has received adequate biographical treatment, but there are studies of *King David I of Scotland: the balance of new and old* (Reading 1985), of *The Reign of William the Lion, king of Scotland* (in *Historical Studies*, vii, 1969), both by G.W.S. Barrow, and of *Alexander III* (London, 1937) by J. Fergusson, who has also written the life of *William Wallace: Guardian of Scotland* (London, 1938). A detailed examination of royal government, 1124–1214, occupies the introductions to volumes I and II of *Regesta Regum Scottorum*, edited by G.W.S. Barrow (Edinburgh, 1960, 1971). The impact of Anglo-Norman influences, the Scandinavian dimension, and the introduction and character of feudalism are dealt with in R.L.G. Ritchie, *The Normans in Scotland* (Edinburgh, 1954), W. Kapelle, *The Norman Conquest of the North: the Region and its Transformation, 1000–1135* (Chapel Hill, N. Carolina, 1979), and G.W.S. Barrow, *The Anglo-Norman Era in Scottish History* (Oxford, 1980). Feudal politics in the part of England nearest to Scotland is the subject of J.C. Holt, *The Northerners* (Oxford, 1961), and J. Le Patourel, *The Norman Empire* (Oxford, 1976), although it devotes few pages to Scotland, is of the first importance for an understanding of the Europe to which Scotland belonged in the late eleventh and earlier twelfth centuries. The Anglo-Scottish world of feudal lordship and interrelated cross-border aristocratic families is thoroughly explored by K.J. Stringer, *Earl David of Huntingdon* (Edinburgh, 1985). Several aspects of Scottish government and society (e.g. the administration of justice and the Anglo-Scottish border) are discussed in detail by G.W.S. Barrow, *The Kingdom of the Scots* (London, 1973).

The Scottish Burghs are investigated by W.M. Mackenzie (Edinburgh, 1949). There is no adequate survey of economic history in this period, but valuable accounts of trading patterns, as well as fresh insights into urban development, may be found in *The Scottish Medieval Town*, ed. M. Lynch, M. Spearman and G. Stell (Edinburgh 1988).

There is no up-to-date study of the church in medieval Scotland, but those by J.A. Duke, *History of the Church of Scotland to the Reformation* (Edinburgh, 1937) and J. Dowden, *The Medieval Church in Scotland* (Glasgow, 1910) may still be used with profit. So also, for the background to changes in the Scottish church, may M.D. Knowles, *The Monastic Order in England* (Cambridge, 1949), D. Nicholl, *Thurston, Archbishop of York* (York, 1964), M. Brett, *The English Church under Henry I* (London, 1975), and C.R. Cheney, *From Becket to Langton* (Manchester, 1956).

Highland history in this period has received scant attention save at local level and in genealogical studies. The publication of essays on *The Middle Ages in the Highlands* by a group of scholars (ed. L. Maclean; Inverness, 1981) ought to mark a turning-point towards better things.

The lack of both general histories and definitive monographs dealing with Scotland in the central Middle Ages contrasts sharply with the conspicuously generous provision of works of basic reference and other collections of essential factual material. Outstanding in this respect for the person coming freshly to the study of Scottish history was *An Historical Atlas of Scotland, c.400–c.1600*, ed. P. McNeill and R. Nicholson (St Andrews, 1975) now out of print. Its place to be taken by a larger and more comprehensive work on the same lines, also edited by P. McNeill. Specialist reference works for the church include J. Dowden, *The Bishops of Scotland* (Glasgow, 1912), not quite superseded by D.E.R. Watt, *Fasti Ecclesiae Scoticanae* (Edinburgh, 1969), with full lists of senior secular clergy and useful notes on diocesan development; for the parish system, I.B. Cowan, *The Parishes of Medieval Scotland* (Glasgow, 1967); and for monasteries, I.B. Cowan and D.E. Easson, *Medieval Religious Houses, Scotland* (London, 1976), prefaced by the best single essay yet published on Scottish monasticism. The educated clergy are treated comprehensively in D.E.R. Watt, *A Biographical Dictionary of Scottish Graduates before 1410* (Oxford, 1979), wider in scope than its title suggests. Papal letters to Scotland before the pontificate of Innocent III have been edited by R. Somerville, *Scotia Pontificia* (Oxford, 1982), covering the period

1100 to 1198. G.S. Pryde, *The Burghs of Scotland* (London, 1965) is little more than an authoritative chronological list, but there is a good deal of extra information provided with the lists in A. Dunbar, *Scottish Kings* (2nd edn, Edinburgh, 1981) and I.H. Stewart, *The Scottish Coinage* (London, 1967). S. Cruden, *The Scottish Castle* (2nd edn, Edinburgh, 1981) and J.G. Dunbar, *The Historic Architecture of Scotland* (London, 1966; 2nd edn, 1980) are monographs as well as reference works, and the same is true of J.M. Gilbert, *Hunting and Hunting Reserves in Medieval Scotland* (Edinburgh, 1979), which prints key documents, and of W.F.H. Nicolaisen, *Scottish Place-names* (London, 1976).

There is no adequate anthology of translated documents (other than narrative sources) to illustrate the period, but some of the leading texts are given in G. Donaldson, *Scottish Historical Documents* (Edinburgh, 1970), while the same author's *The Sources of Scottish History* (Edinburgh, 1978) offers a masterly analysis of medieval documentation. An idea of the character and scope of the narrative sources for the period can best be obtained from the two collections of chronicle material by A.O. Anderson, *Scottish Annals from English Chroniclers* (London, 1908) and *Early Sources of Scottish History* (Edinburgh, 2 vols., 1922), while for relations with England E.L.G. Stones, *Anglo-Scottish Relations, 1174–1328: Some Selected Documents* (London, 1965; re-set 1970) is essential.

Finally it should be noted that much important discussion of Scottish historical problems and questions finds a published outlet in the periodical literature, for example in *The Scottish Historical Review, Innes Review, Scottish Studies, Northern Scotland,* and *Proceedings of the Society of Antiquaries of Scotland.*

Appendices

Appendix A: *Notes on Measures, Money, and Unfamiliar Words*

Medieval Scotland shared many of the measures of length, area, volume, and weight familiar in England, although often with local variation. For weighing, what was called the 'Caithness stone' was supposed to be a standard for the whole country. The mile was probably about 1,976 English yards, giving a furlong of 282 yards. The inch was reckoned as the length of an average grown man's thumb measured from the root of the nail to the first knuckle, or three barley grains laid end to end. The ell was 36 inches thus measured. The Scots acre, as measured long after the end of our period, contained 6,150.4 square (English) yards. It is more realistic to picture the normal acre as an actual stretch of arable one furlong in length and about 21 yards in width. An acre would normally be ploughed in two, three, or four rigs, the earth highest in the middle of the rig and lowest, forming troughs or furrows, on each side. In the twelfth and thirteenth centuries 13 acres made one oxgang or 'bovate' and eight oxgangs (104 acres) one ploughgate ('carucate'). A husbandland, i.e. the normal arable holding of a single husbandman or peasant tenant, consisted of two oxgangs (26 acres). The equivalent of the ploughgate north of Forth and Clyde (except in Lennox where it was the arachor) was the davoch or daugh, from an Old Irish word meaning a vat or large measure of volume. The connexion presumably derived from a measure of seed-corn or else of tribute corn deducted at harvest time. After reaping and before threshing, corn was usually measured by the thrave of 24 or 26 sheaves.

The system of volume measurement in Scotland seems to have been of ancient origin. The boll (in Celtic-speaking areas the *mela* or *mala*) was much used for grain and flour. It was 12 gallons using the normal Scots measure of ale, or about six modern 'Imperial' bushels (approximately 218 litres). Sixteen bolls made a chalder, while a quarter of a boll was called a firlot. Cheese might be measured by the boll, but more commonly by the stone of 15 pounds (in Gaelic the *cudthrom*, literally 'weight'), or by the *cogall*, referring to the wooden vessel into which the cheese was put. Presumably in every parish or sizeable community specimen weights and measures were available as standards, such as the 'ancient measure of flour' which according to a late-eleventh-century document was preserved at the church of Auchterderran in Fife. In burghs each burgess was supposed to keep standard weights and measures. Commonly used, but ill-defined, volume measures were the horse-load (*summa*) and the man's back-load or burthen.

Two interlocking or overlapping systems were in use for quantifying money, both in origin based on weighing gold and silver. Silver was the almost exclusive metal for coinage in our period. The Carolingian system was based on the pound (*libra*) of silver, the shilling (*solidus*) which was the twentieth part of a pound, and the penny (*denarius*) which was the twelfth part of a shilling. In theory, 240 newly-minted pennies weighed one pound. Except for a few foreign coins, some of gold, such as the bezant, or the thirteenth-century ducat and florin, circulating in the hands of merchants, the current coin of Scotland in the earlier middle ages was the sterling, or silver penny, originally made in England in the later Anglo-Saxon period. As far as is known the English penny circulated freely in Scotland but from David I's time it was supplemented, and in the thirteenth century to some extent superseded, by Scottish-minted sterlings. Each sterling penny was identified by the head, in profile, of the king reigning at the time of minting, and as old issues were not infrequently withdrawn the political importance of this carefully managed coinage should therefore not be underestimated. Scottish sterlings were maintained at more or less the same level of fineness and weight as those of England until the second half of the fourteenth century. But although throughout our period there was thus monetary parity between the two kingdoms, it does not follow that Scottish coins were always acceptable in England, whether at face value or at all.

The Carolingian system of £ s. d., still so familiar to us, was primarily a system of accounting, for neither the pound nor the shilling was ever made into a coin. A more specifically Germanic system favoured by the Scandinavians was also much used in Scotland. By this system, precious metal was weighed by the mark or merk, containing eight ores or ounces (*ora* = ounce) each of 20 pennies, so that one merk was two thirds of one pound, or in Carolingian notation 13s. 4d. At some early period (between the eighth and eleventh centuries?) a large area of what is now Scotland, from Shetland and Orkney westward and southward to the Firth of Clyde and even south Ayrshire and western Galloway, had been assessed for taxation and military service in accordance with this Germanic counting system, so that 'ouncelands' and 'pennylands' became a normal feature of the Hebridean and west highland landscape, while 'merklands', perhaps somewhat later in date, are also found. But as with the Carolingian system, the units were mainly used for accounting, and no merk or ounce coins were ever struck. Nevertheless, in medieval Scottish accounts, calculations of rent, valuations, etc., the merk was as common a unit as the pound or the shilling. As regards purchasing power, it may be noted that *c*.1150 a two-year-old ox (chief source of tractive power) might cost 4s. In 1180 an exceptionally valuable horse might be worth five merks (66s. 8d.). In 1279 one penny would buy a day's food and drink for a poor man.

Unavoidably in a book dealing with such a remote-seeming period a number of words have to be used that are either comparatively unknown or at least unfamiliar. Here is a short list of the most important.

Appin (Old Irish, *apdaine*). The jurisdiction of, and hence the territory owned or ruled by, an *ab* or abbot, chief dignitary of a monastic community in the pre-twelfth-century Celtic church. (The district name Appin in Argyll and Perthshire is an example of this word.)

Cain (Old Irish *cáin*, 'law', from Greek *kanon*). Tribute, sometimes annual but often biennial or triennial, due to a lord, especially the king, by virtue of his mere lordship. In later medieval and early modern Scotland familiar as 'kain', a rent often paid in poultry.

Conveth (Old Irish *coinnmed*), also called Waiting. Hospitality (or equivalent) rendered annually to a lord by his vassals.

Demesne (Latin, *dominium*, 'lordship'). That part of a lord's estate held directly by the lord and not let or feued out to tenants. In the case of the king, demesne might refer to whatever lands, rights, and other property within the realm contributed revenue to the crown ('royal demesne').

Feu (Latin *feudum*, from German *vieh* or *feoh*, 'cattle'). Noun: estate or tenement, usually of land, occasionally an office, held heritably of a superior on condition of performing some definite service. Verb: to grant such an estate to a tenant.

Gerseman (formerly *gresman*, 'grass man' or 'grazing man'). Tenant given a cottage and grazing rights, without any arable holding. See also scoloc.

Justiciar. Principal administrative officer of the crown, especially in judicial matters. His sphere of activity lay outwith the royal court and household, and in our period a justiciar was normally assigned to one of three divisions of Scotland, Scotia (north of Forth and Clyde), Lothian (south of Forth and Clyde), and, occasionally, Galloway (the extreme south west).

Mormaer (derived from a Pictish compound word meaning 'great officer' or 'high steward'). Ruler or governor under the king of one of the historic provinces into which Scotland north of Forth was divided (e.g. Mar, Moray). Regarded as equivalent of Anglo-Scandinavian 'earl' and French *comte*, words that superseded mormaer, except in Gaelic usage, during our period.

Mounth (Pictish *monoth*, *monith*, 'mountain'). Old name given primarily to what is now known as the 'Grampians', i.e. the mountain massif lying west–east across Scotland from Ben Nevis to the coast south of Aberdeen. The word survives in the names of several hills and passes in the massif such as Mount Keen, Mount Blair, Cairn o' Mount, Capel Mounth, and Mounth Road.

Neyf (Latin, *nativus*, 'native'). Peasant tenant who, unless formally released or successfully escaping, was attached for life to the estate of his birth.

Scoloc (Old Irish). In origin a member of one of the lesser orders, literally 'scholars', attached to a monastic church in Ireland and Scotland. In our period apparently used of a small-scale tenant on church estates, having a cottage and grazing rights, but no arable land. Equated here and there with gerseman, q.v.

Sheriff (Old English *scir gerefa*, Middle English *shirreve*, 'shire officer'). Officer in charge of a division ('shire') of royal demesne or kingdom, originally closely comparable to thane (q.v.) but from *c*.1100 referring to the usually non-hereditary officials who carried out routine administration of sheriffdoms, especially revenue collection, the convening of courts for freeholders, organizing military levies, and sometimes controlling royal castles.

Teind (= English 'tithe'). Tax consisting of a tenth of the annual increase of agricultural crops and beasts, levied in support of the church and especially of parish churches.

Thane (Old English *thegn*, 'one who serves'). Officer holding, usually hereditarily, an estate forming a distinct portion of royal demesne, or demesne of a bishop or earl, and administering such an estate for the king or other lord as the service by virtue of which he held the estate. Officers of this type, to whom even in Celtic-speaking areas the Old English word *thegn* was applied (the Gaelic equivalent, not a synonym, was *tòiseach*), may be found widely distributed from the region around Inverness as far south as the English north midlands, disappearing in England during the twelfth century, in Scotland surviving somewhat sporadically. The words thegn and toiseach have bequeathed to us the well-known Scots surnames of Thain, Mac(k)intosh, Tosh, and Toshach.

Tocher (Scottish Gaelic, *tocharadh*, 'dowry'). Marriage portion or dowry provided by the bride's family at her marriage and intended to support the children of the marriage; failing whom it would normally revert to the bride's family.

Appendix B: *Chronological Table*

1005	Malcolm II Mackenneth king of Scots
1018	Battle of Carham on Tweed
1034	Duncan I (grandson of Malcolm II) king of Scots
1040	Duncan I killed. Macbeth Macfinlay king of Scots
1054	Macbeth defeated (at Dunsinnan?)
1057	Macbeth killed. Lulach Macgillacomgan king of Scots
c.1057	Death of Edward the Atheling cousin of Edward the Confessor
1058	Lulach killed. Malcolm III Macduncan king of Scots
1061	Malcolm III raids Northumberland
1066	Death of Edward the Confessor king of England. Harold of Wessex king of England. Harold killed at Hastings. William (I) duke of Normandy king of England
c.1068	Malcolm III marries (Saint) Margaret daughter of Edward the Atheling
1070	Malcolm III raids Northumberland.
1072	William I of England invades Scotland and receives homage of Malcolm III at Abernethy on Tay
1079	Malcolm III raids Northumberland
1080	William I sends army to Scotland. 'New Castle' upon Tyne built
1091	Malcolm III raids Northumberland
1092	William II of England takes army to Cumberland, builds castle at Carlisle
1093	Malcolm III, after being refused an audience of William II at Gloucester, raids Northumberland and is killed near Alnwick with his second son Edward (eldest son by Margaret). Death of Margaret. Donald Bán (brother of Malcolm III) king of Scots
1094	Donald Bán defeated. Duncan II Macmalcolm king of Scots. Duncan II killed. Donald Bán restored, sharing rule with Edmund (half-brother of Duncan II)
1097	Donald Bán defeated, dying after mutilation. Edgar Macmalcolm (son of Malcolm III and Saint Margaret) king of Scots
1098	Treaty (?) between Edgar and Magnus king of Norway
1107	Death of Edgar. Alexander I (brother of Edgar) king of Scots
1113	David (brother of Alexander I) marries Maud de Senlis countess of Huntingdon. Selkirk Abbey (afterwards Kelso Abbey) founded with monks from Tiron
1124	Death of Alexander I. David I ki g of Scots
1127	David I accepts Empress Maud as heir of her father Henry I of England

1128   Dunfermline Priory (founded by Malcolm III and Margaret) raised to an abbey. Holyrood Abbey founded

1131   Death of Maud queen of Scots

1135   Death of Henry I of England. Stephen of Blois (grandson of William I) king of England

1136–53   Conflict between Stephen and Empress Maud for possession of the English throne. David I takes Cumberland and Westmorland and claims Northumberland.

1136   First Treaty of Durham between Stephen and David I. Melrose Abbey founded with monks from Rievaulx Abbey

1138   Battle of the Standard near Northallerton. Second Treaty of Durham. Scots retain northernmost counties of England

1149   David I knights Empress Maud's son Henry of Anjou (Plantagenet) at Carlisle

1152   Death of Henry earl of Northumberland only son of David I, 'king-designate' of Scots. Henry's eldest son Malcolm designated king

1153   Death of David I at Carlisle. Malcolm IV (aged 12) king of Scots

1157   Henry II Plantagenet takes four northernmost counties of England from Malcolm IV and fixes Border on Solway–Tweed line

1159   Malcolm IV goes to Toulouse with Henry II by whom he is knighted at Périgueux

1160–4   Malcolm IV subdues Galloway and Argyll

1163   Malcolm IV does homage to Henry II at Woodstock

1165   Death of Malcolm IV. William I 'the Lion' (brother of Malcolm IV) king of Scots

1173–4   Revolt against Henry II in England and on the continent, joined by French and Scots. William I captured at Alnwick (July 1174). Treaty of Falaise between William I and Henry II

1186   William I marries Ermengarde de Beaumont

1187   William I subdues Galloway and defeats and kills Donald Macwilliam, pretender to Scots throne, near Inverness

1189   Death of Henry II. William I obtains cancellation of Treaty of Falaise from Richard I of England ('Quitclaim of Canterbury')

1192   Bull of Pope Celestine III, '*Cum universi*', for the Scottish church

1196   William I subdues earl of Orkney

1209   Lost Treaty between William I and John of England. William's daughters Margaret and Isabel handed over to John on understanding that one of them would be married to John's heir

1212   Renewal of agreement with John, to whom the right to arrange marriage of Alexander, William I's heir, is given. Alexander knighted by John

1214   Death of William I. Alexander II king of Scots

1221   Alexander II marries Joan sister of Henry III of England

1230–1   Dominican and Franciscan friars established in Scotland

1237   Treaty of York between Alexander II and Henry III. Scots claim to northern English counties finally abandoned

1238   Death of Joan queen of Scots

1239   Alexander II marries Marie daughter of Enguerrand de Coucy

1249   Alexander II leads expedition to western isles, dies on Kerrera near Oban. Alexander III (aged 7) king of Scots

1249–58   Minority of Alexander III

1251   Alexander III marries Margaret daughter of Henry III

1263	Expedition of Haakon IV king of Norway to western isles. Battle of Largs (October). Death of Haakon (December)
1266	Treaty of Perth between Alexander III and Magnus king of Norway
1275	Death of Margaret queen of Scots
1278	Controversial homage of Alexander III to Edward I
1281	Marriage of Margaret daughter of Alexander III to Eric king of Norway
1283	Death of Margaret queen of Norway, leaving an only child, Margaret 'the Maid of Norway'
1284	Death of Alexander son and heir of Alexander III. Community of the Realm swears to accept Margaret the Maid of Norway as heir presumptive to Alexander III
1285	Alexander III married Yolande daughter of Robert count of Dreux
1286	Death of Alexander III
1290	Treaty of Birgham between Community of the Realm of Scotland and Edward I. Death of Margaret the Maid of Norway
1291	Edward I obtains overlordship of Scotland at Norham, sets up court to determine succession to throne.
1292	John Balliol king of Scots
1294	War between Edward I and Philip IV king of France
1295	Treaty between John and Philip IV
1296	War between John and Edward I. Defeat, submission, and deposition of John
1297	Risings in north and south-west of Scotland. Battle of Stirling Bridge
1298	William Wallace guardian of Scotland. Battle of Falkirk
1301	Scots argue case for independence before Pope Boniface VIII
1303	Edward I's fourth invasion of Scotland
1304	Submission of many Scots leaders. Surrender of Stirling castle
1305	William Wallace executed (August). Edward I's Ordinance for the government of Scotland (September)
1306	John Comyn killed at Dumfries. Robert Bruce made king of Scots at Scone

Appendix C: *The Royal House*

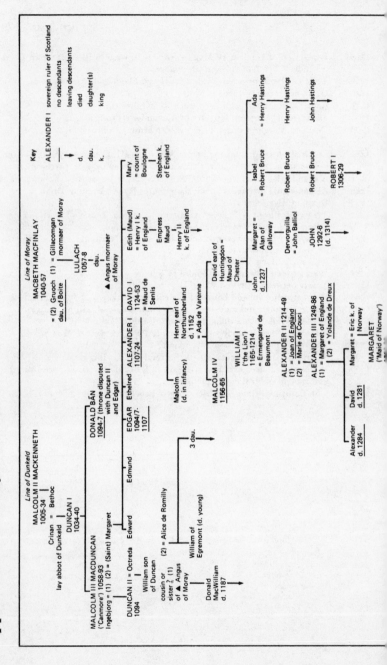

Index

Scottish places are located by region, English places by county, other places by country. Dumfries and Galloway is given as D. and G.